ONE OF THE ADMIRALS

Hans Langsdorff knew that sinking ships was not his only objective. He intended to cause as much confusion as possible. He therefore ordered the name *Graf Spee* painted over and replaced by the name *Admiral Scheer*. At the same time he had the ship's name removed from the cap bands of the crew and also replaced with the *Scheer*'s name.

On the last day of September the *Graf Spee* a/k/a *Admiral Scheer* recorded her first success. Around 1:00 p.m. a steamship was sighted on the horizon. Langsdorff ordered the *Spee*'s plane launched to confirm and identify the sighting. A few minutes later the Arado fired on the S.S. *Clement*.

At first the officers of the *Clement* thought that the approaching warship was the British cruiser *Ajax* as the latter was known to be operating in the area. Only when the Arado began firing did Captain Harris order his ship to send the distress signal. A few minutes later Harris ordered his crew to abandon ship. The unhappy merchant captain and his chief engineer were taken aboard the *Graf Spee* where they were greeted courteously by Langsdorff. "I am sorry, Captain, I will have to sink your ship. It is war."

THE BEST IN ADVENTURE FROM ZEBRA

THE ZONE #1: HARD TARGET (1492, $2.50)
by James Rouch

Across the hellish strip of Western Europe known as The Zone, supertanks armed with tactical nuclear weapons and lethal chemicals roam the germ-infested terrain. War in the mist-enshrouded Zone is a giant game of hide and seek—with a deadly booby prize for the losers!

THE ZONE #2: BLIND FIRE (1588, $2.50)
by James Rouch

In a savage frenzy of blood and fire the superpowers fight the Third Battle of Frankfurt. American Major Revell must delay a Communist column—but only a madman would take on Shilka anti-aircraft tanks with outdated mines and a few Dragon rocket launchers!

THE WARLORD (1189, $3.50)
by Jason Frost

The world's gone mad with disruption. Isolated from help, the survivors face a state in which law is a memory and violence is the rule. Only one man is fit to lead the people, a man raised among the Indians and trained by the Marines. He is Erik Ravensmith, THE WARLORD—a deadly adversary and a hero of our times.

THE WARLORD #2: THE CUTTHROAT (1308, $2.50)
by Jason Frost

Though death sails the Sea of Los Angeles, there is only one man who will fight to save what is left of California's ravaged paradise. His name is THE WARLORD—and he won't stop until the job is done!

THE WARLORD #3: BADLAND (1437, $2.50)
by Jason Frost

His son has been kidnapped by his worst enemy and THE WARLORD must fight a pack of killers to free him. Getting close enough to grab the boy will be nearly impossible—but then so is living in this tortured world!

Available wherever paperbacks are sold, or order direct from the Publisher. Send cover price plus 50¢ per copy for mailing and handling to Zebra Books, Dept. 1756, 475 Park Avenue South, New York, N.Y. 10016. DO NOT SEND CASH.

THE GREAT ADMIRALS OF WORLD WAR II

VOLUME II: THE GERMANS

BY CHARLES E. PFANNES
AND VICTOR A. SALAMONE

ZEBRA BOOKS
KENSINGTON PUBLISHING CORP.

ZEBRA BOOKS

are published by

KENSINGTON PUBLISHING CORP.
475 Park Avenue South
New York, NY 10016

Second printing: August 1985

Printed in the United States of America

To Charles and Victor Salamone. You are the greatest, kids!

CONTENTS

PREFACE

Volume II of *The Great Admirals* focuses on the German naval commanders. When thinking of the German military achievement during the second world war our thoughts immediately turn to their vast effort in Russia, or their massive blitzkriegs in Europe. Of all the aspects of the German military effort, the naval arm was the least prominent in Hitler's thinking. Yet the U-boats at one point in the war almost brought the Allies to their knees and the very names of *Bismarck* and *Tirpitz* caused paralyzing fear among the Allies.

This volume will focus on seven German naval commanders. In the introduction we study the breaking of the German naval code. Grand Admiral Erich Raeder is the subject of chapter one. Capt. Hans Langsdorff, the commander of the *Admiral Graf Spee* is the subject of chapter two. Though not an admiral, he surely would have become one if he had not taken his life after scuttling his ship. In chapter three we study the commander of the pocket battleship *Admiral Scheer*, Adm. Theodor Krancke. Adm. Gunther Lutjens and the exploit of the battleship *Bismarck* is the subject of chapter four. The Channel Dash and Adm. Otto Cilax are examined in the fifth chapter. The commander of the U-boats and Germany's second führer, Grand Adm. Karl Doenitz, is studied in the sixth chapter. In the last chapter we enter into the world of espionage when we study the head of the German military secret intelligence agency, the Abwehr; Adm. Wilhelm Canaris.

This book is our sixth. At this point we would like to tell the readers something about ourselves. Chuck Pfannes lives in Cold Spring, New York. He is married to Lillian and they have three children, Tom, John and Jennifer. Chuck works for a large industrial firm in Dutchess County. World War II has been an interest for Chuck since his high school days. Chuck is an ardent book collector and a collector of scale-model World War II ships. He devotes much of his time to the Boy Scouts. As a Boy Scout leader, Chuck has given much to its development in Cold Spring. In his leisure time he enjoys playing the guitar and singing Irish folk songs.

Vic Salamone lives in Poughkeepsie, New York. He is married to Susanne and they have two children, Charles and Victor. Vic teaches social studies at John Jay Senior High School in Wappinger Falls Central School District. Among the courses he teaches is an elective on World War II. Vic has had an interest in World War II since his graduate studies in history at Fordham University. He holds master's degrees from both Fordham University and Manhattan College. His hobbies include book collecting and piano playing. Vic devotes much of his time to his parish church, St. Martin de Porres where he serves as a lector, eucharistic minister and a religious education teacher.

Victor A. Salamone

Charles "Chuck" Pfannes

September 14, 1983

INTRODUCTION: BREAKING THE GERMAN NAVAL CODE

In the introduction to volume II of *The Great Commanders of World War II: The British*, the cracking of the German Enigma code was analyzed. The authors would now like to carry this story further to include the breaking of the German naval code.

Enigma was a most complex code. As early as 1928 the German army had adopted a machine cipher, an adaptation of a commercial machine called Enigma. The machine was housed in a small, portable box approximately the size of an office typewriter. The basic machine contained a typewriterlike keyboard powered by batteries above which was a series of small windows. The enciphering mechanism consisted of a number of revolving drums, or rotors. Around the perimeter of these drums were the letters of the alphabet. These wheels rotated in the same manner as a typewriter roller and could be manually set in any position. Each wheel (rotor) had fifty-two electrical contacts: twenty-six on one side wired to twenty-six more on the other side. The wiring pattern for each rotor differed.

The machine was relatively simple to operate. When a key was depressed, it made an electrical contact with one of the first wheel's twenty-six letters. The electrical current then flowed through the wiring of three or, in some cases, four rotors. After passing through the rotors the electrical current continued on through a system of complicated loops. From there it returned once more through the rotors. At that point a bulb in one of the windows over the keyboard lit up, indicating that the enciphering position had been reached. One of the rotors was then moved one position so that when the key was depressed again the electrical current followed a slightly different circuit that lit up a different letter of the alphabet. This continued until the message was completed.

Each machine was keyed to a certain position enabling it to be changed once or, frequently, twice a day. Only a machine capable of duplicating the key setting was able to read the message.

Though the code was considered unbreakable, the Polish secret service knew of Enigma some ten years before the Germans unleashed their blitzkrieg against that hapless country. Fortunately, the Poles managed to pass their knowledge on to the British before their country was overrun.

The British cryptologists, a group of scientists and mathematicians, began work on the wealth of information gathered from the Poles. By reconstructing an Enigma machine, the British were able to break the majority of German codes by the summer of 1940. Eventually, the British high command knew virtually every move the Germans were planning and deployed their forces accordingly. The ability to read the German code was dubbed "Ultra."

The Germans were confident that Enigma was unbreakable. But by April, 1940, the Luftwaffe code was cracked followed shortly thereafter by the army code. The German naval code, however, presented the British with a much greater challenge. This code was called Schlusselmachine M (Cipher Machine M). Though operating along the same basic principle of the standard Enigma machine, the naval ciphers remained undecipherable until the middle of 1941. Why?

The answer lies in the fact that although the German navy had also adopted machine ciphering and had in fact procured its machine from the same source, their cryptographic experts had succeeded in introducing a number of technical modifications into the machine, which greatly increased its security and the problem for an enemy cryptanalyst.[1]

The Enigma M Machine was highly versatile and able to handle many different ciphers. That created difficulties for code breakers who constantly searched for patterns in transmissions. Because of the machine's ability to change ciphers so readily, the chances of cracking the code were compounded a hundredfold. A code breaker needs consistency of use in order to pinpoint a pattern. Enigma M did not have that consistency.

The German navy developed thirteen principal ciphers and a number of minor ones. The principal ciphers were: Hydra, Triton, Tetis, Medusa, Aegir, Neptune, Sud, Special Cipher 100, Tibet, Potsdam, Freya, Sleipner and Bertok. Some of the ciphers were used by surface ships, others by submarines. Still others were used exclusively in the Baltic while in the Mediterranean or during special operations such as

Thunderbolt-Cerebus* an entirely different set was utilized.

When in use most of the ciphers were also open for modification. Major modifications occurred monthly, minor ones daily. For all these reasons the German naval high command (*Kriegsmarine*) was confident that their system could withstand the efforts of even the most talented enemy cryptanalysts.

At the beginning of 1941 the German naval ciphers continued to defy all efforts at decoding.

It was realized that only a "pinch," the capture of a naval Enigma machine with current settings and accompanying material would give the necessary start.[2]

Then, on February 23, 1941, the German trawler *Krebs* was disabled during the British raid on the Lofoten Islands. The captain of the *Krebs* was killed before he had time to destroy all confidential material. As a result, the British managed to capture some invaluable cryptographic information as well as a set of spare rollers for a cipher machine.

On May 7 yet another German trawler was captured off Iceland. Though this ship's Enigma machine was destroyed, further useful information was discovered. The red-letter day, however, occurred the next day, May 8. A German U-boat, U-110, was captured and secured before its vital, confidential information could be destroyed. The submarine's Enigma machine and related material and documents were captured intact and quickly dispatched to the code breakers. This wealth of material helped to unravel the mystery of

*The escape of the *Scharnhorst, Gneisenau* and *Prinz Eugan* up the English Channel.

the stubborn naval code. Shortly thereafter Hydra was cracked, followed quickly by Neptune, Sud and Medusa. Others followed in short order.

Though the task of deciphering was endless, it represented the first successful penetration of the Enigma M. More penetrations followed over the next few years. At times there were setbacks, but by the middle of 1943 the British efforts had advanced so far that the whereabouts of virtually all German ships were known, providing those ships utilized Enigma M.

The study of Ultra is almost ten years old now. Most historians agree that its importance is firmly established though there are many more secrets yet to be discovered. For the interested reader, a bibliography of suggested books on the topic of Ultra and code-breaking can be found at the end of this volume. The authors heartily recommend that the reader dig deeper into this most fascinating topic.

1. GRAND ADMIRAL ERICH RAEDER

Any study of Grand Adm. Erich Raeder is a puzzle. He became commander in chief of the German navy in 1928 and remained at the helm until January of 1943. From the Weimar Republic through the early days of the Third Reich and into the world's largest war, Raeder steered the navy away from political involvement and guided its destiny. Though he accepted Hitler's leadership, he refused to allow naval personnel to become party members. Raeder kept alive the great imperial traditions in the navy and went so far as to advocate Sunday church services; yet he directed an arm of the godless Nazi state.

His desire to keep the navy aloof from politics, however, proved his undoing. It gave the army and Luftwaffe leaders an opportunity to cultivate and influence Hitler. Raeder resigned in January, 1943 after the Führer ordered the German capital ships sent to the scrap heap.

What happened to the navy? Why did Hitler order Germany's great battle force dismantled? The answers to these and many more questions lie in the personal history of Grand Adm. Erich Raeder.

Raeder was born in 1876. The German Empire itself was a mere six years old. Otto von Bismarck was at the pinnacle of his power and influence. The Raeders were of middle-class origin. Erich's father was a language teacher at a Hamburg secondary school. He later became headmaster of the Friedrich Wilhelm Realgymnasium at Gruenberg in Silesia. His mother was the daughter of a musician. Early on she instilled in the young man a love for music.

At age eighteen, Erich informed his parents of his desire to pursue a naval career. Meeting with no objection he subsequently became a naval cadet and was posted to a German warship captained by Prince Heinrich. Excelling in his duties, Raeder, along with fifteen other cadets, was selected to attend the naval academy in Kiel for two years. The academy was designed to prepare aspiring young officers for command and staff assignments. The curriculum concentrated on professional training with emphasis on naval history, tactics and languages. In 1904, after selecting Russian as his primary language, the young officer was sent to Russia for a three-month study of the language.

After leaving the naval academy, Raeder served two years in the naval intelligence bureau. From there he was posted as navigation officer on the kaiser's yacht, the *Hohenzollern*. Service on the yacht exposed Raeder to the top leadership of the nation and the navy. After that choice assignment he returned to the line as staff officer to Adm. Franz von Hipper.

During World War I the future admiral took part in the early hit-and-run raids by the German surface fleet up and down the English coast. He quickly earned the respect of his superiors who thought enough of him to ask his advice on strategy and tactics. Raeder participated in the historic Battle of Jutland where the huge dreadnoughts of Germany and England met in the largest naval engagement of the war. Though the Germans managed to inflict greater damage on their opponent, they failed in their attempt to break out of the Baltic and were forced to seek the refuge of their own harbors. There the German fleet languished in inactivity.

Near war's end Raeder was given command of the light cruiser *Koeln*. The *Koeln* was assigned to reconnaissance and anti-mining duty in the North Sea. While carrying out this assignment, Raeder was named a member of the German armistice delegation that met at Spa to lay down terms with the Allies. The harsh terms caused many sailors to revolt. Raeder was appalled by the sailors' mutiny but he was equally revolted by the harsh terms for peace.

To the navy, which had been bred on the words of Kaiser Wilhelm II that "Our future lies on the water,"[1] the treaty marked a death sentence. The great German naval strategist von Tirpitz had declared that the dreadnought was the queen of the sea, the ultimate naval weapon. The provisions of the November 11, 1918 armistice called for the German fleet to steam to British waters and hand itself over to the Royal Navy. At Scapa Flow, the fleet waited patiently for the pundits at Versailles to promulgate the navy's future. The German fleet commanders, not at all optimistic over the navy's future, made preparations for a saving move, the scuttling of the fleet to coincide with the expiration of the armistice.

Once the treaty was signed and before the British could react, the Germans made their move. This self-inflicted destruction somehow made amends for the disgrace of surrender. Adm. Reinhard Scheer commented, "I rejoice over the sinking of the German fleet in Scapa Flow. . . . The stain of surrender has been wiped out."[2]

To many Germans, this defiant act was not the end of the German navy, but, like the Phoenix, it symbolized the birth of a new navy.

A symbol it was indeed. The drafters of the treaty had no intention of allowing Germany to develop a new navy capable of challenging the world's powers again. The terms of the treaty restricted Germany to six battleships, six light cruisers and twelve destroyers. Each battleship, moreover, could weigh no more than ten thousand tons and its main armament was restricted to eleven-inch guns or less. Cruisers were to be no more than six thousand tons with six-inch guns; destroyers were limited in size to eight hundred tons. Torpedo boats were to be no larger than two hundred tons. Aircraft carriers and submarines were strictly forbidden.

The tragedy at Scapa Flow left the German navy with only eight obsolescent, pre-dreadnought battleships, eight ancient cruisers and thirty-two useless destroyers and torpedo boats. Even that, however, was more than was allowable under the terms of the treaty. Basically, the Allies' intent was to make the German navy a coastal defense force with no offensive capabilities whatsoever. To ensure this then, they limited the navy's personnel to fifteen thousand officers and men.

With the war over and the nation fractured by opposition from both the right and left, Raeder turned his energy toward maintaining stability in the highly explosive atmosphere. Shocked by the mutiny of the German sailors, he rationalized that the uprising was the work of the left wing. In his mind, therefore, stability lay with the right wing. Accordingly, he backed the right wing Kapp Putsch in

March, 1920, which attempted to depose the feeble Weimar government. Because he had backed the ill-fated putsch, Raeder was assigned to two years of duty in the naval archives.

The navy, meanwhile, had begun its slow resurrection from the ashes. The first postwar commander in chief was Adm. Paul Behnke. His task was herculean for not only was he faced with the severe limitations, there was also very little capital available for Germany to invest in future growth. Allied reparations saw to that.

Behnke viewed the navy's primary objective as the defense of the Fatherland. To accomplish that he established two squadrons of ships, one in the North Sea and the other in the Baltic. The objective of these forces was to prevent the French and Polish navies from uniting against Germany.

The Versailles Treaty did allow Germany the right to replace older ships with newer ones provided they remained within the limits of the treaty. In 1923 the first new cruiser was launched. Behnke had found ways to evade the treaty limitations. The designs for new torpedo boats looked more like those for destroyers. Submarine development was also initiated in foreign countries under German auspices. In these covert ways Germany's navy was reborn.

In 1924 Behnke was replaced by Admiral Zenker. During the latter's tenure two more cruisers were laid down. In 1926 a book entitled *Strategy of the World War* was written by Vice Adm. Wolfgang Wegener. The admiral constructed a thesis around the idea that if Germany ever became a great power again, England would be her most obvious enemy. In that event Germany had to either construct a large, balanced fleet which could operate from both France and Norway in order to outflank a British blockade, or she must pursue alliances which would neutralize Britain's domination of European trade routes. Zenker read Wegener's book as did the future head of the U-boat service, Karl Doenitz.

Raeder also read the book but dismissed the idea that Germany's prime enemy would again be England. Nevertheless, Wegener's idea of a balanced fleet influenced the future commander in chief, and when he was eventually placed in a position of leadership, he followed Wegener's thesis closely.

As we have already seen, Germany was allowed to replace its outdated ships with newer ones. Zenker was ready to replace one of the pre-dreadnoughts with a more modern version. Because the ship was to be limited in size, it was relatively small for a battleship. The new warship was called the *Deutschland*. Its design was given the nickname of pocket battleship. The *Deutschland* was scheduled for launching in 1931 and would be followed shortly thereafter by her sisters, the *Admiral Scheer* and the *Admiral Graf Spee*.

Even before the *Deutschland* took to the high seas on her maiden voyage, Zenker had been succeeded in 1928 by Admiral Raeder. Following his exile to the naval archives, Raeder had been named flag officer, North Sea Light Forces. Two years later he became flag officer, Baltic. In both positions he began to earn a reputation for a strict moral code and sense of duty. It was these qualities which attracted him to the president of the Weimar Republic, the venerable Field Marshal Paul von Hindenburg who, in 1928, proposed Raeder as the new commander in chief of the German navy.

From the outset, Raeder was determined to keep the navy free of political involvement. He also set about building a highly competent officer corps serviced by well disciplined and trained crews. In addition, Raeder gave his approval to any and all covert activity necessary to improve Germany's weakened position. Thus, he continued to support submarine development abroad, authorized the creation of a fleet of freighters which could double as auxiliary cruisers, and directed that trawlers be turned into mine sweepers. Raeder also advocated and advanced the training of civilian aviators for use in a future naval air wing. As his basic design for the navy, he envisaged a balanced fleet of battleships, cruisers, destroyers and submarines.

In January, 1933, when Hitler became chancellor, Raeder welcomed the accession as a ray of hope for the navy. He did not alter his strategical thinking but, viewing Hitler as a nationalist, was confident of the future. Nevertheless, the commander in chief was very formal with Hitler and insisted from the outset of their relationship that the navy remain non-political. Unfortunately, that stance worked against Raeder and the navy.

In 1934, Raeder began planning larger ships. He considered more ships like the *Deutschland* only larger, with heavier armament. The Versailles restraints continued to haunt him, however. That restraint ended in 1935.

In that year Hitler renounced Versailles and reintroduced conscription. In June of that year an Anglo-German naval treaty was concluded. The treaty allowed the German navy to develop up to thirty-five percent of the strength of the Royal Navy in capital ships and forty-five percent in submarines. This would allow Germany five battleships, five heavy cruisers, eleven light cruisers, two aircraft carriers and sixty-four destroyers. A key clause in the treaty was the one that acknowledged Germany's right to develop a submarine force.

Raeder was pleased with this treaty. Not only did it acknowledge Great Britain's dominance at sea but he felt that it would also avoid a naval armament race with that country.

On September 28, 1935, Germany's first submarine flotilla was born and placed under the command of Capt. Karl Doenitz. Most of the boats that made up the flotilla had been constructed even before the signing of the Anglo-German naval treaty.

During that same year, Raeder also began an expanded shipbuilding program. Within a year the keels had been laid for the giant battleships *Bismarck* and *Tirpitz*. Hitler wanted these ships to displace 80 thousand tons and feature twenty-one-inch guns but Raeder was able to convince him that sixteen-inch guns were more than adequate and that for practicality's sake, the ships should remain within the 40 thousand ton range. This would allow them to utilize existing docking facilities. For the benefit of the rest of the world it was announced that both ships displaced 35 thousand tons, but in reality the *Bismarck* was 41,700 tons and the *Tirpitz* even larger at 42,900 tons. Both ships contained eight fifteen-inch guns.

Meanwhile, the battle cruisers *Scharnhorst* and *Gneisenau* had joined the fleet and by 1937 the light cruisers *Leipzig* and *Nurnberg* had been launched. These were followed in relatively short order by the light cruiser *Konigsberg* and the heavy cruisers *Admiral Hipper* and *Blucher*.

On November 5, 1937, Raeder and his fellow military leaders were summoned by Hitler to an important conference. At this meeting the Führer revealed his future plans. These plans envisaged Germany taking Austria, Czechoslovakia and Poland. Despite the belligerence of Hitler's speech, Raeder was confident that there would not be a war. The year before, when Hitler had marched troops into the Rhineland, Raeder had been concerned for fear of an adverse reaction from the French and British. However, the French had failed to act thereby proving Hitler correct. Raeder wrote, "We admit we were wrong, the Führer was right. We won because we had the stronger nerves and stuck it out."[3]

Raeder hoped that Hitler would forestall any action that might lead to war until the fleet was ready, although he did place the navy on alert in the event of any enemy interference while Germany made its moves.

At the same time, Doenitz was putting his U-boats through maneuvers in the Baltic and Atlantic. The U-boat chief was positive that war with England was inevitable and attempted to bring Raeder around to his way of thinking. But the latter continued to discount the possibility of war, naively believing Hitler's assurances that war was out of the question.

Raeder desired the establishment of a separate air arm. The navy, he said, needed an air arm trained in operations over the sea. Hermann Goering, commander in chief of the Luftwaffe was jealous of his empire, however, and insisted on controlling all air operations. This conflict with Goering never would be satisfactorily resolved but it took the experience of war to prove Raeder correct.

In March, 1938, Austria was annexed. Once more the West failed to react. At the end of May, Hitler summoned his naval chief and revealed to him for the first time that Britain was to be considered one of Germany's future adversaries. Hitler went on to demand an immediate speed-up in warship production.

For his part, Raeder knew that in its present condition the navy was not in any position to contest the British. It would be years before parity could be reached, yet he remained confident that war with Britain would not happen in the near future.

Raeder and the naval general staff immediately began a round of high-level strategic discussions. Big ship advocates on the general staff argued in favor of emphasizing a surface navy. They completely underestimated the ability of the U-boat, believing that British anti-submarine defense was far superior to any effort the submarines were capable of mounting. Doenitz argued against that theory but his voice was in the minority. The conclusion reached was, "For high seas operations in general, surface ships will serve the purpose better than submarines."[4]

The naval staff concluded that for Germany to effectively wage war it required a force large enough to carry out an economic struggle against Britain's Atlantic shipping lanes.

In September, 1938, just one month before France and Britain handed over the Sudetenland to Hitler, Raeder put down the proposals for a new navy. By October, the new plan, dubbed the "Z" Plan (Z for *ziel*, meaning target) had taken shape. The "Z" Plan called for the development of a balanced navy. Submarines would be required but the surface navy took priority. The plan would be expensive and require at least eight years to implement but it held great promise. Time, however, was essential. Raeder warned Hitler that if war broke out in the next year or two the fleet would not be ready. Hitler retorted, "For my political aims I shall not need the fleet before 1946."[5] Thus assured, Raeder once again took Hitler at his word.

The "Z" plan was officially accepted by Hitler in January, 1939 and was given priority over all other construction projects. The plan called for 6 super battleships of fifty-six thousand tons, 2 smaller battleships of forty-two thousand tons, 3 battle cruisers of thirty-one thousand tons, 3 pocket battleships, 2 aircraft carriers, 5 heavy cruisers, 68 destroyers, 90 torpedo boats, and 249 U-boats.

The flaw was that the plan required at least six years of peace to bring it to a successful conclusion. Any war before that time would find the German navy too weak to challenge the might of the Royal Navy.

Though many of the naval staff officers, including Doenitz, did not believe that Britain would remain quiet in the face of German expansion, Raeder still accepted Hitler's assurances that Britain would not intervene. Doenitz considered the "Z" Plan inadequate. First of all he was not convinced of Britain's complacency in the face of additional German moves. Secondly, he reasoned, the plan should have given priority to submarines and small surface raiders that could menace the Atlantic shipping lanes. Raeder and the balance of the staff, however, were big ship oriented and Doenitz's arguments fell on deaf ears.

In April, 1939, Hitler abrogated the Anglo-German naval treaty without even consulting Raeder. Many naval leaders took this as a sure sign that war was coming soon, but Raeder, although taken totally by surprise and greatly troubled, was once more reassured by Hitler that he had no intention of going to war in the near future. The non-aggression pact with the Soviet Union further convinced him of Hitler's desire to avoid hostilities.

Raeder found himself becoming increasingly disenchanted with those around Hitler. He never did become close to any of the party's leaders. He hated Goering, whom he considered an enemy, particularly in light of the latter's position of not allowing the navy its own air arm. Goering's position was that if the navy wanted air support, it could simply ask the Luftwaffe for it. Their animosity, however, went deeper than that. Goering frequently attempted to undermine Raeder's position, berating him because he went to church, questioning his political beliefs, and invariably giving false information about the navy to Hitler.

Raeder despised Goering for other reasons as well. One of these was the part the Luftwaffe chief had played in destroying the reputation of War Minister von Blomberg and Colonel General von Fritsch, chief of the general staff. The former had unwittingly married a prostitute; Fritsch had been falsely accused of being a homosexual.

Raeder even considered resigning in 1938 but stayed on despite his troubles with the SS. He specifically considered Reinhard Heydrich, head of the SD*, an implacable enemy. The fact that Heydrich was a former naval officer whom Raeder had dismissed for conduct unbecoming an officer was the root of that hatred.

Raeder also disliked Foreign Minister von Ribbentrop whom he considered totally incompetent. When war did eventually begin, the admiral blamed von Ribbentrop for feeding Hitler erroneous ideas about England.

On September 1, 1939, the German blitzkrieg was unleashed against Poland. Two days later the British and French declared war on Germany. Upon receipt of that declaration Raeder commented, "The surface forces . . . can do no more than show that they know how to die gallantly."[6] Though this sounded defeatist,

---

Sicherheitsdienst—responsible for external security.

Raeder was just the opposite. He met with his staff to revise battle plans. The admiral immediately dispatched the surface fleet to do its duty. The two old, pre-World War I battleships *Schleswig-Holstein* and *Schlesien* were sent to the Baltic where their eleven-inch guns could be used against the Polish coastal forts at Hela and Westerplatte.

Raeder had already sent the *Admiral Graf Spee* and the *Deutschland* into the Atlantic along with two supply tankers, *Altmark* and *Westerwald*. Their primary function was to keep the Allied fleet off balance by hitting where least expected. The operational zone for the *Graf Spee* was the South Atlantic; the *Deutschland* prowled the North Atlantic. Raeder, however, had to restrain his ships from commerce raiding because Hitler had refused to allow them to attack in hopes of concluding a peace settlement after Poland's demise. Finally, after much prompting from Raeder, Hitler yielded to the request for action.

Meanwhile, work on the "Z" Plan ships was suspended. Only the two nearly completed battleships and a cruiser* were to be finished. Construction of the two giant battleships was halted as was the lone aircraft carrier. No replacements larger than destroyers would be available but submarine construction was allowed to continue.

At the beginning of the war Germany's navy consisted of two battle cruisers, *Scharnhorst* and *Gneisenau*; three pocket battleships, *Deutschland, Admiral Scheer* and *Admiral Graf Spee*; two heavy cruisers, *Admiral Hipper* and *Blucher*; six light cruisers, thirty-four destroyers and torpedo boats, and

*Battleships *Bismarck* and *Tirpitz* and cruiser *Prinz Eugen*.

fifty-seven submarines. Two larger battleships and a heavy cruiser were nearing completion. Raeder found himself caught in a bind. Promised peace, he now faced war against the mightiest navy in the world: the Royal Navy. It was his unfortunate lot to go to war without having built up the forces needed to successfully prosecute the war. Nevertheless he plowed ahead for the sake of his country.

As the chapter on Admiral Doenitz will concentrate on the U-boat war, rather than be repetitive, this chapter will place emphasis on the surface war with only passing reference to the submarine struggle.

The immediate problem confronting Raeder was Hitler's restrictions. Doenitz wanted to wage unrestricted submarine warfare, but the admiralty ordered him to forbid his U-boats from sinking ships unless they zigzagged, were blacked out, or radioed the position of the U-boat to a warship. The sinking of the liner *Athenia* at the beginning of the war by *U-30* did not mean that Raeder had given Doenitz permission to practice unrestricted warfare. In fact, the *Athenia* was sunk only because she was blacked out and following a zigzag course. Therefore, the captain of the *U-30* had little option but to consider the *Athenia* a belligerent. In spite of this, Hitler ordered additional restraints, even going so far as to order that no French ships were to be attacked.

As the war progressed and hardened, however, Raeder was able to change Hitler's cautious attitude. By the end of September he had convinced the Führer to give approval to the sinking of any merchant ship that made use of its radio when stopped. He also managed to have the order protecting French ships rescinded. By November, most of the restrictions were lifted, allowing the navy to prosecute the war in its own manner.

Meanwhile, the pocket battleship *Graf Spee*, under the able command of Capt. Hans Langsdorff, began its war cruise on September 30 as it opened fire and sank the British merchantman, *Clement*. For the next two months the *Graf Spee* racked up one success after another in both the South Atlantic and Indian Oceans.

On November 21, the *Scharnhorst* and *Gneisenau* sailed into the Atlantic via the Iceland-Faroes Passage. Two days later the *Scharnhorst* destroyed the British auxiliary cruiser *Rawalpindi*.

Eventually, the *Graf Spee*'s luck ran out. A British force under Commodore Henry Harwood located her off the River Plate at dawn on December 13. By 6:20 the battle was on. The next morning found the *Graf Spee* seeking asylum in Montevideo, Uruguay with the British cruiser squadron on station just beyond that nation's territorial waters. Because Montevideo was a neutral port, Langsdorff felt he was free to remain there to repair the damage his ship had received in the battle.

But the government of Uruguay caved in to British pressure and refused to allow the German ship to remain in port indefinitely. Faced with the prospect of doing battle against what he felt were overwhelming odds, Langsdorff ordered the pocket battleship scuttled. Then the captain of the *Graf Spee* committed suicide. Raeder concurred with Langsdorff's actions although he deeply regretted the captain's death.

While the capital ships ranged the high seas, closer to home, Raeder ordered the mining of Britain's coastal waters and harbor entrances. The magnetic mine was Germany's greatest weapon during these early months of the war. The deployment of magnetic mines could produce a state of affairs comparable to a blockade. Their effectiveness was deadly. Though their production was limited, by December, 1939, the mines were responsible for the loss of 67 allied merchant ships with a gross tonnage of 252,237. By the following March, the total had risen to 128 ships. In addition, the mines had destroyed 3 British destroyers and 6 auxiliary warships. Cajus Bekker has said, "It can be confidently stated that during the first winter of the war the mine represented the most important threat to allied shipping plying to and from the United Kingdom."[7]

What created difficulties for the British was the fact that conventional mine-sweeping methods were not effective against the magnetic mine. The British had to find some way of neutralizing its deadly effect. They soon realized that if they demagnetized a ship's hull it would not attract the mine. In addition, they devised a method of making the mine explode prematurely.

News of the British success caused Raeder to insist that the Luftwaffe help in the mining effort before the enemy could put their countermeasures into effect. This created a deeper rift between Raeder and Goering. The Luftwaffe commander refused to participate until an overwhelming number of mines had been produced. He reasoned that only an all-out effort would make it worthwhile. Raeder shot back that by that time it might be too late. Lack of coordination hurt the effort. It was but one more cause to support Raeder's arguments for a separate air arm for the navy.

As the new year rolled around, Raeder could be justifiably proud of the navy's performance. Though lacking sufficient numbers, the U-boats tallied a remarkable record. The magnetic mines were proving costly to the British and the *Admiral Graf Spee* had proven the theory that a surface raider could create havoc and cause the enemy to disperse their forces. The lone sour note was the loss of the *Graf Spee*.

The loss of the pocket battleship brought to light a major problem, Hitler himself. The Führer had earlier told Raeder, "On land I am a hero. At sea I am a coward."[8] Hitler was deeply rankled over the destruction of the *Graf Spee*. The loss only served to magnify the fear he experienced any time a capital ship sortied. He would worry to the point of being unable to sleep. To Hitler, ships were not expendable, their loss would give the enemy too much prestige. Because of these fears he placed heavy restraints on the ships to the point of hindering their freedom of action. The problem became quite acute in 1941 following the loss of the *Bismarck*, but its seeds were planted by the debacle off the River Plate.

Raeder was destined for trouble because of Hitler's interference. In one breath he ordered aggressive action but in the next he cautioned restraint. He wanted his ships to be aggressive to the point of questioning the courage of the officers who refused battle, but his own excessive caution tied the hands of the same commanders. This problem would eventually lead to a showdown between Hitler and his naval chief. But that was in the future. For now, Raeder was about to embark on the navy's greatest venture, the conquest of Norway.

For Germany, Norway held a special significance. First of all, most of Germany's iron ore was imported from Sweden. This ore was transported to Germany by way of the Norwegian port of Narvik. A blockade of Norway would drastically reduce Germany's arms production. Secondly, any student of the first world war could easily see what the British had achieved by blockading the exit to the North Sea from the Baltic.

Norway therefore held a crucial strategic position and Raeder wanted to exploit it. He desired ports in Norway that would enable the navy to outflank a British blockade while providing bases on the Atlantic for U-boats to range against British trade.

Hitler, however, favored Norwegian neutrality. He felt secure that the British would not violate international law. Events were to prove him wrong.

On November 30, 1939, Finland went to war against the Soviet Union. As the world stood by in amazement, the gallant Finns fought the Red army to a standstill. The Allies quickly proposed plans to send aid to Finland by way of Narvik. Such a proposal would prove disastrous to Germany's iron ore supply. But Winston Churchill, the first lord of the admiralty, had his eyes fixed on that very target. In fact, he proposed the mining of the waters along Norway's coast in order to halt the iron ore trade even though that act not only violated Norway's neutrality, but international law as well. Therefore, both Raeder and Churchill had their gaze riveted on Norway.

Raeder found an ally in the person of the pro-German head of the Norwegian Nazi party, Vidkun Quisling. Quisling made contact first with the Nazi philosopher and chief ideologist, Alfred Rosenberg, who in turn brought the Norwegian to Raeder. On December 24, 1939, Raeder had an audience with Hitler during which he introduced Quisling to the Führer. Though still reluctant, Hitler did commission a preliminary study on a potential military move in Norway. On January 27 he ordered more detailed plans developed. A code name was assigned: Operation Weserbrung. It was not, however, until after the *Altmark* affair that planning began in earnest.

The *Altmark* was the support ship for the ill-fated

Graf Spee. Aboard the *Altmark* were 299 British merchant seamen who had been taken prisoner by the pocket battleship. On February 14, 1940, the British spotted the *Altmark* heading into neutral Norwegian territorial waters. Churchill ordered the *Altmark* intercepted and its prisoners freed. On the sixteenth, Capt. Philip Vian of the destroyer *Cossack* located the German ship sheltering in Jossing Fjord. Despite protests from the Norwegians and their assurances that the Germans had no prisoners and that the *Altmark* was unarmed, the British were not to be denied. Vian boarded the ship and found both prisoners and weapons. Hitler fumed at the British audacity while Norway duly sent protests to London. As a result. Hitler was now convinced that Norway must be conquered. Obviously the British had no regard for Norwegian neutrality and it was doubly evident that Norway was in no position to resist.

Operational command of the proposed move against Norway was given to Gen. Nikolaus von Falkenhorst. Lacking accurate intelligence and knowledge of Norway's topography, Falkenhorst bought a Baedeker travel guide for that country. After studying the guide he concluded that Norway's five major ports—Oslo, Stavanger, Bergen, Trondheim and Narvik—would have to be taken quickly.

On March 1, Hitler issued a directive making Weserbung an official operation. The directive stated, "The situation in Scandinavia makes it necessary to prepare for the occupation of Denmark and Norway."[9] Thus Denmark was added as a necessary adjunct to the occupation of Norway.

Meanwhile, the British were placing the finishing touches on their own plans to send aid to Finland via Narvik. On March 10, Prime Minister Neville Chamberlain assured Finland that in two days the forces would be dispatched. Unfortunately, Finland was unable to hold out that long and sued for peace with the Russians. This act pulled the rug out from under the British plan. With their pretext for occupying Narvik gone, the British postponed any move.

Nevertheless, Raeder continued to prod the Führer into action. On March 26 and again on the twenty-ninth he urged Hitler to accept an early date for the operation. The latter finally. accepted April 9 as D-day.

Allied plans were moving along as well. The failure to aid Finland caused France to change leaders. The Daladier government was replaced by one headed by the more forceful Paul Reynaud. Both Reynaud and Churchill thought along the same lines and knew that Germany's trade had to be hit and hit hard.

Churchill reviewed his plan for mining Norwegian territorial waters in order to make travel along its coast a hazard. April 5 was selected as the date for the mining operation to begin but it was later changed to the eighth. This placed the Germans and the Allies on a collision course.

On April 2 the *Scharnhorst* and *Gneisenau* sortied. Their role was to tie down the British home fleet while the landings were proceeding in Norway. The German plan called for ten destroyers to land two thousand troops at Narvik while the *Hipper* and four destroyers landed seventeen hundred more at Trondheim. Meanwhile, the light cruisers *Koln* and *Konigsberg* were to put nine hundred more men ashore at Bergen. The light cruiser *Karlsruhe* accompanied by the depot ship *Tsingtau* were to land eleven hundred more troops at Kristiansand and Arendal. At Oslo, two thousand troops covered by the *Blucher* and pocket battleship *Lutzow** would land. The Luftwaffe was to provide air cover while the army captured these key ports.

The first confrontation occurred on the morning of April 8. The British were busily preparing their mining operation when the destroyer *Glowworm* came across the *Hipper* off Trondheim. The resulting uneven struggle concluded with the *Glowworm*'s destruction thus making the British destroyer the first casualty of the Norwegian campaign. The *Glowworm*'s captain, however, was determined not to let his ship die without drawing blood. He set the burning ship on a collision course with the German cruiser. Though damaged, the *Hipper* was able to continue on with her assigned duties. For his daring action the British captain, Commander Roope, was awarded a posthumous Victoria Cross.

On the ninth, the British battle cruiser *Renown* sighted the *Scharnhorst* about fifty miles off Narvik. The weather was stormy but the British admiral, Whitworth, was determined to prevent the German warship from advancing into the Atlantic. Vice Adm. Gunther Lutjens was under orders, however, to lure the enemy away from the Norwegian coast so he turned and ran, with the *Renown* in hot pursuit. The *Renown* fired her main battery and put three shells into the *Gneisenau*, knocking out her forward eleven-inch turret and damaging the fire control system.

Thanks to the combination of bad weather and superior speed, the German ships eventually outran the *Renown*. What's more, the two battle cruisers had

*Formerly known as *Deutschland*. The name was changed at Hitler's orders as he felt that the loss of a ship bearing the name *Deutschland* would be a tremendous propaganda victory for the enemy.

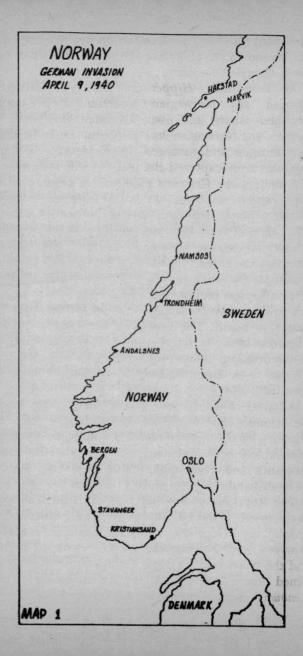

NORWAY
GERMAN INVASION
APRIL 9, 1940

HARSTAD
NARVIK
NAMSOS
TRONDHEIM
SWEDEN
ANDALSNES
NORWAY
BERGEN
OSLO
STAVANGER
KRISTIANSAND
DENMARK

MAP 1

prevented the *Renown* from using her guns against the invasion force at Narvik. Thus the German troops easily occupied the port.

At Trondheim, *Hipper* and her four destroyers silenced any Norwegian batteries while troops swarmed ashore and easily captured the port. At Bergen, the Norwegian coastal defense forces fired on the Germans and damaged the *Konigsberg*. Despite this, the army captured the port in swift fashion.

Although the Germans managed to capture all of their targets, at Oslo they nearly suffered a major disaster. The *Blucher* and *Lutzow* steamed headlong into Oslo Fjord but the alert gunners of the Norwegian defense force opened fire on the ships at point-blank range. The *Blucher* was quickly crippled. The shore batteries then fired torpedoes and finished off the hapless cruiser resulting in a heavy loss of life not only amongst the ship's crew, but also amongst the troops on board. The captain of the *Lutzow* quickly withdrew from the narrows of the fjord and landed the remaining troops ten miles down the fjord. Thanks to aid from the Luftwaffe, Oslo fell later, on the ninth.

Admiral Raeder was pleased with the navy's performance despite the loss of the *Blucher* and the crippling of the *Konigsberg*. The day had proven an admirable success. Denmark had capitulated without resistance and every major Norwegian port was in German hands, as were their vital airfields.

The Royal Navy, however, was not ready to throw in the towel. It moved towards Norway determined to smash the Germans. The battleships *Rodney, Warspite* and *Valiant*, the aircraft carrier *Furious*, and the heavy cruisers *York, Devonshire* and *Berwick* joined Admiral Whitworth's force consisting of the *Renown, Repulse* and two destroyer flotillas and headed for Narvik.

On the morning of the tenth, the British Second Destroyer Flotilla entered Ofot Fjord enroute to Narvik with the intent of smashing the German ships there. Two German destroyers were quickly sunk and three others seriously damaged. Six transports were also sunk. Five other German destroyers quickly counterattacked and smashed the British destroyers *Hardy* and *Hotspur*. But the Germans did not press their attack home and by 6:30 a.m. the first Battle of Narvik was over as the British forces retreated down the fjord. The balance sheet showed two destroyers lost on either side, but the Germans had suffered damage to three others against only one for the British and had lost six supply ships and an ammunition ship.

Meanwhile the rest of the German warships began to move out from Norway on their way back to Germany. En route the *Karlsruhe* and the *Lutzow* were torpedoed by a British submarine. In the interim, the *Hipper* had joined forces with *Scharnhorst* and *Gneisenau*. After evading heavy air attacks, all three ships reached home on the evening of the twelfth. The *Lutzow* also made Germany without further damage but not so the light cruisers *Konigsberg* and *Karlsruhe*. The former was sunk by British aircraft at Bergen; the *Karlsruhe*'s damage from the British submarine was so extensive that her captain ordered her sunk by his own forces.

On the thirteenth, the British once more attacked at Narvik. The *Warspite* accompanied by nine destroyers moved up Ofot Fjord. One by one they smashed the defending German destroyers, sinking eight in all. Luckily for the Germans the British were not accompanied by the landing force originally designated for Narvik.

The following day, British landings began at

Trondheim and of course Narvik. The landing at Trondheim failed miserably as the Luftwaffe obliterated the British effort. The troops were evacuated on April 27.

At Narvik the Allies met with more success. On May 28 they finally captured the port. But their losses in other places coupled with the crisis brought about by the German attack on France caused them to evacuate Narvik on June 8.

Richard Humble offered the following comments on the Norwegian campaign and the Navy's role:

> "The German navy had done its job in landing the army in Norway; the army completed its task superbly; and the Germans clinched their triumph in Norway with a final victory at sea."[10]

The victory that Humble refers to occurred early in June. The *Scharnhorst, Gneisenau, Hipper*, and four destroyers had sortied northward from Kiel. They had orders to proceed to Harstad near Narvik and bombard the British base there. While moving north they made contact with a British force. At 4:00 p.m. on the eighth the *Scharnhorst* attacked the British aircraft carrier *Glorious*. In the uneven fight the *Glorious* was sunk along with her escorting destroyers *Ardent* and *Acasta*. But the *Scharnhorst* did not escape unscathed. Although the damage was slight it reduced her fighting efficiency. Therefore, after the ships returned to Trondheim, it was decided twelve days later to bring the damaged battle cruiser back to Germany. To divert attention from the *Scharnhorst, Gneisenau* and *Hipper* made a feint toward Iceland to draw off any patrolling British warships. The ruse worked. The *Scharnhorst* beat a hasty retreat back to Germany. Though *Gneisenau* was struck by a torpedo, the covering operation was a total success; all three warships eventually reached home. This marked the end of the Norwegian campaign.

Although Raeder had ample reason to be proud of the fleet's efforts he did level criticism at Admiral Marschall's handling of the surface ships during the campaign. Miffed by the rebuff, Marschall resigned and was replaced as fleet commander by Admiral Lutjens. Other than that, Raeder was completely satisfied. The navy now had bases in Norway from which it could range out into the Atlantic and attack British shipping. It had also saved Germany's ore supply from dwindling to a stop. But the cost was not cheap. The *Blucher, Konigsberg* and *Karlsruhe* had been lost along with ten destroyers and four U-boats. In addition, the *Scharnhorst, Gneisenau, Hipper* and *Lutzow* all required repairs.

Not only had the navy received the bases in Norway, but with the fall of France the Biscay ports of Brest, Lorient and Saint-Nazaire fell into German hands. The German navy was now free of the dangers the Imperial Fleet had faced during the first world war. With bases in Norway and France the war against England's shipping lanes was now tipped in Germany's favor. For the U-boats the summer of 1940 was a happy time. The same could be said for the surface fleet.

Since November, 1939, Raeder had anticipated the prospect of an invasion of England and had ordered the naval operations staff to investigate the problem. In May, 1940, he brought the staff assessment to Hitler but the German leader was reluctant to take plans for an invasion seriously. In fact, after France surrendered he cut the army by a full one-fifth.

The naval plan was called Operation SeaLion. Despite Hitler's original rebuff Raeder continued preparations. In a later discussion with Hitler, the admiral emphasized the need for aerial supremacy but the naval staff had not yet consulted the Luftwaffe.

In July the army began to show an interest in SeaLion. British tenacity coupled with their attack on the French fleet in early July convinced the Germans that an invasion of England would have to be taken seriously.

Actually Raeder hoped that SeaLion would be a last resort. He hoped that by cutting off their imports, bombing their cities and mining their coast, England could be convinced that continued resistance was futile.

On July 16, Hitler issued Directive 16, the execution of SeaLion but only after the Luftwaffe had gained control of the air. For SeaLion the navy's role would be limited to providing light flotilla escorts, troop carriers and invasion barges. The capital ships would not be utilized because most of them were still in drydock undergoing repairs to the damage sustained in Norway. The burden of the invasion would therefore fall on the Luftwaffe.

On August 13, during a conference with Hitler, Raeder pressed for a decision. Would SeaLion go forth or not? Though Hitler conceded that the operation should be a last resort, he wanted to confer with the army and air force leaders to assess the results of the bombings before reaching a decision.

For his part Raeder was acutely aware that he did not possess a large number of transports. This limitation restricted the area of any landing. The proposed invasion point would be a modified assault along a narrow strip by six infantry divisions followed by six more ten days later. This was contingent, however, on attaining aerial supremacy.

Deep down Raeder hoped Britain would capitulate

before an invasion became necessary. But by September 15, the Luftwaffe losses were so heavy that Hitler decided to postpone SeaLion indefinitely.

While Raeder was preoccupied with SeaLion, a force of raiders was preying on enemy ships. With the cancellation of the "Z" Plan at the outbreak of the war, Raeder had ordered the conversion of merchant ships into armed commerce raiders. By the spring of 1940 the first of these ships was ready and the admiral began to deploy them along the trade routes on a deadly mission to sink merchant shipping.

Taking their cue from the bygone days of the swashbuckling pirates, these disguised merchant raiders were fast and durable. Masters of disguise, they sailed under flags of different nations and used false names. They constructed fake deck contours in order to deceive and mask their deadly armament. On deck would be false containers and disguised crew members.* But these vessels were deadly ships containing the firepower of a cruiser. They were appropriately called auxiliary cruisers.

The objective of these ships was to lure unsuspecting victims into close range, then sink them. The most famous of these raiders was the *Atlantis*, the Rattlesnake of the Ocean. By the end of 1940 this ship alone had accounted for the destruction of thirteen enemy ships. Other raiders also made successful voyages, some lasting over a year. The *Orion* and *Komet* ranged into the Pacific where they compiled a fantastic record. During a five-month period the *Widder* sank ten ships.

The first nine months of the auxiliary cruiser was a distinct success. Then, by the end of the year, the

*They even had crewmen disguised as women to deceive unsuspecting victims as to the true nature of their intentions.

heavy ships damaged during the Norwegian campaign were ready to play their part in the attack on Britain's trade.

The *Admiral Scheer* and the *Hipper* were the first to sail, followed later by the *Scharnhorst* and *Gneisenau*. The *Scheer* left port on October 27. Under cover of bad weather she broke through the Denmark Strait and made her way into the Atlantic. A few days later she made her first kill. Later that same day the *Scheer* stumbled across a British convoy. The pocket battleship sank the escorting auxiliary cruiser and five of the convoy's ships before they scattered. Three more merchant ships were damaged. Then Captain Krancke turned the *Scheer* for the South Atlantic where it began an amazing voyage.*

The presence of the *Scheer* caused the British to suspend convoys temporarily. When the next convoy did sail it was covered by a battleship.

Following on the heels of the *Scheer*, the *Hipper* broke through the Denmark Strait on December 6. The *Hipper*-class cruisers were magnificently designed warships with one significant flaw: Thanks to a relatively small fuel supply, their range was severely limited. Finding no victims in the western Atlantic, the cruiser hovered off the West African coast where on Christmas Eve she came upon a troop convoy of twenty ships heading for the Middle East. The next day the *Hipper* attacked but the British escorts were strong and included the aircraft carrier *Furious*. In the resulting duel both sides suffered slight damage but the *Hipper*'s was in a crucial spot. An engine that had previously caused trouble was hit. It was therefore imperative that she return to base. Slipping past the

*For a more detailed account of the voyage see the chapter on Admiral Krancke.

British blockade, the *Hipper* made Brest safely on December 27 after a most unsatisfactory cruise.

The turn of the year found the *Scheer* the lone capital ship still at sea. Also at large were the auxiliary cruisers *Thor*, *Atlantis*, *Komet*, *Orion*, *Pinguin* and *Kormoran*.

Meanwhile, the mighty battle cruisers *Scharnhorst* and *Gneisenau* under the command of Admiral Lutjens left Kiel on December 27. They immediately ran into a particularly severe storm during which the *Gneisenau* was damaged slightly. As a result, both ships returned to port. Their next attempt was made on January 23, 1941.

The British, meanwhile, were waiting. The commander of the home fleet, Adm. Sir John Tovey, had been warned by the admiralty on the twentieth to expect another breakout at any time. He dispatched two cruisers to cover the Iceland-Faroes Passage between Iceland and the Faroe Islands. On the twenty-sixth the German warships were sighted steaming into the passage. The German ship's radar alerted them to the British presence so Lutjens reversed course and moved north. After refueling, the German ships made another attempt on February 3 by breaking through the Denmark Strait. This effort was successful and the two battle cruisers made straight for the convoy routes.

During the next six weeks, the battle cruisers managed to sink a total of twenty-one merchant ships.* Then Lutjens received orders to cover the return of the *Scheer* and *Hipper* to Germany. Accordingly, he made for Brest, arriving safely on March 22. Intent on bringing the *Scharnhorst* and

*The cruise of the *Scharnhorst* and *Gneisenau* is covered in greater detail in the chapter on Lutjens.

Gneisenau to bay, the British allowed the *Hipper* and *Scheer* to slip past their patrols independently and to successfully return to Germany.

Before returning to Germany, however, the *Hipper* made a second cruise which was distinctly more successful than the earlier one. Patrolling off the African coast on February 11 she came upon convoy SLS-64 containing nineteen unescorted merchantmen. With no enemy warships to stop her the *Hipper* quickly sank seven ships before a raider report from one of the surviving ships alerted the British to the presence of the German ship. Low on fuel and in danger of being found by British warships, the *Hipper* returned to Brest on February 14 in need of a complete overhaul. It was decided to bring her home to Germany via the Denmark Strait.

After leaving Brest on the fifteenth, the *Hipper* moved toward Greenland where she refueled from a supply ship while waiting for bad weather. Then, under the cloak of heavy clouds, she traversed the Denmark Strait and arrived in Kiel on March 28, just prior to the *Scheer*'s successful dash through the strait.

The High Seas Fleet had performed magnificently. However, as Richard Humble put it, "The successes of Hitler's High Seas Fleet had almost reached their zenith. The past twelve months had seen triumphant cruises by battle squadrons and by lone raiders, backed by the establishment of a beautifully running supply system."[11]

Despite their success, though, Raeder's fleet had yet to clash with the British battle fleet but he was preparing the greatest sortie yet for the German surface fleet, Rheinubung (Operation Rhine). The mighty battleship *Bismarck* was ready for action. Along with the *Prinz Eugen*, the *Bismarck* was making preparations to sail and link up with the *Scharnhorst* and *Gneisenau* in what would be virtually an invincible force.

Rheinubung called for the *Bismarck* and her consort to form the right-hand pincer with the left pincer comprised of the two battle cruisers sitting at Brest. Raeder felt that the combined striking power of this force would cause the British to strip their convoys of the battleship escorts thus making them sitting ducks for the U-boats and auxiliary cruisers.

Even if the British refused to strip their convoys of battleship protection, the combined might of the German surface force could challenge anything the British had to offer. Raeder was confident. There was only one fly in the ointment. Would the *Scharnhorst* and *Gneisenau* be ready to put to sea in time to join the *Bismarck* and *Prinz Eugen* sometime in April?

Scharnhorst was in dire need of a major engine overhaul that would confine her to port until June, but her equally formidable sister was ready. Although the two battle cruisers remained at Brest their proximity to British air bases made it a hazardous place. The base was well protected, however, making it virtually impossible for the R.A.F. bomber command to hit a target. Therefore, *Gneisenau* was temporarily moved into the open harbor while an unexploded torpedo dropped during one of the many British attacks was cleared. Temporarily exposed, the ship made an ideal target, one which Churchill wanted exploited.

On April 6, the *Gneisenau* was struck by a torpedo, damaging her so extensively that eight months later she was still undergoing repairs.

Rheinubung had been dealt a major setback, the *Bismarck* and *Prinz Eugen* would have to make their voyage alone. Though disappointed, Raeder remained optimistic that the battleship and cruiser still constituted a formidable force of their own.

There was another reason why Raeder was so anxious to send the *Bismarck* and *Prinz Eugen* into the Atlantic before the *Scharnhorst* and *Gneisenau* could be made ready. He knew that in June Hitler intended to launch Operation Barbarossa, the invasion of Russia. Once that happened, the army and Luftwaffe would receive priority over the navy. A victory at sea would serve to keep Hitler's interest riveted on the navy.

But Raeder was opposed to Hitler's attack on Russia without having first conquered England. The admiral placed his hopes on bringing England to her knees on an all-out effort in the Mediterranean. He and his staff pinpointed two key points, Gibraltar and Suez, which, if captured, would hurl the British out of the Mediterranean and free the Italian fleet for decisive operations in the Atlantic. For the latter to be free to maneuver, Gibraltar had to fall.

At the same time, if Suez were captured, Raeder reasoned, Turkey and the Balkans would easily fall into Axis hands. In addition, England's trade route to India and the Far East would be severed thereby adding to her slow strangulation.

Through the summer and fall of 1940 and into the winter the Mediterranean therefore became a hotly contested battle zone, the Italian fleet versus the Royal Navy. Contrary to popular myth, the Italian fleet was modern, powerful, and a formidable force indeed. Following the postponement of SeaLion, Raeder demanded a total effort against the British fleet for a strong effort in the Mediterranean was an integral part of his worldwide strategy. He continued to insist on operations against Gibraltar, the Canary Islands and the Suez Canal. His arguments made a lot of sense but Hitler was difficult to convince.

Hitler did recognize the advantages of operations in the Mediterranean and offered aid to the Italians. However, they refused all offers from their ally, hoping to defeat the Royal Navy on their own. Their dreams were dealt a severe blow in February of 1941, when Gen. Sir Richard O'Connor's small desert force captured over one hundred thousand Italian troops and pushed the rest halfway across Libya. But even prior to that the Axis plans for the Mediterranean were in deep trouble. The previous October the Germans had attempted to woo the Spanish dictator, Francisco Franco, whose aid was deemed essential for an assault on Gibraltar. That attempt fell flat as even Hitler himself was unable to obtain a commitment from Franco. The general was most reluctant to join the Axis as long as the British showed signs of continuing the struggle.

Another severe blow followed in November. On the eleventh of that month planes from the British carriers *Illustrious* and *Eagle* launched an attack against the Italian fleet at Taranto Harbor. The attack was a total success and put much of the Italian fleet, including over half the battleships, out of commission.

Despite Raeder's knowledge of Hitler's move against the Soviet Union following the summer of 1940 and the admiral's subsequent efforts to lobby against the plan, the Führer insisted on moving ahead despite the fact that England continued to hold out. On December 18, Hitler officially issued Directive 21, Operation Barbarossa. Despite this, on December 27 Raeder tried one more time to dissuade Hitler from his intentions by openly protesting the directive.

Directive 21 really ended any hopes for fighting and winnning a single front war in the Mediterranean and in the Atlantic sea lanes.[12]

Nevertheless, Raeder was not through. As long as Barbarossa was not initiated there was still hope. He coerced the Japanese into attacking Singapore in order to pin down the British military strength in the Far East and threaten their commerce system in the Indian Ocean.

Then came a ray of hope. General Rommel arrived in Africa and began an offensive in the spring of 1941, completely routing the British and hurling them back to Egypt. This was followed by a German campaign in the Balkans. Raeder seized this opportunity to pressure the Italian naval commander in chief to use his fleet more aggressively. The result was the disastrous Battle of Cape Matapan. Undaunted, Raeder continued his efforts to convince Hitler of the importance of North Africa, but the Führer's interest that spring was focused in another direction.

Rommel's Afrika Korps continued to push the British into Egypt. In the Balkans, Yugoslavia and Greece fell to the Germans. In May the Luftwaffe captured the island of Crete by the exclusive use of paratroops. The Royal Navy put up a staunch defense which prevented the Germans from ferrying reinforcements to Crete but the Luftwaffe gave the British fleet a severe mauling, sinking three cruisers and six destroyers. In addition, two battleships, one carrier, six cruisers and seven destroyers were damaged.

Simultaneous with the activities in the Mediterranean, the epic voyage of the *Bismarck* began. The complete story of this voyage will be related in the chapter on Admiral Lutjens. On May 27, the *Bismarck* was surrounded and sunk by battleships of the British home fleet.

The auxiliary cruisers were also beginning to suffer. By the end of 1941 the raiders no longer harassed the high seas at will. One by one they either returned to port or were sunk. Among the latter was the legendary *Atlantis* which met its end at the hands of the H.M.S. *Devonshire* on November 22, 1941 following a record twenty months at sea with a score of twenty-two ships sunk.

Less than a month after *Bismarck*'s untimely demise, the German army unleashed its blitzkrieg against the Soviet Union. Raeder faced increasing pressure now that the Soviet Union was added to the list of Germany's enemies. The navy had to assume the vital job of preventing supplies from reaching Russia from the outside. U-boats could be sent to the arctic waters but what about the surface fleet? Where was it?

The *Scharnhorst, Gneisenau* and *Prinz Eugen* were at Brest. The *Tirpitz*, sister ship to the *Bismarck*, was in Germany. The balance of the high seas fleet was either in the Baltic or in the Norwegian fjords.

The ships at Brest lived a precarious existence. To the British the three warships represented a menace that had to be eliminated or at the very least immobilized. Therefore, during the latter portion of 1941 Brest became the number one target for the bomber command.

The danger to the ships at Brest convinced Hitler that Norway was the safest place for the surface fleet. Coupled with his continuing obsession with the idea that the British would eventually invade Norway, it served to firm up his conviction to have the fleet transferred there.

Raeder agreed that the *Tirpitz* should move to Trondheim but he expressed doubts that the force at Brest could be safely returned to Germany up the English Channel under the very noses of the enemy as Hitler suggested. Originally, the admiral planned to send this force on an Atlantic cruise in March or April. The critical fuel situation mitigated against such a lengthy cruise and he was forced to modify his plans. So he had little choice but to concede that the Brest fleet be transferred to Norway. But Raeder insisted that the ships not return by way of the English Channel, rather they should take a route around the north of Iceland.

While the debate regarding the fate of the Brest fleet raged on in the highest circles, Raeder found himself faced with a further extension of the war. The United States had been sending England enormous amounts of supplies following the passage of the Lend-Lease Act in the winter of 1941. The German navy had been hampered by the severe restrictions laid down by Hitler. Raeder urged Hitler to lift the restrictions on attacks against American ships but the Führer refused for fear of unduly antagonizing the United States. Increased American activity, however, eventually resulted in inevitable clashes. On October 10, 1941, the American destroyer *Kearny* was torpedoed by a U-boat while escorting a convoy. On the thirty-first of that same month, the destroyer *Reuben James* was sunk by a U-boat. The restrictions were finally lifted on December 11 as Germany fulfilled its pledge to the Japanese by declaring war on the United States The Japanese had attacked the American fleet at Pearl Harbor on December 7. U-boats were immediately dispatched to the East Coast of the United States.

In the interim, Hitler had overruled Raeder's decision to bring the Brest ships to Norway via the Icelandic route. He wanted the fleet returned as soon as possible and that meant the gamble to sail up the English Channel. In bold style, Hitler argued away all protests of the hazards of such an operation. The Luftwaffe, he insisted, would provide a carpet of aerial protection. In addition, the Führer was counting on the element of surprise. Raeder had no choice. Hitler's orders could not be transgressed.

During the waning hours of February 11, 1942, the three German warships left Brest. Although both the *Scharnhorst* and *Gneisenau* were damaged during the effort, in company with the *Prinz Eugen* they managed to reach Germany after one of the most audacious operations of the war. England was totally embarrassed. Not since the Spanish Armada in Elizabethan days had an enemy fleet dared to move through the English Channel.

The fleet was now just where Hitler wanted it. It could be easily moved to the "Zone of Destiny," as Hitler called Norway.

One of the main reasons for assembling a strong naval force in Norway was to halt Allied convoys to Russia. When Russia had been attacked by Germany, British Prime Minister Winston Churchill had promised the Russians as much material as possible. In December, with America now in the war, vast shipments of goods began in earnest. In order to move the supplies, a system of arctic convoys was developed. It was the responsibility of the German navy to halt these convoys.

The battle zone was the world's coldest waters, the Barents Sea, an area constantly buffeted by sub-zero winds from the polar ice cap which at times reach hurricane force. These create waves that reach a height of seventy feet and a wind-chill factor of minus one hundred degrees Celsius. Sea spray thrown up by an advancing ship would freeze instantly as it landed on the deck. God help the sailor who fell overboard for the icy waters would kill a human within minutes. Fog is commonplace where the warmer waters of the Gulf Stream meet the arctic cold. In summer, the midnight sun makes battle possible at any time, day or night.

Raeder knew that his prime task was to prevent the Allied convoys from reaching Murmansk, Russia's far northern port. The admiral, however, found himself once again locking horns with his old antagonist, Hermann Goering, over the role of the Luftwaffe in the northern area. Raeder recognized that air reconnaissance was crucial in order to locate the Allied convoys but the Norway air fleet, Luftflotte V, had been severely depleted since June of the previous year. He spent an inordinate amount of time complaining to the Führer about the defects in air reconnaissance, not only for the surface fleet but for the U-boats as well. If only the navy had developed its own air arm as Raeder had wished as far back as the 1930's.

In the autumn of 1941 the shift of the fleet northward began. First the *Lutzow* was dispatched to Trondheim. Unfortunately, en route she was attacked by a flight of R.A.F. bombers and crippled, requiring her return to Germany for repairs. In mid-November Raeder sent five destroyers to the north. He also ordered Doenitz to establish a U-boat patrol to cover the approaches to the Barents Sea and Murmansk.

At the conference of January 12, 1942, during which the Channel Dash was organized, the decision to transfer the *Tirpitz* to Norway was also made. The fact that there had been seven successful convoys to Russia rankled Hitler.

By mid-January the *Tirpitz* was on its way north. In February, after the successful return of the *Scharnhorst, Gneisenau* and *Prinz Eugen,* the latter was sent to Norway along with the *Admiral Scheer.* Unfortunately, on the twenty-third, the heretofore lucky *Prinz Eugen* was torpedoed by the British submarine *Trident*. Despite her damage, the cruiser made it to Ass Fjord where she joined the *Tirpitz* and *Scheer*.

Admiral Tovey, commander in chief of the British home fleet, was certain that the German concentration in the northern waters was a prelude to a sortie in the near future. He therefore recommended that the next two convoys, PQ12 and the returning QP8* be accompanied by the home fleet. Tovey's instincts proved correct. On March 8 a British submarine sighted the *Tirpitz* and three destroyers heading north from their base. Bad weather prevented the fleets from making contact and late on the eighth the *Tirpitz* and her escorts turned for home. The British, monitoring the German wavelength, were apprised of the *Tirpitz*'s move and sent a heavy air attack against the German battleship on the ninth. With her superior speed, the *Tirpitz* zigzagged violently and skillfully and evaded every enemy bomb. By March 13 she was safely back at her berth thus ending her first sortie.

Churchill was disappointed that the British had missed an opportunity to cripple the mighty ship. He said, "No other target is comparable to it."[13] For his part Raeder was relieved that the *Tirpitz* was safe but it had been a close call. More than ever he realized that air protection was essential. Help soon arrived as Luftflotte V was reinforced with bomber units. Raeder designated the British aircraft carriers as the bombers' primary target. But he still wanted more air protection and once again pushed for the completion of Germany's own aircraft carrier, the *Graf Zeppelin*.

On March 21, the *Hipper* was sent to Trondheim.

*PQ was the designation for convoys to Russia, QP for those returning.

Its arrival coincided with the sailing of convoys PQ13 and QP9. PQ13 had the distinction of becoming the first of the arctic convoys to run afoul of the Germans. First an arctic storm hit the convoy on the twenty-fourth, causing it to scatter. The scattered merchant ships were sighted by the Luftwaffe reconnaissance planes which quickly radioed their position. By the twenty-eighth the scattered ships had been hit from the air, on the sea, and from underneath. On April 1 the survivors made it to Murmansk but only after having lost two ships to the Luftwaffe, two to U-boats, and one to German destroyers. The arctic butcher's bill was just beginning to be tallied.

Russia placed heavy demands on the British for additional supplies. On April 8, PQ14 sailed. This convoy made it to Murmansk with the loss of only one ship. As a result Hitler ordered Raeder to give the stopping of Allied convoys top priority. Future convoys would not have it so easy.

PQ15 sailed on April 26, followed two days later by QP11. The Luftwaffe was up in force and sank three of PQ15's twenty-five ships. Though the rest of the merchantmen eventually made it through, the British lost a destroyer.

On May 21, PQ16, with thirty-five ships, sailed. Two days later QP12 left Murmansk. Not only was the Luftwaffe ready, but the *Scheer* and *Lutzow* were out hunting the target. For five days German dive bombers harassed the convoy. The British escorts did their job by keeping the German ships away from the convoy but the Luftwaffe sank six merchantmen. This made the navy even more determined than ever to stop the next convoy. Doenitz was ordered to send more U-boats to the north.

By June, Allied forces were facing danger in both North Africa and Russia. Rommel had captured

Tobruk, Malta appeared about to fall, and the British were retreating toward Suez. In Russia, the German steamroller was ready to launch its summer offensive. To counteract the anticipated German offensive, massive amounts of supplies were required by the Russians. Another arctic convoy was vital. PQ17 had to sail as soon as possible.

By now Raeder was determined to commit the entire High Seas Fleet against the next convoy. Dubbed Operation Rosselsprung (Knight's Move), he divided his forces into two groups, one at Trondheim and the other at Narvik.

The Trondheim group consisted of the *Tirpitz*, *Hipper* and six destroyers. At Narvik were the *Lutzow*, *Admiral Scheer* and six more destroyers. The Luftwaffe was directed to concentrate their attacks on the enemy aircraft carriers while the surface ships dealt with the escorts and merchant ships.

Hitler modified Raeder's plan somewhat by suggesting that the Luftwaffe attack the enemy carriers before the fleet sailed, fearing that enemy planes might cause damage to the surface ships.

Raeder's plan was as follows. Once the Luftwaffe located the convoy, the Narvik group would move to Alten Fjord near North Cape while the Trondheim group moved up to Narvik. Once Hitler was completely satisfied that it was safe for the fleet to sail, both groups would rendezvous one hundred miles north of North Cape where, as one powerful force, they would descend on the hapless convoy.

PQ17 containing thirty-three merchant ships sailed on June 27. It was escorted by six destroyers, four corvettes, four trawlers, two anti-aircraft ships and two submarines. Close cover was provided by the American cruisers *Tuscaloosa* and *Wichita* and the British cruisers *Norfolk* and *London*. A distant cover consisted of the American battleship *Washington* and the British *Duke of York*, the British carrier *Victorious* and the cruisers *Nigeria* and *Cumberland*. PQ17's destination was Archangel, not Murmansk since the latter had been recently damaged during a German air raid.

On July 1 both the Luftwaffe and the U-boats located the convoy. By the fourth the convoy had lost three ships but it continued ploughing ahead toward Archangel, still hopinng for success.

On the evening of July 4, however, with success in sight, the convoy received orders to scatter. Why?

On the second, Raeder had set Rosselsprung into motion. By the following day the Britsh knew that the *Tirpitz* was loose. The very thought of that sent shivers down their spines. Lacking detailed intelligence of the battleship's whereabouts, they feared that the convoy was headed directly toward it. This fear gave way to panic and caused the scatter order to be issued. The scattered ships were easy pickings for the Luftwaffe and U-boats. Ironically, the surface fleet did not have to fire its guns. Instead, its very presence made victory possible. Out of thirty-three ships in PQ17, twenty-three were sunk, ten by U-boats and the rest by the Luftwaffe. Enough weapons to equip an entire army were lost. The Allies had suffered a crushing defeat.

The fear of Hitler's High Seas Fleet had inflicted a major naval disaster on the Allies without the German warships having to fire a shot.[14]

The horrible losses caused the Allies to temporarily suspend the Russian convoys.

Heavy Russian demands eventually pressured the British to attempt another convoy in early September, PQ18. Hoping to benefit from the lessons of PQ17, the Allies intended to make a successful run. This convoy would be the strongest yet. Though it lost thirteen ships, the Germans suffered the loss of forty-one aircraft and four U-boats.

The returning convoy, QP14 was escorted by a carrier. Only two ships were lost out of fifteen. Raeder had his doubts that the Luftwaffe still controlled the air over the Barents Sea so he vetoed the employment of surface ships against this convoy.

Following PQ18's arrival at Archangel, the Allies suspended the Russian convoys once more, but only because every available fighting ship was needed for the first Anglo-American landing on a hostile shore, dubbed Operation Torch, the invasion of Northwest Africa. The arctic convoys would have to wait until escort vessels were again free for duty. This would not be before December.

The German surface fleet's inactivity was galling and stemmed from a number of reasons. High on the list was Hitler's excessive caution and fear of losing another surface ship. The losses of the *Graf Spee* and *Bismarck* had left an indelible imprint on his mind. Fuel shortages also hindered the fleet. Diesel fuel was plentiful but not all the ships were fitted with diesel engines. Nevertheless, Raeder was still desirous, if not obsessed, with the notion that the surface fleet had to prove itself against enemy convoys. He therefore made plans to utilize the ships against the homebound convoys feeling that these would be easier targets. But the suspension of the convoys thwarted these plans and kept the fleet idle.

As Raeder searched vainly for alternative plans, toward the end of the year the Allies reviewed the possibility of resuming the Russian convoys.

On December 15, 1942 the first of a new series of convoys sailed for Murmansk. The PQ designation was discarded and this new convoy used a JW code. In addition, the Allies had decided to split the convoy into two sections numbered JW-51A and JW-51B. Escorting the former would be seven destroyers and five smaller vessels for fifteen merchantmen. After sailing on December 15, it arrived safely in Murmansk on Christmas Day. One week later, JW-51B sailed. It too was protected by destroyers, six of them, and five smaller ships. This convoy was not as lucky as its predecessor. It was sighted by a U-boat almost immediately after sailing. The submarine reported the convoy's position and description. Raeder viewed this as an opportunity to send the *Hipper, Lutzow* and their escorting destroyers in for the kill.

Raeder ordered Admiral Kummetz to initiate Operation Regenbogen (Rainbow), and to destroy the convoy. Kummez's force put to sea at 6:00 p.m. on December 30. His plan called for a pincer move against the lightly escorted convoy. What the Germans did not know was that the convoy was escorted from a distance by the British cruisers *Sheffield* and *Jamaica*.

The weather in the battle area was horrendous. Visibility was so poor that visual sighting was virtually impossible. The respective fleets moved toward each other each unaware of the other's presence. After reaching radar range, one of the British destroyers made the initial contact. After being ordered to investigate the contact by the escort commander, Captain Sherbrooke, the British destroyer found itself under fire from the German destroyers. The time was 9:15 a.m. on December 31. The Battle of the Barents Sea was on.

The British escorting force was comprised of the destroyers *Onslow, Orwell, Obdurate, Obedient* and *Achates*. A sixth ship, *Oribi*, had been delayed in sailing due to engine trouble and never did catch up. The entire force was commanded by Capt. Robert Sherbrooke.

Kummetz commanded the German force from his flagship *Hipper*. When his destroyers opened fire he swung the ship toward the sound of the guns but found the visibility so bad that he could not distinguish friend from foe. Soon afterward he made out a British destroyer advancing toward him. Fearing a torpedo attack he fired several broadsides which fell wide of the mark.

Undaunted, Sherbrooke ordered his destroyers to attack the *Hipper*. The British ships advanced at high speed, swung broadside to simulate a torpedo attack and forced Kummetz to break off his attack and steam away. But Sherbrooke had not fired his torpedoes. Once they were gone, his primary threat against larger ships would be gone with them so he merely threatened the German ships. In addition, Sherbrooke had left the *Achates* behind with orders to make smoke and mask the convoy.

At 9:57 Kummetz decided to turn on his attackers, but two defiant British destroyers barred the way. At 10:20 the *Hipper*'s eight-inch guns fired on the British destroyers, seriously damaging Sherbrooke's flagship, *Onslow*, and injuring the commander himself. Nevertheless, the two destroyers continued to feint at the German force. Then, with victory in sight, Kummetz ordered the *Hipper* to move away from the crippled British force thus throwing away certain victory. The threat of the British torpedoes had preyed on the German admiral's mind and he refused to risk his ship. If the *Hipper* were sunk or heavily damaged, the Führer would be furious.

Meanwhile, on the other side of the convoy, the *Lutzow*, under Captain Stange, and accompanied by three destroyers, began to close on the convoy. Sherbrooke split the force, defying the *Hipper*, and sent two destroyers to the threatened area. Before they could arrive, however, Stange ordered the *Lutzow* to move off because the weather made it difficult to distinguish friend from foe. Stange's caution robbed Operation Regenbogen of its last chance for success.

At 10:45 the *Hipper* decided to vent its wrath on the only enemy ship in sight, the faithful *Achates* who continued to lay a blanket of smoke over the convoy during the entire battle. The *Hipper* reduced the *Achates* to a burning wreck in a short time. But by now the *Sheffield* and *Jamaica* had arrived on the scene.

The two British cruisers fired on the *Hipper*, scoring three hits, flooding a boiler room and reducing her speed. Taken by surprise by the larger caliber shells falling around his flagship, Kummetz moved off immediately for the final time. A few minutes later two German destroyers loomed up out of the gloom and crossed in front of the *Sheffield* and *Jamaica*. The *Sheffield* quickly blew the *Eckholdt* out of the water and drove the other German ship off.

While the *Hipper* was dueling with the British cruisers, Stange had second thoughts about the convoy and maneuvered the *Lutzow* closer for the kill. Just then, with British shells raining down on his flagship, Kummetz signalled all vessels to withdraw. The Battle of the Barents Sea was over. Sherbrooke's four "O" Class destroyers had not fired one torpedo, but the threat of a torpedo attack had added to the German admiral's confusion. The British lost the *Achates*; the Germans suffered damage to the *Hipper* and the loss of the *Eckholdt*.

Although it had lasted only four hours, the confused Battle of the Barents Sea was history.

Licking their wounds, the German ships returned to Alten Fjord. Kummetz blamed the fiasco on the bad weather but this did not explain why the British were able to perform so much better. They had to cope with the same weather. Kummetz's indecision and Stange's inactivity doomed the plan, handing victory to the British.

Hitler was furious. The end of 1942 did not find Germany enjoying the fruits of victory as anticipated. The Sixth Army was trapped at Stalingrad, Rommel was in retreat across Libya and a large Anglo-American force was in Tunisia. On top of this bad news came the poor performance of the surface fleet in the Barents Sea.

On January 6, Raeder had a meeting with Hitler during which the Führer exploded. His mood increased in fury as his monologue droned on. Like a beaten puppy dog, Grand Admiral Raeder simply stood there and took the guff from the crazed dictator. During the monologue Hitler dropped a bomb: "I have made the following decision, and order you forthwith to inform the admiralty that it is my unalterable resolve. The heavy ships are a needless drain on men and materials. They will accordingly be paid off and reduced to scrap. Their guns will be mounted on land for coastal defense."[15]

Hitler continued to rant on. During the harangue Raeder had no chance to deliver his own report. He just stood there motionless. "I considered it beneath my dignity to challenge the details of this completely fabricated story,"[16] he later said.

After all, he knew that the basic reason for the failure of Regenbogen was the restriction imposed on the ships' captains by none other than Hitler himself. His orders that they refrain from exposing themselves to a major risk were incredible. Their very existence could only be justified by deploying them in an aggressive manner. Hitler felt that any loss would be detrimental to Germany's operational policies. Thus they were required to proceed with the utmost caution. They were prohibited from fighting an opponent of equal strength. It was the Führer, after all, who kept tight control over the movement of capital ships. How could a ship go into action with orders to avoid contact if strong enemy forces were anticipated? Throughout Hitler's one-and-a-half hour long tirade, Raeder's thoughts kept returning to Hitler's responsibility for the debacle in the Barents Sea thanks to his order to avoid unnecessary risks. The order placed an undue burden on a captain as he plotted his strategy. There was little doubt that it had restricted Kummetz and Stange on the Barents Sea.

After Hitler's tirade, Raeder asked to see the Führer privately. According to Cajus Becker, Raeder told Hitler he felt "responsible for the navy's reputation, and after all the assertions the Führer had made, now and in the last few days, he no longer felt he was a suitable person to hold the supreme command of this navy."[17]

Hitler attempted to dissuade Raeder from resigning, saying that he had not meant to condemn the entire navy, only the heavy ships. But Raeder felt that the insult had cut too deep. He did ask that the change of command take place on January 30, the tenth anniversary of Hitler's assumption to power. By this he hoped to impress upon the public that he was voluntarily resigning to make way for a younger man.

In the interim Raeder did all in his power to dissuade Hitler from paying off the surface fleet. He and his staff prepared a five thousand word memorandum emphasizing the deterrent effect on the Allies that retention of the capital ships would have.

In part, it said:

> The scrapping of our surface ships would raise a
> shout of jubilation from the enemy and bring
> great disillusionment to the Axis powers,
> particularly the Japanese. It would indicate both
> weakness and a failure to understand the over-
> whelming importance of naval warfare above all
> in the approaching final phase of the war.[18]

Scrapping the ships, the memorandum went on to say,
would give the Allies a victory without effort.

These arguments fell on deaf ears. Hitler was
determined to scrap the big ships and reassign the
crews to either U-boats or coastal defense batteries.

Raeder proposed two candidates as his successor,
Admiral Carls or Admiral Doenitz, head of the U-boat
force. Hitler accepted Doenitz who became
commander in chief on January 30. Eventually,
Doenitz was able to convince Hitler of the folly of
completely scrapping the surface ships and, for the
most part, they were given a reprieve.

Raeder was given the honorary position of inspector
general of the navy where his services were never
called on again except for a few ceremonial functions.
In August, 1943 he attended the funeral of King Boris
of Bulgaria. But other than a few mere state
ceremonies, he stood helplessly by and watched the
war turn from bad to worse.

In May, 1945 Raeder was captured by the Russians.
He and his wife were confined in a villa near Moscow
where their treatment was most proper.

In the fall of 1945 Raeder was brought to
Nuremberg to stand trial as a war criminal. There
were many charges leveled against him. Among these
was the accusation that he instigated Japanese

aggression by urging Hitler to induce the Japanese to seize Singapore from the British as part of an overall plan to bring the British commonwealth to their knees. The primary charge against Raeder, however, was that of war crimes, the so-called Commando Order, and the use of unrestricted submarine warfare. The latter charge was dropped after the written testimony of Admiral Nimitz and the British admiralty admitted that their own submarines also had orders to sink any ship on sight, without regard to visit and search. Nimitz further testified that it was not the practice of American submarines to rescue survivors if such an act constituted undue hazard to the submarine. The Commando Order, however, was another matter.

The Commando Order was issued by Hitler on October 18, 1942, two months after the British attack on Dieppe. This order was designed to discourage such raids in the future by giving the German military the authority to treat sabotage and terror units as bandits. Actually, it was in reaction to orders taken from British commandos who had participated in the raid on Dieppe. The orders issued to the British commandos were brutal.

> Your value to the war effort as a live and effective killer is great. . . . The only way to achieve this is never to give the enemy a chance. . . . Remember you are not a wrestler trying to render your enemy helpless, you have to kill. And remember you are out to kill. . . . While he is doubled up in pain get him on the ground and stamp his head in.[19]

Raeder's guilt in this matter was his forwarding of the infamous order giving a license to murder anyone accused of being a saboteur. At his trial Raeder testified that he considered the Commando Order just reprisal for the British order.

Although defended by a brilliant Hamburg lawyer, Walter Siemens, Raeder was nevertheless sentenced to life imprisonment. When he heard the verdict the admiral implored the tribunal to change it to death by firing squad.

Following his conviction Raeder's head was shaved and he was sent to Spandau Prison in Berlin to join the other German war criminals. His wife, who had committed no crime whatsoever, was retained under arrest by the Russians until September, 1949. In March, 1950 the couple was allowed to see each other for the first time since 1945 but were allowed only fifteen minutes together.

Life in prison was harsh, particularly when it was the Russians' turn to stand guard.* Raeder was forbidden to talk to the other prisoners and was allowed to write only one letter a month to his family. He was not even allowed to attend funeral services for his only son.

At the age of eighty, to his immense surprise, Admiral Raeder was paroled thanks to the untiring efforts of his lawyer, Siemens. He lived long enough to write his memoirs and, along with Doenitz, he attended a ceremony in Wilhelmshaven marking the dedication of the Naval War Memorial. Admiral Raeder passed away in 1960.

Grand Admiral Raeder was neither martinet nor toady to Hitler's will. He was a German patriot, a man who probably would have been more at home in Imperial Germany than the Third Reich. He never

---

*The Americans, British, French and Russians rotated guard duty.

did accept the Nazi doctrine and in fact managed to retain church services as part of naval life even though he was highly criticized by certain party members for his convictions. A little known fact was that Raeder had helped many Jews to escape the horror of the holocaust.

Raeder's great fault was his naïvete. He believed Hitler's statements that there would be no war. As a result the admiral prepared the "Z" Plan, a plan that needed time above all to be successful. Unfortunately, Raeder was not allowed the time to build his balanced navy. Furthermore, Raeder never really had the ear of Hitler. Because of this he was unable to save the big ships in January, 1943. His successor, who did have Hitler's ear, was able to accomplish what Raeder could not.

However, Raeder did lead the German navy for fifteen years, 1928 to 1943, and will forever be remembered for this feat, if nothing else.

2. CAPTAIN HANS LANGSDORFF

Following Germany's defeat in World War I, the victorious Allies imposed unusually harsh restrictions on the defeated nation under the guise of a fancy sounding name: the Treaty of Versailles. Among other items, the treaty severely restricted the size of Germany's armed forces. The navy was denied submarines, the number of ships was minimal and those that were allowed were restricted in size and armament. Consequently, the German navy faced a rebuilding job with one hand tied behind its back.

Fortunately, a handful of forward-minded officers refused to throw in the towel. If the Treaty of Versailles would not allow an adequate number of ships, those vessels that were approved would have to make up in quality what they lacked in quantity. These same officers were not averse to violating the terms of the treaty by falsifying records regarding the tonnage of surface ships or building a small U-boat arm and training crews in foreign countries.

Perhaps the most dramatic example of the attempt to circumvent the terms of Versailles were the so-called pocket battleships. Brilliantly designed utilizing the very latest shipbuilding technology, the pocket battleships were actually nothing but oversized heavy cruisers. The Naval Disarmament Conference of 1928 limited the size of heavy cruisers to ten thousand tons and a main armament of eight inches.

That same year the first of the Deutschland Class cruisers was laid down. The German naval high command had no intention of honoring the ten thousand ton-eight inch guidelines.* The Deutschlands were three in number. The first, named for the Fatherland, gave its name to the entire class and was launched in 1931. The second, named for Adm. Reinhard Scheer, one of Germany's finest commanders in World War I and commander of the battle cruisers at the Battle of Jutland, was launched in 1933. The following year saw the launching of the final ship of the class, the *Admiral Graf Spee*, in honor of World War I Adm. Maxmillian Graf von Spee who, after a brilliant victory over the British at Coronel, lost his life when his small fleet was overwhelmed at the Battle of the Falklands.

The Deutschlands were impressive ships indeed. Mounting six eleven-inch guns each, their designed speed was twenty-six knots, a relatively high speed for heavy ships of the day. Only the *Deutschland*† failed to exceed 12,000 tons, weighing in at 11,700 tons, 400 tons lighter than her sisters.

In addition to the emphasis on speed and armament, the German ships included another feature vital to the plans for their ultimate

*For additional treaty violations see Raeder, chapter one.

†Hitler later changed the name to *Lutzow* for fear that a ship named for Germany would be sunk.

deployment. Their radius of operation before requiring fuel was a truly whopping nineteen-thousand miles, far in excess of their contemporaries in other navies. In theory, those enemy ships that could not be outgunned by the Deutschlands could be outrun. At the time there were but five ships in the navies of Germany's potential enemies that could match the pocket battleships. England had the battle cruisers *Renown, Repulse* and *Hood*; the French the modern battleships *Straasbourg* and *Dunkerque*. These five alone had the capability to both outrun and outgun the pocket battleships, but they lacked the German range.

To their consternation, the British did not realize until it was too late just how swift and powerful Germany's new cruisers were. As for their range, this was a feature that German ship designers considered one of the most vital factors. Thanks to years of being unable to compete on an even keel with the British ability to construct a large and balanced fleet, Germany had become masters of Kreuzerkrieg, i.e. cruiser warfare. Simply put, Kreuzerkrieg was the tactic of sending lone raiders out into the oceans of the world to prey on enemy merchant shipping. For the most part the Germans utilized disguised merchant ships converted to auxiliary cruisers via the addition of medium-caliber guns skillfully hidden on the deck. However, frequently the German navy dispatched warships to act as raiders. During World War I the cruiser *Emden* made a remarkable record in the Pacific. Other warships, including those of von Spee's squadron, roamed the oceans of the world sinking enemy merchant ships and wreaking havoc by completely disrupting shipping lanes. Consequently, when a German ship was designed, its potential operational range was one of the factors taken into consideration. During World War II the contradiction to this was Germany's Hipper Class cruisers* whose range was extremely limited.

During the Spanish Civil War, all three Deutschlands spent a period of time on the intervention patrol. There they made an impression on the British with their graceful lines and heavy armament. However, the full potential of these ships remained a closely guarded secret. To their dismay, it was only after WWII began that the British were able to realize the full extent of the menace posed by Germany's latest class of cruisers.

Being the newest ship of the class, the *Graf Spee* was chosen to be Germany's representative at the Spithead Review in May, 1937. This gala was in honor of the coronation of George VI as king of England. From there, the ship returned home and spent the next two years exercising in the Baltic and off Norway.

At the beginning of 1939, the *Graf Spee*'s first commander, Captain Patzig, was relieved by Capt. Hans Langsdorff. The new captain had come up through the ranks of the German navy. As a young junior officer in the Imperial Navy of the kaiser, Langsdorff had seen action in World War I. The between-war period was spent alternating between sea duty aboard destroyers and cruisers and frequent intervals of shore duty in a series of staff assignments. Command of one of the pocket battleships, particularly the latest one, marked Langsdorff as an officer on the rise. With such a choice command it would not be long before he attained flag rank. Admiral Raeder, commander in chief of the German navy, thought highly of Langsdorff and was watching

Hipper, Prinz Eugen and *Blucher*.

his career closely with an eye for bigger and better things.

During the summer of 1939, the *Graf Spee* sat idle at Wilhelmshaven while her crew was busily engaged overhauling the ship's machinery, hauling supplies aboard, and manhandling shells for the ship's guns and storing them in the magazines. The hard work was broken sporadically by brief forays into the Baltic to conduct gunnery and maneuvering exercises. This activity gave birth to a multitude of rumors amongst the crew: There would most certainly be war against England; The ship was preparing for a round-the-world flag-showing cruise. Captain Langsdorff did nothing to refute the numerous rumors. He was already privy to the secret orders regarding his ship's mission. He alone knew the *Spee*'s destination and was under strict orders not to share the contents of his orders until the ship was well out to sea where there was no chance of the secret being revealed.

On August 3, 1939, a German tanker slipped her berth and set a course towards the Iceland-Faroes Passage. This relatively routine event went virtually unnoticed as merchant ships arrived and departed the busy port almost daily. But Captain Dau of the *Altmark* had secret orders as well.

On August 19, all shore leave for the *Spee*'s crew was abruptly cancelled and all hands were recalled to the ship. In the early morning hours of the twenty-first, the ship's anchor rattled aboard and the *Graf Spee* left Wilhelmshaven behind.

There were three potential routes to the Atlantic for German ships leaving base. The first, between the Faroe and Shetland Islands was in close proximity to the British naval base at Scapa Flow. To avoid curious patrolling British ships, German captains almost always shunned this route. The northernmost route to the Atlantic was the Denmark Strait between Greenland and Iceland. Fog-shrouded and often buffeted by storms and littered with floating ice, this route, although perilous, served the German navy well. However, since Germany and the Western nations were still nominally at peace, Langsdorff chose the third route into the Atlantic. This was the Iceland-Faroes Passage.

Three days after sailing, the *Graf Spee* moved through this passage and entered the broad expanse of the Atlantic Ocean. Unbeknownst to her crew, while they were in the heart of the passage the *Spee*'s sister ship, *Deutschland,* hauled in her anchor and in company with the tanker *Westerwald* headed for the Denmark Strait. The naval high command was not anxious to keep the sailing of the *Spee* a total secret. In fact, it might serve their plans better if she were sighted in the Iceland-Faroes Passage. They were, however, extremely anxious to keep the *Deutschland*'s passage into the Atlantic a secret. Thus the selection of the Denmark Strait for the latter's route.

Langsdorff's orders called for him to take the *Graf Spee* to the South Atlantic, avoid contact with strange ships, and await further orders. Hitler's intentions were no secret to naval command nor for that matter Langsdorff. He knew that war was imminent and that it would be simply a matter of time before the *Graf Spee* received instructions to commence hostilities.

Once in the Atlantic, Langsdorff, in keeping with his orders, set a course almost due south. By the twenty-eighth the *Graf Spee* was northwest of the Azores. That day the crew sighted a ship on the horizon making directly for them. Shortly thereafter, the two ships were side by side and the tanker that had left Wilhelmshaven two weeks prior to the *Graf Spee* hove to. Langsdorff ordered his own ship to stop.

Almost immediately fuel hoses were stretched between the two ships and the *Altmark* began to pump the precious oil into the *Spee*'s fuel bunkers.

The refueling operation over, the two ships parted company temporarily and Langsdorff made off into the Atlantic.

On September 1, Germany invaded Poland and plunged the world into World War II. Two days later Britain and France honored their commitment to Poland and declared war on Germany. Langsdorff learned that Germany was at war when the *Spee* intercepted a transmission from the British admiralty ordering its ships to commence hostilities against Germany. Far out in the Atlantic, the captains of the *Graf Spee* and the *Deutschland* eagerly awaited permission to initiate action of their own. They waited in vain.

Hitler, in hopes that peace with the Allies was still a possibility, refused to antagonize them further by making war against their merchant ships. Despite Raeder's pleas, Hitler refused to waver.

Day after day the *Graf Spee*, in company with the *Altmark*, made for its predetermined patrol area as Langsdorff paced the deck impatiently awaiting the word that would unleash his ship. How long could he remain hidden without being sighted? he mused. On September 11 the *Graf Spee* had a narrow escape in this respect. While refueling from the *Altmark*, the ship's Arado seaplane which Langsdorff had sent aloft on a routine patrol, sighted the British cruiser *Cumberland* steaming peacefully along some miles away. Fortunately, the British were not expecting to find a German warship in those waters and the *Graf Spee* avoided detection.

On the thirteenth, the *Graf Spee* reached her patrol area in mid-Atlantic between the African coast and

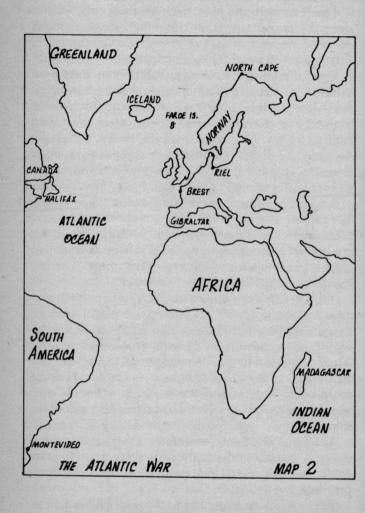

THE ATLANTIC WAR

MAP 2

Pernambuco on the easternmost tip of South America. There the ship steamed back and forth for a week while Langsdorff impatiently awaited further orders. On the twentieth the *Spee* refuelled from the *Altmark* once more. After the two ships parted, Langsdorff resumed the tedious task of steaming back and forth, taking care to avoid detection.

On the evening of the twenty-fifth, the *Graf Spee* received a signal giving the disposition of British warships in the South Atlantic. Langsdorff was amused that Berlin had taken such pains to keep him informed. For the previous two weeks his own radio operators had been monitoring the transmissions of British ships and Langsdorff's information was more current than that of the desk jockeys in Berlin.

September 26 was the fateful day. At midmorning Langsdorff was handed an urgent signal from Naval Headquarters: "Commence active participation in the trade war."[1] At last the *Spee* and *Deutschland* had their hands untied. Immediately after noon, Langsdorff informed Captain Dau of the *Altmark* that the *Graf Spee* would now operate on its own and scheduled another refuelling operation for October 14 at a predetermined area even though the ship had the ability to operate for six weeks without refuelling. Then Langsdorff set a course for the area of Pernambuco, Brazil. From there, he planned to move south along the coast of South America where there was a good likelihood of intercepting British merchant shipping.

As soon as the *Spee* was well under way, Langsdorff donned his dress uniform and ordered as many men as could be spared to assemble on deck. He then proceeded to announce that it was the ship's objective to seize or sink as many enemy ships as possible. The announcement was met with a resounding cheer.

Langsdorff knew that sinking ships was not his only objective. He intended to cause as much confusion as possible. He therefore ordered the name *Graf Spee* painted over and replaced by the name *Admiral Scheer*. At the same time he had the ship's name removed from the cap bands of the crew and also replaced with the *Scheer*'s name.

On the last day of September the *Graf Spee* a/k/a *Admiral Scheer* recorded her first success. Around 1:00 p.m. a steamship was sighted on the horizon. Langsdorff ordered the *Spee*'s plane launched to confirm and identify the sighting. A few minutes later the Arado fired on the S.S. *Clement*.

At first the officers of the *Clement* thought that the approaching warship was the British cruiser *Ajax* as the latter was known to be operating in the area. Only when the Arado began firing did Captain Harris order his ship to send the R-R-R signal.* A few minutes later Harris ordered his crew to abandon ship. The unhappy merchant captain and his chief engineer were taken aboard the *Graf Spee* where they were greeted courteously by Langsdorff. "I am sorry, Captain, I will have to sink your ship. It is war."²

After a futile attempt to sink the *Clement* by scuttling and torpedoes, Langsdorff ordered the ship's guns to open up. At approximately 3:30 the *Clement* became the first of the *Graf Spee*'s victims to plunge to the bottom of the sea.

Langsdorff turned south once more. His guests were given a meal, and a razor with which to shave. Langsdorff then sent a signal to Pernambuco asking that the *Clement*'s lifeboats containing the balance of

---

*When a ship was attacked by a surface raider it used the distress signal R-R-R for raider. S-S-S was the universal signal for those ships under attack by a submarine.

her crew be picked up. He did not, however, sign the transmission with his ship's name. Less than three hours later a Greek freighter was stopped by the *Spee*. Captain Harris and his engineer were transferred after Langsdorff had exacted a promise from the Greek captain that he would not use his wireless until he was at least six hundred miles removed from his present position. The promise was kept but when the Greek ship did radio a report of the incident, it was to announce an encounter with the German warship *Admiral Scheer*.

The following day the *Clement*'s lifeboats were picked up and word was out that the *Admiral Scheer* was loose in the South Atlantic. As yet, the *Deutschland* had failed to make contact with an enemy ship, so the British admiralty labored under the impression that only one raider was at large and began to form their hunter groups accordingly. Force F, the cruisers *Berwick* and *York*; Force G, *Cumberland* and *Exeter*; Force H, *Sussex* and *Shropshire*; Force I, *Cornwall* and *Dorsetshire* and the carrier *Eagle*; Force K, *Renown, Ark Royal* and destroyers; Force L, *Dunkerque* and the carrier *Bearn*; Force N, *Straasbourg* and the carrier *Hermes*. Additional battleships and cruisers were hastily dispatched from England to escort convoys, thereby weakening the home fleet. Forces G, H, and K were directly under the command of Admiral Lyon, commander in chief, South Atlantic. By sinking only one ship, Langsdorff had caused a disruption of the entire Allied navy.

Following the sinking of the *Clement* and the stopping of the Greek *Papolagos* further south, Langsdorff moved east, away from where he had last been reported.

It was four days before Langsdorff registered his

next success. Around 6:30 a.m. on October 4, between Ascension Island and St. Helena, the *Spee*'s lookouts sighted smoke. Langsdorff ordered an intercepting course. At the same time he had the French tricolor run up the mast. A short while later the *Spee* approached her next victim head-on to reduce her silhouette. When he was within eighteen hundred yards, Langsdorff swung his ship broadside, lowered the French flag and ran up the German ensign. At the same time the luckless merchant ship was ordered to stop and not to use her wireless or the *Spee* would open fire. The captain of the *Newton Beech* complied at once.

When the *Spee*'s boarding party climbed aboard the *Newton Beech* they found that she was loaded with a cargo of corn for England. This time, however, Langsdorff decided to keep the merchant ship in company with the *Spee* temporarily. The *Newton Beech* would make an excellent accommodation for future prisoners, accommodations that were severely lacking aboard the *Graf Spee*.

At dawn on the sixth, Langsdorff ordered the Arado launched to search new prey. Unfortunately, after covering a wide area, the plane returned and reported that nothing was in sight. Undaunted, Langsdorff continued to head his ship towards the Gulf of Guinea. The next morning, the captain's breakfast was interrupted by word that smoke had been sighted.

A few hours later the familiar signal, "Do not transmit or we will open fire," was received by the *Ashlea*. The ship's commander, Captain Pattinger, described the incident this way:

I went on the bridge and saw a man-of-war coming towards us on our starboard bow. She seemed to be coming from the direction of the Cameroons. Her fighting top gave me the impression she was either the *Dunkerque* or *Straasbourg* so I carried on.[3]

This fatal error in identification cost Captain Pattinger his ship with its cargo of sugar. After ordering the *Ashlea*'s crew transferred to the *Newton Beech*, Langsdorff ordered the merchant ship sunk.

Following this incident Langsdorff reversed course and headed northwest. The next day he was forced to face the inevitable. The need to sail at a reduced speed so that the *Newton Beech* could maintain pace was simply too dangerous. Accordingly, despite the lack of space aboard his own ship, Langsdorff ordered all prisoners transferred. Once this was accomplished, the *Newton Beech* was scuttled.

For the next two days the *Graf Spee* continued to search for victims. In the late afternoon of the tenth, smoke was again sighted. Once more Langsdorff approached the target bows-on, making identification difficult at best. A short time later the *Graf Spee* and the S.S. *Huntsman* lay hove to. The *Huntsman* was rather large for a merchant ship and carried a crew of eighty-eight. There was simply no way the *Spee* could add that many prisoners to the crews of the *Ashlea* and *Newton Beech*. Langsdorff decided to make the *Huntsman* a prize.

After the capture of the *Huntsman*, Langsdorff attempted a ruse. Confident that the *Clement*'s lifeboats had been found and her captain safely landed, it was a foregone conclusion that the British were aware of the presence of a raider in the South Atlantic. Langsdorff therefore had one of the *Spee*'s radio operators make the S-S-S distress signal using the *Huntsman*'s radio. In this way Langsdorff hoped that when the *Huntsman* was found to be overdue at her destination, the enemy would assume she had been sunk by a submarine. Then the *Huntsman* was dispatched to a preselected rendezvous point under a prize crew while the *Graf Spee* set off for a midocean meeting with the *Altmark*.

Captain Dau had much to report. The day preceding the capture of the *Huntsman*, the *Altmark* had been sighted by a scout plane from the *Ark Royal*. Fortunately, the British plane had apparently been deceived by the fact that the *Altmark* was disguised as the Norwegian freighter *Songe*. As a result, Dau's ship had been allowed to proceed unmolested.

There was also news of the *Deutschland*. The *Graf Spee*'s sister had made her first score. Unfortunately, the ship happened to be the American *City of Flint*. The U.S. ship was allowed to proceed to the Russian port of Murmansk but reported her encounter with the German ship as soon as her captain was certain he was out of range of the *Deutschland*. Although the incident might have been disastrous for German plans, in fact it proved to be just the opposite.

Still under the impression that only one German raider was loose, the British were thrown into a state of confusion because they were concentrating their search in the South Atlantic. Then came word of a raider astride the West Indies-England trade route. Additional warships were ordered to join the hunt, but the force was diluted when Raeder sent the *Gneisenau* and *Koln* on a feint into Norwegian waters. The British were thus obliged to keep the home fleet in a state of readiness in the event the latter ships attempted to break into the Atlantic.

On the sixteenth, the *Graf Spee* and *Altmark* rendezvoused with the *Huntsman*. Langsdorff had already made up his mind that the freighter was a luxury he could not afford. The prisoners aboard the *Huntsman* were transferred to the *Altmark* and the British ship was sent to the bottom of the sea.

Langsdorff parted company with the *Altmark* and took his ship to explore a new hunting ground. Although he continued to concentrate on the Capetown-Freetown trade route, the *Spee*'s captain decided to search the area south of St. Helena.

On the twenty-second, the new hunting ground paid its first dividend. The freighter *Trevanion* was sighted by the *Graf Spee*'s scout plane. Langsdorff was a strong proponent of using this new method to locate potential victims and the tactic reaped huge rewards.

About three hours after the initial sighting the *Graf Spee* overhauled the unsuspecting steamer. The ship turned out to be the *Trevanion,* bound for England with a cargo of concentrates. Despite being ordered to stop, the *Trevanion* began transmitting R-R-R. Langsdorff ordered the *Graf Spee*'s machine guns to rake the bridge of the helpless victim. Fortunately, no one was injured but the *Spee*'s action convinced the *Trevanion*'s captain to cease transmitting. After transferring the *Trevanion*'s crew to the *Spee,* Langsdorff set off once more in pursuit of game. Thus far, even though he had an impressive string of kills, they had been bloodless victories. Not one enemy life was lost as a result of Langsdorff's actions.

Another week passed without a sighting. During that time the *Graf Spee*'s wireless operators intercepted signals indicating a great deal of British activity. The search for the German raider was intensifying. At the same time the British reduced the Capetown-Freetown shipping traffic. As a result, the *Graf Spee* was unable to locate any more victims. However, Langsdorff had already settled on another hunting ground. First, though, another rendezvous with the *Altmark* was called for.

On the twenty-ninth the *Graf Spee* topped off her bunkers before heading for her newest patrol area. Langsdorff had decided to sow the seeds of confusion in the Indian Ocean. After scheduling another rendezvous with Dau, the *Altmark* and *Graf Spee* parted company again.

Just as the British were beginning to get wise to the fact that there were in fact two raiders operating in the Atlantic, the number was reduced to one. Fearing harm to a ship bearing the name *Deutschland,* Hitler ordered that ship recalled to Germany where she was rechristened *Lutzow.* The *Deutschland*'s return home via the Denmark Strait went undetected by the British who continued to search for both raiders. Now Langsdorff was ready to stir the kettle even more. Unbeknown to the British, the Atlantic was about to be devoid of raiders. Instead, there would soon be every reason to believe that a third raider had made an appearance, thanks to Langsdorff.

After a two-day journey through the "Roarin' Forties," south of the Cape of Good Hope, the *Graf Spee* burst into the warm waters of the Indian Ocean on November 3, Langsdorff intended to patrol the area of the Mozambique Channel between Madagascar and the African mainland. Unfortunately, shipping in this area was sparse and it was twelve days before the *Graf Spee* sighted a potential victim.

At midmorning on the fifteenth, the freighter *Africa Shell* was ordered to halt by what the freighter's captain thought to be a French man-of-war. Once he realized his mistake, Captain Dove ordered his ship to run for it. A warning shot from the *Graf Spee* quickly made Dove realize the futility of the situation. The *Africa Shell* engines were ordered to stop.

While the *Africa Shell*'s lifeboats made off toward shore at Langsdorff's suggestion, Captain Dove was taken aboard the German ship. Langsdorff had already decided to return to the Atlantic and knew that his presence would be reported when the latest victim's lifeboats reached shore. That would be sufficient to confuse the enemy by alerting them to the presence of a German warship in the Indian Ocean. Another determining factor in Langsdorff's desire to return to the Atlantic was the slim pickings in the Indian Ocean.

The *Graf Spee* turned south on her tracks. On the seventeenth, with the captain on the bridge, the *Graf Spee* plunged into the Roarin' Forties. Three days later she was back on the prowl in the South Atlantic.

In Berlin, Admiral Raeder continued to apply pressure on the British. The day after the *Graf Spee* returned to the South Atlantic, the battle cruisers *Scharnhorst* and *Gneisenau* sailed from Wilhelms- haven. Two days later they encountered the armed merchant cruiser *Rawalpindi* in the Iceland-Faroes passage. The two German warships made short work of the outmanned *Rawalpindi* and made off toward Norway. The British were therefore required to stretch their fleet resources to the limit to ensure that the *Scharnhorst* and *Gneisenau* did not make an attempt to break out into the Atlantic to join the undetermined amount of raiders already there. Once more, Atlantic shipping was disrupted.

Meanwhile, on the twenty-seventh, the *Graf Spee* began refuelling from the *Altmark* once more. Because of the warships' success and the *Altmark*'s ability to avoid detection, confidence among both crews was at a peak and spirits were running high.

While the *Graf Spee* was topping off her fuel bunkers and transferring supplies, the British were tightening the noose around Langsdorff and his ship. The *Cumberland* and *Exeter* were at the Falklands. The *Ajax*, flagship of Commodore Henry Harwood, was patrolling near the River Plate. Off Rio de Janeiro was the New Zealand cruiser *Achilles*. These four ships comprised Force G. Force H (*Shropshire* and *Sussex*) was guarding the area around the Cape of Good Hope. Near Pernambuco was the most powerful enemy force in the area, Force K, made up of the *Renown* and *Ark Royal*.

Langsdorff now decided to disguise the *Graf Spee*. A dummy wooden funnel was added to make it appear that the ship had two funnels. A fake plywood turret was added forward in the style of British cruisers. After a fresh coat of paint was applied, from a distance the *Graf Spee* could be easily mistaken for the *Renown*. Captain Dove of the *Africa Shell* was fortunate enough to have the run of the ship, he and Langsdorff having developed a mutual trust. Dove passed the long days observing the *Graf Spee*'s crew at work. At the same time, Langsdorff was unusually generous with information and made it a point to explain most of his actions to his captive. It was one of the ironies of war that although Dove and Langsdorff were technically enemies, they thoroughly enjoyed each other's company.

On the twenty-ninth, the *Graf Spee* and *Altmark* parted company again. Langsdorff did not have to wait long for his next success. A few minutes after noon on December 2, smoke was sighted on the horizon. Despite the knowledge that British warships were probably in the area, Langsdorff decided to investigate. Ninety minutes later the *Graf Spee* fired a shot across the bows of another merchant ship. Langsdorff ordered the signal sent demanding that the victim not use her wireless. But the captain of the

Doric Star ignored the warning. Using a wireless set salvaged from the *Newton Beech*, the German radio operators attempted to jam the *Doric Star*'s R-R-R but could not be certain that they had succeeded.

The *Doric Star* was Langsdorff's largest prize to date. A ship of over ten thousand tons, she was making her way to England from New Zealand with a cargo of meat. Langsdorff considered taking the ship as a prize but the latter's crew had already sabotaged her engines. Undaunted, Langsdorff ordered the ship scuttled.

Unfortunately, the *Spee*'s radio operators' efforts to jam the *Doric Star*'s transmissions had failed. The British station at Simonstown picked up the transmission. A signal was quickly sent to all British naval units in the South Atlantic informing them of the *Doric Star*'s latest position and that she had been attacked by a raider.

The *Spee*'s wireless operators were able to intercept the signal from Simonstown. Accordingly, Langsdorff set off at high speed away from the area. Around the same time, the steamer *Taiora*, having monitored the *Doric Star*'s transmission, had altered course away from the area of the latter's demise. Her new course took the steamer right across the path of the *Graf Spee*. As a result, just after dawn the following morning, the *Taiora* met up with the pocket battleship.

Half an hour after the sighting, Langsdorff ordered the merchant ship to stop and not to use her wireless. However, although the *Taiora* began to reduce speed, she began transmitting a distress signal. Langsdorff ordered the *Spee*'s secondary armament to open fire. The *Taiora*'s bridge was heavily damaged and she appeared to have ceased transmitting. But as soon as Langsdorff ordered a cease fire, the *Taiora* began transmitting again. Once more the *Graf Spee*'s guns roared. This time the *Taiora*'s radio cabin was destroyed and all wireless activity ceased abruptly. Three of the *Taiora*'s crewmen had been wounded during the firing, the first three casualties inflicted by Langsdorff's ship. Fortunately, all three wounded seamen survived.

As the wounded seamen lay in the *Graf Spee*'s sick bay having their wounds attended to, Langsdorff strode through the door. He had come to apologize for having wounded the three men. "We do not make war on civilians," he said, "but you use your telefunken (radio), so I have to open fire."[4]

After the *Taiora* was sunk by one of the *Spee*'s torpedoes, Langsdorff set out for another rendezvous with the *Altmark*. Once he had refuelled, Langsdorff planned to try his hand at the shipping lanes off the River Plate, the main route between South America and Europe. Langsdorff felt that, with luck, he could find a number of easy victims in that area. After that, he planned to make for the southern end of the Capetown-Freetown route where he intended to deliberately make his presence known even if it meant stopping a neutral ship. In this way he hoped to deceive the British into thinking that the *Graf Spee* was headed for the Indian Ocean once more. But Langsdorff had no intention of rounding the cape again. Instead, after setting off the alarm, he would head straight for Germany and home.

On November 6, the *Altmark* and *Graf Spee* sat side-by-side for the final time. The prisoners from the *Graf Spee*'s latest series of victims were transferred to Dau's tanker. However, in a reversal of his earlier stand against having prisoners on board his own ship, Langsdorff directed Dau to transfer the captains and other key officers of the sunken British ships back to the *Graf Spee*. They would return to Germany on the warship while their crews faced a hellish voyage in the holds of the *Altmark*.

While the refuelling operation and transfer proceeded, the crews of both ships swapped the latest gossip and rumors. Not one of them ever dreamed that this would be their final meeting or that the successful hunting team would shortly be broken up by the loss of one of them.

The two ships parted company the next day. Soon afterward, the *Graf Spee*'s lookouts sighted victim number nine. The *Streonshalh* was a relatively small freighter bound for England with a cargo of wheat. By this time the warship's crew had the routine down to a science. The usual signals were sent: Halt and Do not use your wireless. The captain of the *Streonshalh* complied almost at once. Following the traditional thorough search of the victim for anything of value and the transfer of her crew to the *Graf Spee,* the freighter was sunk. Langsdorff resumed course for the River Plate.

While Langsdorff took his ship in search of new victims, Commodore Harwood was in the process of consolidating his forces. The commodore knew that the River Plate area was an inviting target for German raiders and suspected that Langsdorff would eventually yield to temptation and try his hand in that area. Because the *Graf Spee* a/k/a *Admiral Scheer* a/k/a *Deutschland* had been reported in most of the other heavily travelled shipping lanes, the timing was probably right for an appearance off the River Plate. Accordingly, Harwood ordered the *Exeter* and *Achilles* to rendezvous with his flagship (*Ajax*) in that precise area. Harwood's instincts proved right.

By December 12, the small British fleet was assembled and waiting. Harwood planned to patrol a wide area to the east of the River Plate. He met with the captains of his three ships, Bell of *Exeter*, Parry of *Achilles* and Woodhouse of *Ajax*, and outlined his plan of action. If the enemy were sighted, the *Ajax* and *Achilles* with their six-inch guns would operate as a team while the *Exeter*, mounting eight-inch guns, engaged the enemy independently from another angle. All Harwood needed now was for Langsdorff to put in an appearance. The British commander's wish was fulfilled even sooner than he dared hoped.

Langsdorff was a tired man. Almost four months at sea had taken its toll. Thousands of miles from home, alone in waters swarming with enemy ships, the need to be constantly on the alert, the fate of his country's proudest warship and its crew resting directly on his most minute decision—all had exacted a tremendous price. Captain Dove of the *Africa Shell* suspected that Langsdorff's nerves were stretched taut just by observing his actions. Nevertheless, Langsdorff masked his tension admirably.

An hour before dawn on the thirteenth, the *Graf Spee*'s radar began to register a contact. Langsdorff immediately passed the order to make directly for the target. Almost an hour passed before the ship's lookouts sighted masts on the horizon. In another ten minutes the silhouette of a ship began to take shape. Langsdorff seemed unconcerned when the sighting confirmed the ship ahead to be H.M.S. *Exeter*.

Once the target was confirmed as a warship, the *Spee*'s officers asked their captain what his intentions were. Langsdorff replied that he was prepared to fight. At that moment he thought the *Exeter* might be escorting a convoy of merchantmen. Langsdorff knew the British cruiser was no match for the *Graf Spee*; the German's superior speed could be used to avoid contact with the *Exeter* while, at the same time, the longer range of the *Spee*'s guns could be utilized to full advantage. In any event, alone the *Exeter* posed little threat to the *Graf Spee*. Anxious to get at the convoy, Langsdorff pressed on.

Shortly afterward, two other warships were sighted steaming in line with the *Exeter*. At first it was thought that the two new sightings were destroyers either in company with the *Exeter* or part of a convoy escort. As the ships began to take on a more distinct silhouette, however, it was confirmed that they were light cruisers.

Langsdorff now found himself in the teeth of a dilemma. He could engage the enemy ships or run. If he chose the latter, he could not hope to outrun the *Ajax* and *Achilles* who were capable of superior speed. The two light cruisers could follow his every move and report them until heavier units of the British fleet could be brought into action. Then, too, there was always the possibility that the enemy might score a lucky hit.

Langsdorff's other option was to fight it out in hopes that he could inflict enough damage on the enemy warships to slow them down and prevent them from shadowing him. The *Graf Spee* could again lose itself in the broad expanse of the Atlantic. The *Graf Spee*'s secondary armament was almost equal in size to the main armament of the *Ajax* and *Achilles,* and its eleven-inch guns far outweighed the main battery of the *Exeter*. Langsdorff knew that he could not hope to reach Germany through the North Atlantic and Denmark Strait with a pair of enemy cruisers constantly reporting his position. The route home would be swarming with heavy enemy units. Therefore, he chose the only option he felt was realistic. Langsdorff elected to fight.

The three British cruisers did not sight the German ship until some time after the *Graf Spee*'s lookouts had identified the *Exeter*. As soon as the *Spee* was sighted, however, Harwood's ships began to maneuver into position in compliance with the battle plan. As the antagonists approached head-on, the *Exeter* swung away from the *Ajax* and *Achilles* and moved out so she could engage the *Graf Spee* from the German's starboard side.

With both sides approaching each other at high speed, the range decreased rapidly. At 6:14 the *Spee* opened the Battle of the River Plate by unleashing the first salvo. Her third and fourth salvos straddled the *Exeter*. Langsdorff had wisely elected to concentrate his main armament on the potentially more dangerous foe rather than split his fire between the divided enemy force. Because of this, the *Exeter* soon began to take a fearful punishment.

Four minutes after the *Graf Spee* opened the battle, the *Exeter* began to reply. Meanwhile, the *Spee*'s secondary armament had opened up on the remaining enemy cruisers. The *Achilles* was quickly damaged by splinters from near misses. At the same time, Langsdorff began laying smoke to make it more difficult for the British to spot his ship. The accuracy of the *Ajax* and *Achilles* suffered due to their inability to see through the smoke.

While Langsdorff was fending off the attack by the two smaller cruisers, the *Spee*'s eleven-inch guns continued to pound the *Exeter*. Fires had been started in the British ship by the first near misses. Now the *Spee*'s gunners had the range and were scoring direct hits. A shell tore off the front armor on *Exeter*'s B turret putting it totally out of commission. Splinters from the explosion riddled the bridge. With the exception of Captain Bell, who was wounded by flying steel, almost everyone on the bridge was killed. Another direct hit wrecked the wheelhouse, knocked out the steering and all communications to the engine room. Nevertheless, both A and Y turrets were hitting back, and those in a position to see watched hits being made on the *Graf Spee*.

At 6:36 Langsdorff reversed course to avoid running completely by the enemy ships. As she swung around, the *Graf Spee* continued to pound the *Exeter*. The A turret suffered the same fate as had B turret. Down below, fires raged out of control in the British cruiser. A direct hit tore a sixteen-foot hole in her side and the ship began to take on water. Then the communications system was knocked out and contact with Harwood was lost. Fortunately for the *Exeter*, however, her engine room remained unharmed.

The *Exeter* was a wreck. Listing to starboard and slightly down by the bow, the gallant ship continued to fight until her remaining turret was put out of action by a hit that severed the electrical system. With his ship out of control and unable to fight back, Bell broke off the action at 7:30. His main concern now was not fighting the enemy but saving his ship.

In the interim, the *Ajax* and *Achilles* had begun to find the range. Harwood had deliberately reduced the number of guns able to fire by heading straight for the *Graf Spee*. As a result, only the forward turrets of his ships could be brought to bear. Then, at 7:16, Langsdorff turned toward the crippled *Exeter*, intent on finishing her off. To counter this move, Harwood turned both his ships broadside and opened up a withering fire on the *Graf Spee*. Although there was little chance of a six-inch shell sinking the pocket battleship, hit after hit began to register on Langsdorff's ship. During this encounter the captain himself was wounded in the arm. He had already been wounded in the shoulder. Despite his wounds, though, Langsdorff continued to remain at his station on the bridge.

Thanks to the tenacity of the *Ajax* and *Achilles,* Langsdorff was forced to call off his attempt to polish off the *Exeter* and to turn his attention elsewhere. He countered Harwood's move by swinging the *Graf Spee* broadside and letting loose with the *Spee*'s eleven-inch main armament.

At 7:24, the *Ajax* fired four torpedoes from long range. The *Graf Spee*'s lookouts spotted the torpedo wakes immediately and Langsdorff was able to maneuver his ship to comb their wakes. All torpedoes missed. After swinging back broadside, the *Graf Spee* exacted retribution.

At 7:30, the *Ajax* shuddered from a direct hit by an eleven-inch shell. The shell penetrated Harwood's sleeping quarters, destroyed the cabin and passed out to explode deeper in the ship. Another hit knocked out the X and Y turrets. Others started fires. With his damaged flagship receiving the full attention of the *Graf Spee*'s main guns, Harwood ordered the *Achilles* to lay a blanket of smoke. Then, under cover of the thick, black blanket, the *Ajax* turned away.

Unknown to Harwood, Langsdorff had already decided to break off the action. The *Graf Spee*'s damage was more extensive than the British thought. Her galley and bakery were both destroyed making it impossible to feed the crew. Numerous splinter holes punctured the ship's hull along with two larger holes in the forward deck. In addition, the *Graf Spee* had expended nearly two-thirds of her ammunition during the battle.

After making a thorough inspection of the damage, Langsdorff decided that his ship was unseaworthy. He could not break back to Germany for three reasons.

First, of course, was the inability to feed the crew. Secondly, the holes in the ship meant that the *Graf Spee* could not under any circumstances face the wintry gales and high seas of the North Atlantic. Finally, there was the lack of ammunition. Langsdorff knew that if he attempted to break back to Germany he would be shadowed by British ships every step of the way. Without an adequate supply of shells for his guns, Langsdorff could not hope to fight his way through the gauntlet of enemy ships bound to be lining the route home. Therefore, Langsdorff decided to seek temporary refuge in the nearest neutral port.

Then there was the wounded to consider. Thirty-seven members of the *Graf Spee*'s crew had perished during the battle and an additional fifty-seven were wounded. Among the latter were several whose serious wounds were beyond the ability of the ship's medical facilities to cope with.

The nearest neutral port happened to be Montevideo, Uruguay. The next closest port was Buenos Aires, Argentina but that was over one hundred miles beyond Montevideo. Langsdorff selected the latter because of its proximity. He was deeply concerned with the safety of his ship and the welfare of the wounded. Therefore, he set a course for the port at the mouth of the River Plate.

The *Ajax* and *Achilles* dutifully followed the *Graf Spee*. After reviewing the damage reports from Captain Bell, at 1:00 p.m. Harwood ordered the *Exeter* to head for the Falklands. Earlier, he had ordered the *Cumberland* to leave Port Stanley and head for the River Plate at full speed.

Around 11:00 a.m., the *Graf Spee* passed close to the S.S. *Shakespeare*. Langsdorff simply could not resist the possibility of taking another victim. As he passed he ordered the *Graf Spee*'s turrets swung around toward the merchant ship. At the same time the *Spee* signaled the *Shakespeare* to have her crew abandon ship. Then Langsdorff sent a signal to the *Ajax* asking that the British ships pick up the *Shakespeare*'s lifeboats. Perhaps if they delayed, the *Graf Spee* could make good its escape. The captain of the *Shakespeare* refused to comply. Unwilling to take innocent lives, Langsdorff simply continued on course instead of blowing the freighter out of the water.

During the twelve-hour voyage to Montevideo, Langsdorff refused to rest. He visited the wounded and congratulated them on their courage. After that he took a thorough tour of the ship making a more detailed assessment of the damage. Then the captain returned to the bridge and continued to exercise direct command of the ship.

Disappointed with the outcome of the battle, angered over the loss of so many of his crew, and frustrated with being unable to shake off his tenacious shadowers during the three-hundred-mile voyage to Montevideo, around 5:15 Langsdorff swung the *Graf Spee* around and fired a full salvo at his pursuers. The salvo fell short and the *Graf Spee* resumed course. But the fate of his ship continued to prey on Langsdorff's mind. An hour-and-a-half later he again attemped to exact vengeance from his pursuers. Three more salvos were fired at the *Ajax* and *Achilles*. These were also short but by now the *Graf Spee* was approaching the territorial waters of Uruguay. Anxious not to offend the Uruguayan government, Langsdorff decided that the day's hostilities were finally at an end. Just before midnight, the *Graf Spee* dropped anchor at Montevideo.

Virtually forgotten during the battle were the merchant officers confined deep in the bowels of the *Graf Spee*. During the battle there was much speculation as to what was actually taking place. Each time the *Graf Spee* fired or ceased fire for a few moments, a new wave of rumors swept through the prisoners' quarters. They were, however, unified in one thought. What a dreadful fate to have survived the sinking of their own ships only to be killed by a shell from one of their own warships lucky enough to score a hit on their prison. They had little to fear though. Langsdorff had ordered them confined in one of the safest places on the ship.

After the battle, the seaman responsible for the captives informed them that they would soon be free since the *Spee* was heading for neutral Montevideo. A new wave of speculation made the rounds. Was the German ship heavily damaged and unable to make a long voyage? Had she sunk the entire British force and simply making a stopover for fuel and supplies?

Early the next morning the German ambassador to Uruguay, Dr. Langman, arrived aboard the *Graf Spee*. He was followed in short order by the German naval attache in Buenos Aires who had come to assess the damage. Langman berated Langsdorff for seeking refuge in Montevideo instead of continuing on to Buenos Aires. The Uruguayan government, he said, was weak and could not be counted on to stand up to the British government. On the other hand, Langman continued, the Argentine government, although neutral, was more sympathetic to the German cause.

Langsdorff listened with interest to Langman's arguments. Meanwhile his crew was busily engaged repairing as much battle damage as the ship's facilities permitted. The wounded were quickly transferred to a hospital ashore. The grim task of making funeral arrangements for his thirty-seven dead crewmen also occupied Langsdorff's time. Nevertheless, he told Langman that he would need at least fifteen days to effect repairs and make the *Graf Spee* seaworthy again. Langman agreed to pass the request along to the Uruguayan government.

After Dr. Langman left, Langsdorff sent for Captain Dove for the *Africa Shell*. When Dove arrived he was taken aback by Langsdorff's haggard appearance. The German captain explained that he had been in battle with three British cruisers and had been forced to seek refuge in Montevideo. He wished Dove well and informed him that he and his comrades would soon be freed as they were now in a neutral port. The two captains then shook hands and Langsdorff asked Dove if there was anything he could do for him. Almost as an afterthought, Langsdorff picked up two cap bands bearing the name of the *Graf Spee* and handed them to Dove as a souvenir of his ordeal.

Encouraged by Langsdorff's warm send-off, Dove asked for a more comprehensive detail of the battle. Langsdorff strolled over to his map table and proceeded to give Dove a detailed blow-by-blow description of the battle. "My men—young boys and men—fought magnificently," he said. "The British commander was a brilliant strategist. He divided my fire from the start. I could have sunk her (*Exeter*) but the others pressed me so hard that they made me divide my fire again. I had three ships to fight and I couldn't take my eyes off them.

"The *Exeter* was magnificent. They only had one gun left and they fought me with that. When you fight brave men like that there is no enmity.

"I thought they were trying to drive me out into the guns of bigger ships."[5]

While Langsdorff was bidding farewell to Dove, a Uruguayan naval inspection team was assessing the *Graf Spee*'s damage. International law permitted warships of a belligerent nation to remain in a neutral port for a maximum of seventy-two hours to take on supplies, fuel or repair battle damage. Langsdorff had requested fifteen days.

Ashore, the political maneuvering went on in earnest. Langman insisted that the *Graf Spee* be allowed the requested period in port. His counterpart, the British ambassador, Millington-Drake, pressured the Uruguayans to invoke the seventy-two hour rule. After hearing the report of their naval inspection team, the Uruguayan government did just as Langman had predicted and caved in to Millington-Drake's pressure, announcing that the *Graf Spee* could only remain in port for seventy-two hours beginning that moment. As the *Graf Spee* had already been on port for over twenty-four hours, in effect, Langsdorff was being granted an additional day. However, as far as he was concerned, it was not enough. That evening, the *Cumberland* arrived and took up patrol with the *Ajax* and *Achilles*.

The following morning, December 15, the funeral for the *Graf Spee*'s thirty-seven dead crew members was held. Langsdorff attended in a rumpled dress uniform that gave mute testimony to his weariness and the burden he carried. The funeral was attended by the surviving members of the ship's crew, the German diplomatic delegation and a handful of German civilians residing in Uruguay. Also present were a score of the recent captives of the *Graf Spee*. One of the latter came forward and laid a wreath on the grave inscribed, "To the memory of brave men of the sea from their comrades of the British Merchant Service."[6]

As the coffins were lowered into the ground, the German delegation raised their hands in the Nazi salute. All, that is, except Langsdorff. To Langman's anger, the captain raised his hand to his cap and gave the traditional naval salute.

When he returned to his ship, Langsdorff was handed an intelligence report stating that the *Renown* and *Ark Royal* had arrived and were on station a few miles out to sea. One of the ship's lookouts even insisted that he had actually seen the upper works of the *Renown*.

In reality, only the *Ajax, Achilles* and *Cumberland* were steaming back and forth offshore. After the battle the British had ordered the *Renown* and *Ark Royal* to leave Pernambuco, refuel at Rio, and make straight for the River Plate, but they could not reach the area until the seventeenth at the very earliest. The *Dorsetshire* and *Shropshire* were ordered up from Capetown but they were even further away and could not reach the River Plate until after the *Ark Royal* and *Renown*. As a result, Harwood was concerned over the relative weakness of his force. If the *Graf Spee* elected to break out, his force was no stronger than it had been at the beginning of the battle. Therefore, it was in his best interest to have the *Graf Spee* remain in harbor until such time as reinforcements could arrive. This was in direct contrast with Millington-Drake's arguments that the German warship be ordered to leave port within seventy-two hours.

Shortly after arriving at Montevideo, Langsdorff had sent off a lengthy report to Berlin giving details of the battle and outlining his options. He could break out, fight his way through the blockade, and attempt to reach Germany. An alternative was to attempt to slip through the blockade in darkness and make his way along the coast to Buenos Aires where he could request a more sympathetic government to grant his ship internment. As a last resort, he could scuttle the ship. At that point Langsdorff leaned toward fighting his way out.

In Berlin, Hitler and Raeder agreed that the propaganda value of the *Graf Spee* being sunk was too valuable to the enemy. Therefore, the breakout idea was vetoed. They preferred to have the *Graf Spee* interned in Argentina. However, Raeder did inform Langsdorff that if circumstances warranted it, he had permission to scuttle the *Graf Spee* to prevent it from falling into enemy hands.

This exchange of signals took place before Langsdorff was misled into believing that the *Ark Royal* and *Renown* were waiting offshore to ambush him. He had already informed Captain Dove that he had no intention of asking his crew to commit suicide. Thus, Langsdorff had a decision to make.

The following day, the British steamer *Ashworth*, which had been at anchor in Montevideo, suddenly raised steam and moved out of the harbor. In a reversal of his earlier tactic, Millington-Drake, at Harwood's insistence, was now attempting to keep the *Graf Spee* confined to harbor. Harwood preferred to wait for the arrival of reinforcements. International law governing the behavior of belligerent warships also stated that a warship of one belligerent nation could not leave a neutral harbor until at least twenty-four hours after the sailing of an unarmed vessel of an opposing nation. The Uruguayan government was puzzled and also angered by Millington-Drake's actions and lodged a firm protest. But the British ambassador was prepared to order yet another ship to sail if necessary to buy time for Harwood.

Langsdorff was unconcerned with the sailing of the British steamer. He had already written to Langman outlining his intention to scuttle the *Graf Spee*.

Therefore, it mattered little if he violated international law or not.

On December 17, shortly after noon, members of the *Graf Spee*'s crew began transferring to the German steamer *Tacoma*. Hidden in the boats that appeared to be shuttling supplies to the warship, the operation left the impression that the *Graf Spee* was preparing for sea. In the meantime, Langsdorff had requested that two Argentine tugs sail up from Buenos Aires and rendezvous with the *Graf Spee* at sea.

At 5:00 p.m. the *Graf Spee*'s anchors rattled aboard and the mighty ship began to slowly move out to sea accompanied by the *Tacoma*. The *Spee*'s secret papers were burned in the fire boxes of the boilers. Important equipment was smashed beyond repair to prevent anything of value from falling into enemy hands.

Thousands lined the shores of the mouth of the river eager for an eyewitness view of the anticipated forthcoming naval battle. At sea, Harwood was informed of the *Graf Spee*'s sailing almost immediately. He quickly sent all three of his ships to action stations and the *Ajax, Achilles* and *Cumberland* took up their positions. Harwood planned to use the same tactic that had served him so well four days previously. The exception was that in place of the battered *Exeter* was the undamaged *Cumberland*.

The great battle, however, was not to be. As soon as the *Graf Spee* crossed the three-mile territorial limit, Langsdorff ordered the ship to stop. During the brief voyage he seemed to be his old self again as he trod the deck of his beloved ship issuing orders. The destruction of vital equipment continued for a while longer. Satisfied that the explosive charges were in place and that nothing of value remained for the enemy, Langsdorff ordered the handful of men remaining on board to transfer to the waiting Argentine tugs. At 8:40 p.m., Langsdorff was the last man to leave the *Graf Spee*. Fifteen minutes later a huge explosion shook the ship. A tower of fire over a hundred feet high rose above the *Graf Spee*. Subsequent explosions set the ship blazing from stem to stern. Racked by explosions, her bottom blown out, burning furiously, the once-proud *Graf Spee* settled into the mud.

The *Tacoma* returned to Montevideo where the bulk of the *Graf Spee*'s crew were interned. The remaining crewmen sailed with the tugs to Buenos Aires. The next day Captain Langsdorff assembled his remaining crew. He praised their courage, assured them that they would receive good treatment in Argentina and bid them a sad farewell. Then, after giving them the naval salute, he left his crew behind for good.

That evening Langsdorff held a dinner party for his remaining officers. During the course of the gathering the captain seemed to be returning to his old self. Around midnight, after everyone had left, Langsdorff sat down in his room and wrote a letter to his wife and one to his parents. Finally, he penned a note to the German ambassador to Argentina outlining the reasons for his action.

"I alone bear responsibility for scuttling the pocket battleship *Admiral Graf Spee*," the letter read. "I am happy to pay with my life for any possible reflection on the honor of the flag. I shall face my fate with firm faith in the cause and future of the nation and of my Führer."[7]

Shortly after 8:00 a.m. the next morning, one of the *Graf Spee*'s officers found Capt. Hans Langsdorff dead. After sealing the letter to the German ambassador he had wrapped himself in the ensign of the Imperial Navy and shot himself. To the very last he refused to be associated with Nazism.

The initial success of the *Graf Spee* encouraged the Germans to continue sending raiders into the Atlantic. The *Admiral Scheer* later haunted the same hunting grounds as the *Graf Spee*. Many lessons had been learned from Langsdorff's epic voyage, lessons that were put to good use by later captains.

As for Langsdorff himself, he was a throwback to the days of chivalry. A gentleman to the last, he earned the respect of his crewmen and foes alike. The fact that he had been able to sink nine enemy merchant ships without causing the loss of one life was a truly amazing feat, probably unsurpassed by any raider in history. But Langsdorff did not feel that war should be made against civilians who had no control over irresponsible governments warring with each other. He feverently held to this conviction. Even though he would certainly have been promoted to admiral had he been able to return to Germany as a national hero, it is doubtful that he would have gotten along in the Nazi regime. Gentlemen simply did not survive the mad world of Nazi Germany.

It was particularly ironic that his ship, the *Graf Spee,* named for the admiral who had gone down with his ship at the Battle of the Falklands, should meet its own doom in the South Atlantic at the hands of a squadron of warships based in the Falklands.

Nevertheless, when the great sea commanders of the century are mentioned, Capt. Hans Langsdorff name will be mentioned in the same breath, and justifiably so.

As a postscript to the death of the *Graf Spee,* the *Altmark* made its way through the North Atlantic and Denmark Strait to Norway. En route, Dau held his prisoners in squalid conditions, treated them cruelly, and behaved like a jailer instead of a humane captor. The British navy discovered the *Altmark* hiding in a Norwegian fjord and intercepted the hell ship. Capt. Philip Vian took the destroyer *Cossack* alongside the *Altmark*, boarded her, freed the prisoners, and killed a number of the *Altmark*'s crew. The *Altmark* was allowed to continue on its way following the action but Vian's refusal to honor Norwegian neutrality, even though Dau had violated it, convinced Hitler that Norway had to be invaded.

3. THEODOR KRANCKE

Theodor Krancke is perhaps the least known of the leading German admirals of World War II. Yet he is undeserving of this obscurity for, excluding the two commanders in chief, Doenitz and Raeder, Krancke's contribution to the German naval effort was rivalled by none. He played a key role in the planning for the Norwegian campaign, spent almost two years as the navy's representative at Hitler's headquarters, and closed out his career as naval commander in chief west with responsibility for all naval operations in France and Belgium with the exception of U-boats.

Krancke had risen through the various ranks of the German navy until in 1937, he was promoted to captain and placed in charge of the naval academy. He spent two years developing budding officers for the new German navy but, like all naval officers, longed for a seagoing command. His opportunity came on November 1, 1939 when he was appointed commander of the pocket battleship *Admiral Scheer*. Krancke took up his command immediately only to see the *Scheer* go into dry dock a few weeks later for an extensive refit. Krancke was a captain without a ship.

Meanwhile, the commander in chief of the navy, Admiral Raeder, had for some time been casting a covetous glance at the natural harbors along the west coast of Norway. From these harbors, ships had relatively free access to the Atlantic and could, if events warranted it, interrupt shipping to Russia. Raeder planned to broach the possibility of procuring use of these harbors with Hitler at the earliest opportunity. There were, however, only two ways the navy could gain access to the Norwegian ports: either by diplomatic means or war.

There had already been a number of feasibility studies prepared for a potential attack on Norway. None of the plans seemed workable and following the onset of war with France and England, Norway was put on the back burner.

On January 23, 1940, after a meeting with the Norwegian traitor Vidkung Quisling, Hitler ordered another study made. Because the operation would obviously be primarily a naval show, Hitler gave Raeder responsibility for developing the plan. The commander in chief plucked Krancke from the idle decks of the *Admiral Scheer* and appointed him senior member of a three-service planning team whose task was to develop a feasible plan for attacking Norway. After careful study, Krancke suggested that Germany not plan to attack the entire country. The Norwegian armed forces being relatively weak, Krancke recommended attacking only the major cities along the coast in strength and securing them against attack from the interior. Then, with their major ports and communication centers occupied, the Norwegians would surrender. It was the first practical plan Raeder had read.

On February 16, the *Altmark* affair* convinced Hitler that the British had no intention of honoring Norway's neutrality. The Führer ordered the army to appoint a commander to devise a plan for the conquest of Norway. The army appointed Gen. Nikolaus von Falkenhorst.

When Falkenhorst took up his new command a few days later, he reviewed Krancke's plan. It was obvious that any attack against Norway would require a complicated sea movement. Krancke had planned to utilize the entire fleet. The general took Krancke's plan, made a few minor modifications and submitted it to Hitler. The Führer was impressed and ordered Falkenhorst to proceed with plans for the attack. Krancke was appointed senior naval advisor.

On April 9 and 10, the entire German fleet landed troops at Oslo, Trondheim, Stavanger, Bergen and Narvik. The struggle for Norway was over quickly with the exception of the Battle for Narvik. Raeder had his bases in the North Sea.

In June, Krancke once more stepped onto the deck of the *Admiral Scheer*. He was amazed at the transformation that had taken place in his absence. The armored control tower was gone and in its place was a lighter mast similar to the *Deutschland*'s. She also sported a new funnel cap which resembled that of the Hipper-class cruisers. It was a strange silhouette that greeted Krancke on his return to the *Scheer*.

Another change that had occurred in Krancke's absence was the influx of new crew members. Germany could not afford to allow experienced seamen to sit idle while their ship underwent a refit. Thus, many of the *Scheer*'s crew had been dispersed

*See Langsdorff, chapter two.

throughout the fleet. Krancke was faced with the task of turning the new recruits into a homogeneous fighting team for he was aware that the job that lay ahead was a dangerous one that required every man's skill to be honed to a fine edge.

For the next few months the pocket battleship carried out maneuvers in the Baltic. There was gunnery practice, torpedo practice and, above all, anti-aircraft gunnery exercises, the last of which proved especially prudent. During the *Scheer*'s periods at Wilhelmshaven, the R.A.F. made repeated attempts to damage her through bombing attacks. The *Scheer*'s highly accurate anti-aircraft fire destroyed the bomber's aim and the ship was spared any damage. The inability of the British bombardiers to hit the ship resulted in many of her crewmen believing that the *Scheer* was a "lucky ship." Sailors are a notoriously superstitious lot anyway.

The beginning of October found the training exercises complete and the *Scheer* moved to Gotenhagen. The new crew members were familiar with their duties by now and had adapted to the ship's routine in good fashion. Provisioning for the long voyage that lay ahead began in earnest:

> Munitions of all calibers were taken on board, and machine parts, tool cases and supplies in such quantities that it almost began to look as though the *Scheer* were going to establish another dockyard somewhere. Lorry after lorry came driving up with foodstuffs. Between decks, cases and sacks began to pile up until there was hardly room to pass.[1]

As usual when a ship was preparing to set out to sea, rumors abounded about the *Scheer*'s ultimate destination. However, only Captain Krancke knew for certain what lay ahead and had in fact known for some time.

During the months at sea and in port, the men of the *Scheer*'s crew had come to like and admire their captain. His businesslike attitude was tempered by a jovial personality and a willingness to turn a blind eye to minor accidental discretions.

George Pollock has written, "Krancke was one of Germany's outstanding naval officers. He was not only a first-class seaman, he was also a brilliant strategist and tactician. At first glance he looked austere, but his face was not without humour. In appearance he would have passed for a typical senior Royal Naval officer, except for the fact that he habitually smoked black cigars."[2]

It was the black cigars that caught the fancy of the crew. Whenever Krancke appeared on the bridge with the long, black cylinder clenched between his teeth, a sense of serenity seemed to settle over the ship. Surely, if the captain was so relaxed, danger was not imminent.

Krancke's orders called for the *Scheer* to break out into the Atlantic, attack British shipping, and disrupt the enemy's lines of supply. He was determined at all costs to avoid the fate of the *Graf Spee*.

Immediately after breakfast on October 23, the order went through the ship to prepare for sea. A short time later the powerful ship slipped her mooring and began what was to be a historic voyage, although no one on board, Krancke included, could anticipate their ultimate success at that moment. As soon as land was out of sight, Krancke assembled all hands and announced their destination: the Atlantic shipping lanes via the Denmark Strait.

Krancke was banking on the bad weather in the

NEWFOUNDLAND

NEW YORK

AZORES

GIBRALTAR

CANARY
ISLANDS

BERMUDA

CAPE VERDE

FREETOWN

ASCENSION

RIO de JANEIRO

ST. HELENA

MADAGASCAR

ATLANTIC
OCEAN

CAPE TOWN

MONTEVIDEO

FALKLAND
ISLANDS

THE ATLANTIC WAR

MAP 3

strait to mask his breakout into the Atlantic. Unfortunately, on the voyage north, the weather remained clear and the sea calm. As a result, Krancke took the ship to Stavanger, Norway until the weather could be counted on as an ally.

The *Scheer* remained at Stavanger for two days until the meteorological officer announced that the weather was beginning to turn. Krancke then decided to risk the voyage through the Denmark Strait.

Since the earlier breakout of the *Deutschland* (*Lutzow*), the British home fleet had increased its vigilance in the Denmark Strait. At least two cruisers were on constant patrol in those waters intent on thwarting the effort of any German ship to break out. Fortunately for Krancke, the British ships were not yet equipped with radar though his own ship sported a relatively primitive radar apparatus that had been installed during the recent overhaul. As a result, the German ship had the capability to spot an enemy ship in bad weather. In contrast, the visibility had to be perfect before an enemy ship could locate the *Scheer*.

By the time the *Admiral Scheer* entered the Denmark Strait the weather had deteriorated drastically. Great breakers pummeled the *Scheer* and tossed her about despite her twelve thousand tons. Two men were swept overboard as huge waves crashed over the ship. Tossed from side to side, the ship's furniture and fixtures began to break loose from their mountings. Below decks were a mess. Men were pummeled by loose lockers, crates and other equipment. Despite the howling gale, Krancke was pleased. Certainly in this weather it was impossible for the enemy to see the *Scheer*.

As the *Scheer* approached the exit to the strait the weather began to improve. On November 2 the ship broke out into the Atlantic to clear weather. Krancke now set off in search of enemy shipping.

November 5 dawned bright and clear. Krancke ordered the ship's Arado seaplane launched to search for victims. The first attempt was in vain but returning home from the second effort, the plane's pilot wagged his wings indicating that something had been sighted.

Sure enough, convoy HX-84 was just over eighty miles distant. The convoy was en route to England from Halifax.

At this point in the war, England was critically short of destroyers with which to escort convoys. Consequently, many convoys were escorted by converted merchant ships known as armed merchant cruisers. Convoy HX-84 was escorted by just such a ship, the *Jervis Bay*. This ship had been hastily fitted with a handful of gun mountings and drew convoy escort duty.

Krancke was faced with a dilemma. If he moved in to attack the convoy, nightfall would be almost upon him before the *Scheer* could make up the distance separating her from her prey. On the other hand, by morning the convoy would be over two hundred miles closer to England and the protection of the British fleet. Krancke decided to attack. He rang down the engine room for full speed ahead.

Around 2:30 p.m. the *Scheer*'s lookouts sighted smoke on the horizon. On the bridge of the warship Krancke was puzzled. They were not due to make contact with the convoy for another few hours. Could the Arado's pilot have mistaken the convoy's position? All hands were sent to battle stations as the *Scheer* headed to investigate the contact.

The ship was the five-thousand-ton refrigerator ship *Mopan*. The *Mopan* was a relatively fast ship and had thus elected to sail alone instead of plodding along at

116

the snail's pace of a convoy the top speed of which was only as good as that of the slowest ship. The unfortunate *Mopan* paid a heavy price for her captain's independence.

Krancke ordered the *Sheer*'s gunners to fire a shot across the *Mopan*'s bows. At the same time his signalmen ordered the British ship to stop. The *Mopan* complied and came to a halt. As the convoy was the more important target, Krancke ordered the *Mopan* quickly dispatched by gunfire rather than taking the time to put a prize crew aboard and sail the ship back to Germany. Once the British crew was safely off and aboard the *Sheer*, the *Mopan* was sunk by gunfire and the *Sheer* set off in pursuit of her primary objective.

Around 4:30 the *Sheer*'s crew was once more rewarded with the news of smoke on the horizon. Even though the ship had remained at action stations all hands were now notified that further action was imminent. Unfortunately, the precious daylight was waning. Darkness was the ally of the convoy.

Krancke turned his ship toward the smoke. Soon the masts of the convoy became visible. As the *Sheer* bore down on the vulnerable convoy one ship appeared to turn out of line and head directly for the warship. On the bridge Krancke watched this unusual maneuver through his binoculars. There was only one conclusion to draw from the enemy ship's behavior. She had to be an armed merchant ship. Krancke had no way of knowing that this brave little ship comprised the convoy's sole escort.

On board the *Jervis Bay,* as soon as the strange warship was sighted, Captain Fegen altered course to intercept and keep his ship between the enemy and the convoy. Krancke attempted to deceive the Englishman by exchanging recognition signals but Fegen would have none of it. There were no friendly warships in the vicinity and he knew it. The *Jervis Bay*'s captain therefore fired a prearranged series of colored flares indicating that the convoy was to scatter. At the same time, he attempted to mask the helpless merchant ships by laying down a heavy smoke screen.

Krancke was anxious to get at the convoy but could not ignore the threat posed by the *Jervis Bay*. Even though the merchant ship was heavily outgunned her few guns could cause serious harm to the *Scheer* with a lucky hit. The *Jervis Bay* had to be eliminated before the convoy could be attacked.

It was an uneven battle from the very beginning. On the third salvo the *Scheer*'s eleven-inch shells began to score on the outgunned auxiliary cruiser. At the same time, Krancke kept his ship out of range of the smaller caliber British guns. For twenty-two minutes the *Jervis Bay* kept up the uneven struggle and drew the full attention of the pocket battleship. Captain Fegen kept his burning ship between the enemy and his precious convoy for twenty-two minutes during which the thirty-eight ships of the convoy scattered to all points of the compass.

The fate of the *Jervis Bay* was a foregone conclusion. Blazing from stem to stern, her guns out of action, over half of her crew either dead or wounded, including the brave Captain Fegen, the gallant ship slipped beneath the waves. The way was now open for the *Scheer* to concentrate on the convoy. But the prey was fast eluding the fox and darkness was closing in. Using both the main and secondary armaments, the *Scheer* began to fire at any target in sight. In the next few hours five merchant ships succumbed to the might of the Scheer's guns. Seven more were badly damaged. Only the onset of darkness prevented the score from being heavier. A few days into her voyage, the *Scheer* had already accounted for seven enemy ships.

Krancke's officers implored him to pursue the fleeing merchant ships. They argued that when daylight came the helpless ships could be picked off one by one. Krancke, however, was immune to their pleas. Waiting around in the North Atlantic for British warships to find him was not the primary objective. One of Krancke's objectives, though, had already been achieved.

The British recalled the next two convoys to Halifax and postponed their sailing for almost two weeks. At the same time the battleships *Rodney* and *Nelson* were sent to seal off the Iceland-Faroes Passage in the event the *Scheer* attempted to break back to Germany. The cruiser patrols in the Denmark Strait were beefed up. In addition, the battle cruisers *Hood, Renown* and *Repulse* and the cruisers *Naiad, Dido* and *Pheobe* were sent to blockade the Bay of Biscay in case the *Scheer* attempted to make for a French port. Finally, all normal convoy traffic was temporarily halted.

Krancke was satisfied with the results of the attack on the convoy. True, under different circumstances more ships might have been sunk but that was a moot point. Let the British chase their tails around the North Atlantic searching for a raider. Of one thing Krancke was absolutely certain. They would not find the *Admiral Scheer* there. By the time the British dispositions were complete the *Scheer* was en route to the South Atlantic at full speed, leaving in her wake a completely disrupted North Atlantic shipping lane. Normal traffic was not resumed until mid-November.

Krancke's destination was a rendezvous with the supply ship *Nordmark*. Just prior to leaving Germany the captain had volunteered the services of his crew to aid in loading supplies aboard the tanker. Amid much grunting, sweating, heavy lifting and complaining, the *Scheer*'s crew wondered aloud why they, crewmen of a proud pocket battleship, were being pressed into service manhandling cargo for a lowly merchant ship. Now these same grumblers were about to witness first-hand the fruits of their toil. The *Scheer* was scheduled to meet her supply ship almost directly astride the Tropic of Cancer in mid-Atlantic.

As the battleship raced south, the crew began to notice a drastic change in the weather. Left behind were the turbulent, cold and stormy waters of the North Atlantic. The *Scheer* was entering warmer waters. On November 12, the ship neared the rendez-vous point. Waiting there was a strange ship, not the *Nordmark*. The *Scheer*'s lookouts quickly reported their observations to the bridge were Krancke sat non-chalantly smoking one of his Brazilian cigars. The sight of their captain's lack of concern eased the concern of the alarmed lookouts. Obviously the captain knew something that they did not. If the ship ahead were not friendly, Krancke would most certainly have already sent the ship to action stations.

Krancke did indeed know the identity of the strange ship. She was the German tanker *Eurofeld*. The out-break of war had found the *Eurofeld* at sea with a cargo of oil. Unfortunately, her overworked engines were in dire need of overhaul and the German naval command knew that the ship had little chance of reaching Germany safely. The tanker was therefore directed to seek refuge in the Spanish-controlled Canary Islands and await further orders.

Eventually, the naval high command decided to utilize the *Eurofeld* as a supply ship for surface raiders. Thus, as summer was drawing to a close, the *Eurofeld* received orders to make for a midocean rendezvous point and await further orders. Waiting at the rendezvous was the auxiliary cruiser *Widder*. The *Widder* refuelled from the *Eurofeld* and continued on to Germany. Unfortunately, the *Widder* lacked the necessary spare parts to repair the *Eurofeld*'s engines. As a result, the tanker was forced to hover in the area of the rendezvous awaiting the arrival of other German ships.

When the startled captain of the *Eurofeld* saw a warship making directly for his ship he initially thought it to be a British cruiser as he was totally ignorant of the fact that a pocket battleship was operating in the area. A quick exchange of signals, however, eased his fears.

Krancke sent a boat to fetch the *Eurofeld*'s captain. After a cordial exchange of greetings the captain of the *Scheer* assured his visitor that the facilities on the *Scheer* were more than adequate to repair the *Eurofeld*'s engines.

On the fourteenth, a familiar ship approached the rendezvous. At first the German lookouts were confused since the approaching ship flew the Stars and Stripes and on her bows was painted the name Prairie. But the silhouette was unmistakable. The new arrival was the *Nordmark* disguised as an American ship. Krancke quickly set all available crew members to the task at hand. Refuelling operations commenced at once while a constant stream of boats shuttled back and forth between ships carrying fresh meat and vegetables from the *Nordmark*'s refrigerated hold. Shells for the *Scheer*'s powerful guns were carefully hauled aboard the warship. The transfer of supplies lasted for over two days. Then, the operation completed, Krancke set another rendezvous point and ordered the *Nordmark* to proceed there. At the same time the *Eurofeld* was directed to rendezvous with the auxiliary cruiser *Thor* deep in the South Atlantic.

For the next week the *Scheer* hovered around the shipping lanes of the West Indies. The temperature of the sea water was much higher than it had been in the North Atlantic and the interior of the ship resembled a steam oven. Krancke was liberal regarding dress codes. As a consequence, in an effort to remain comfortable, men stripped their shirts and sported all sorts of non-regulation uniforms.

On November 24 Krancke's patience paid off. The *Scheer* sprang to life as action stations was sounded. Lookouts had sighted smoke and Krancke ordered the *Scheer* to investigate. As the *Scheer* ploughed ahead at full speed, a freighter was quickly sighted. Instead of issuing the customary warning not to use the radio, Krancke deliberately allowed the by-now retreating ship to transmit an R-R-R and its position. R-R-R was the universal maritime signal for a ship under attack by a surface raider. Once the transmission was complete, Krancke ordered the *Scheer*'s gunners to fire a shot across the target's bows while a signal was sent ordering the fleeing ship to stop and cease using its radio. The hapless merchantman complied at once.

The ship turned out to be the refrigeration ship *Port Hobart*. In addition to her cargo of perishables, the *Port Hobart*'s decks contained crates of spare airplane parts destined for the Royal New Zealand Air Force. To Krancke's dismay, however, the *Port Hobart* also carried passengers. Among these were seven women. Providing accommodations aboard the *Sheer* would be difficult for the prospect of having women aboard had never occurred to anyone.

Because the *Port Hobart* was a relatively small vessel with deck cargo of no value to Germany, Krancke decided not to waste a prize crew on her. Once the passengers and crew were safely aboard the warship, he ordered the *Port Hobart* sunk by gunfire from point-blank range.

Krancke's decision to allow the *Port Hobart* to use its radio before signaling it to halt was an integral part of his future plans. The interception of the *Port Hobart*'s signal giving its position set into action a chain of moves. The British sent the carrier *Formidable* and the cruisers *Berwick* and *York* to patrol between Freetown and the West African coast. The carrier *Hermes* and the cruiser *Dragon* moved out of St. Helena. The cruisers *Cumberland* and *Newcastle* were sent to the South Atlantic. The most significant enemy move, however, was the rerouting of all merchant traffic to the area of the Cape Verde Islands. This was precisely what Krancke had hoped for as that was where he intended to take the *Scheer* next.

After arriving in the new hunting grounds the *Scheer* settled down to the monotony of cruising in search of potential victims. With his enemies searching for him in the area last reported, Krancke felt relatively secure. On December 1, the merchant ship *Tribesman* was sighted by the *Scheer*'s lookouts. Krancke ordered his ship to steer a parallel course until it could be determined if the sighting was in fact a merchant ship. There was every chance that it could be a warship or auxiliary cruiser. Once he was assured that the *Scheer* was indeed shadowing a merchantman, he ordered the ship to move off ahead of the target at high speed. He planned to intercept at the onset of darkness.

One of the officers on the bridge questioned Krancke's decision to wait until dark. The captain replied, "Well, I was thinking that it would be a good idea if we waited until the gentlemen had their dinner in peace and were sitting down to a hand of poker."[3]

Just before 9:00 p.m. the *Scheer* altered course to position itself across the enemy's bows. Within minutes the *Tribesman* hove into view. Via the ship's blinker, Krancke ordered the merchant ship to heave to and not to use its wireless. This was followed immediately by a shot across the bows of the victim and the snapping on of the *Scheer*'s searchlights.

The captain of the *Tribesman* refused to be intimidated. Using his lone gun he opened fire on the *Scheer* and altered course to run. Krancke was not amused. He knew that the fleeing merchant ship could not inflict serious damage on his own ship unless she scored a direct hit, but at the same time, he was determined not to allow the defiant enemy to escape. Consequently, the *Scheer*'s guns opened up and almost immediately began to score hits. After taking a number of hits in a brief span of time, the captain of the *Tribesman* got the message and ordered his ship to stop.

After the *Scheer*'s boarding party reported back, Krancke decided that the *Tribesman* was also not of sufficient value to waste a prize crew. He ordered scuttling charges placed in the holds of the ship. Once her crew was safely transferred, the charges blew out the bottom of the *Tribesman*, which quickly settled beneath the waves.

The most recent victim's crew posed still another problem for Krancke. The captured crewmen were primarily Indians who refused to eat unless their rice was cooked in a particular manner. After a few futile attempts by the *Scheer*'s cooks and the refusal of the Indians to eat, Krancke allowed a few of the captives to cook for the rest of their comrades. Once this was accomplished, the Indians became peacefully resigned to their fate.

For the next week the *Scheer* continued to patrol

without success. Eventually, Krancke decided that it was time to seek other hunting grounds. After another rendezvous with the *Nordmark,* the *Scheer* headed for the area of the equator.

Krancke felt the pickings would be better if he patrolled the main shipping routes between Brazil and Africa and Brazil and Europe. Once he reached the new area he found his instincts had been correct.

On December 17, the *Scheer*'s lookouts sighted another merchant ship. As the warship moved swiftly into position, the enemy ship sighted her and began transmitting R-R-R. Krancke ordered a shot fired across the victim's bows. After the second shot, the retreating ship stopped and ceased transmitting, but the damage had already been done. British shore stations acknowledged receipt of the signal.

The luckless ship turned out to be the refrigerator ship *Duquesa.* Her cargo was nine thousand tons of meat and over nine hundred tons of eggs destined for England. Unwilling to destroy such a valuable cargo, Krancke decided to take the *Duquesa* as a prize. Her crew was exchanged for a prize crew from the *Scheer* and the freighter headed off for the rendezvous point.

When the British shore stations picked up the *Duquesa*'s report of a raider, their naval forces sprang into action. *Dorsetshire* and *Neptune* sailed from Freetown; *Hermes, Dragon* and *Pretoria Castle* moved out from St. Helena. South from the Azores sailed the *Formidable, Berwick* and *Norfolk. Cumberland, Enterprise* and *Newcastle* searched the area between Rio and Montevideo. None of the British patrols managed to come near the *Scheer.*

Krancke patrolled the hunting area for another few days before setting off for another rendezvous with his supply ship. The Germans had designated their meeting point in mid-Atlantic, Point Andalusia. On

December 27, the *Scheer* reached Andalusia where the *Nordmark*, *Eurofeld* and the recently captured *Duquesa* were waiting along with the raider *Thor*.

The next few days were spent refuelling and distributing the *Duquesa*'s precious cargo. The ships' crews had all the fresh meat they could eat. Fresh eggs, an extreme rarity on ships at sea for any length of time, were in abundance. Eggs were on the menu at virtually every meal. Among the crew there was much speculation about how many eggs there were in nine hundred tons.

On January 4, the Norwegian whaling ship *Norstad*, captured by the raider *Pinguin* in the Antarctic, arrived at Point Andalusia manned by a German prize crew. After refuelling and being supplied with fresh meat and, of course, eggs, the *Norstad* sailed for Germany.

The next day Krancke ordered the small German fleet to disperse after setting a date for another rendezvous. By the tenth the *Scheer* was patrolling the waters off the Gulf of Guinea in search of new victims. On the thirteenth Krancke ordered the ship stopped so that a new coat of camouflage could be painted. From a distance, the camouflage altered the *Sheer*'s features and served to confuse enemy lookouts as to her actual size and silhouette. The next day Krancke and the *Scheer* were off seeking new victims.

On the eighteenth, another ship was sighted. Once more Krancke decided to utilize the tactic that had proven so successful with the *Tribesman*. He paralleled the other ship's course until dark when the *Scheer* moved in front of the latest victim. As the unsuspecting ship hove into sight, the *Scheer* fired a shot across her bow and challenged her. At the same time, the approaching victim was ordered not to use her wireless.

The latest victim complied at once and stopped dead in the water. The ship was the Norwegian tanker *Sandefjord* with a cargo of thirteen thousand tons of oil. Once more Krancke decided to take the ship as a prize for not only could the oil be put to good use, but the *Sandefjord* had one other valuable feature. She had plenty of room for prisoners and Krancke was anxious to rid the *Scheer* of the bothersome Indians and women captured earlier. After a prize crew was placed aboard, the *Sandefjord* was dispatched to Point Andalusia.

That night there was little rest for the *Scheer*'s crew. Shortly after the departure of the *Sandefjord* the lights of another ship were sighted. Krancke decided not to intercept immediately for he had received reports of a convoy in the area escorted by warships. In addition, there were the British patrols to worry about. Therefore, he resolved to wait until a better assessment of the situation could be made.

Around 3:00 a.m., the masts of yet another ship were sighted just as the first target turned away. The distance between the two strange ships prohibited taking action against both so Krancke decided to pursue the original target.

A short time later the freighter, having spotted the *Scheer*, requested a recognition signal. Krancke gambled on a bluff and ordered his signalman to answer: Stop, I have secret orders for you. Almost immediately the freighter reversed course and headed directly for the *Scheer*.

The unfortunate ship was the Dutch *Barneveld*. On board were three British naval officers who convinced the Dutch captain that the approaching warship was a Cumberland-class cruiser. Krancke's decision to pause and apply new camouflage had paid off. Only after the *Scheer* was within three thousand yards did the

Dutch captain realize his error but by then it was too late. The twelve-inch guns of the pocket battleship were pointed directly at his ship. The British officers, once they realized their mistake, implored the *Barneveld*'s captain to use his wireless and send the R-R-R signal. Unwilling to risk his ship and the lives of his crew, the Dutch captain, after berating his British guests for the mistake that had resulted in their current hopeless state of affairs, ordered his ship to stop.

The *Barneveld* was carrying a cargo of military equipment for the British forces in Egypt. Krancke was eager to be off after the other ship sighted a few hours earlier so he hastily dispatched a prize crew to the *Barnveld* while the *Scheer* wheeled about and was off.

A few hours later the other ship was sighted once more. Like his Dutch counterpart, the freighter's captain believed the *Scheer* to be a patrolling British cruiser. Accordingly, when ordered to stop, he complied at once without using his radio. This ship was the *Stampack* en route to England from Bombay with a cargo of cotton. Krancke felt that this ship held little value and thus decided to sink her. After transferring her crew, explosive charges strategically placed in the freighter's hold were set off.

The cargo of cotton, however, held the ship up and prevented her from sinking. Krancke decided that perhaps his crew could use some long-overdue torpedo practice so he ordered the *Stampack* sunk in that manner.

The first torpedo missed completely, much to Krancke's displeasure. He ordered a second fired. This torpedo malfunctioned and reversed course 180 degrees as it approached the target. From his vantage point on the bridge Krancke stared in horror as the errant torpedo headed directly for the *Scheer*. With the ship at a standstill there was no chance to maneuver out of the way. Suddenly, less than ten yards from impact, the torpedo plunged straight to the bottom of the ocean. Had it struck, it would most certainly have marked the end of the *Scheer*, for although the torpedo would probably not have sunk the pocket battleship, there was no place where the ship could seek refuge and repair extensive damage. A third torpedo struck home and the *Stampack* followed the errant torpedo to the bottom of the ocean.

Following this harrowing experience, Krancke took the *Scheer* back to the *Barneveld*, which was also sunk, this time by gunfire. Then the *Scheer* headed for Andalusia after accounting for three victims in less than twenty-four hours.

The *Nordmark* and *Duquesa* were already waiting when the *Scheer* arrived at Andalusia. Krancke utilized the respite afforded by the refuelling and reprovisioning operation to plan his future conduct of operations. In addition to the *Scheer*, the auxiliary cruisers *Thor* and *Kormoran* were operating in the South Atlantic at that time. The *Pinguin* was making its presence felt in the antarctic where it had recently captured an entire fleet of Norwegian whaling ships. The presence of these other raiders in the South Atlantic increased the chance that a patrolling British warship would locate one or the other. Therefore, Krancke decided to seek out a less risky area of operations.

In the Indian Ocean, the auxiliary cruiser *Atlantis* was the sole German warship. Accordingly, Krancke hit on the idea of increasing activity in that area. He informed naval headquarters of his intentions and quickly received authorization to carry out his plan.

Before setting off, however, there were items that

required attention. The *Nordmark* received a fresh coat of paint and was disguised as the U.S. ship *Dixie*. All passengers and prisoners were transferred to the *Sandefjord* which had joined the gathering of ships at Andalusia. As many supplies as possible were transferred to the other ships from the *Duquesa* including, of course, huge quantities of eggs. Krancke was beginning to feel that the *Duquesa* had just about outlived its usefulness. Therefore, he ordered her prize crew to wait at the rendezvous to supply the *Pinguin* and then scuttle the *Scheer*'s floating delicatessen. This was eventually accomplished on February 20.

Meanwhile, on January 28, the *Scheer*'s crew bid their comrades farewell as Krancke set a course southward. As the *Scheer* plunged ahead at full speed, the water temperature began to drop and make the atmosphere below decks more habitable. Eventually the climate turned cold. In contrast to a few days previously when they went about shirtless, the *Scheer*'s crew now found themselves bundling up against the chill of the extreme southern end of the Atlantic.

As the *Scheer* approached the tip of Africa, Krancke took precautions to ensure that the ship would not be surprised by enemy warships based at Capetown. Fortunately, just before turning eastward, a gale began to whip up. The *Scheer* plunged forward in the direction of the "Roarin' Forties" as the gale increased in intensity. During the two-day voyage around the Cape of Good Hope, the *Scheer* battled heavy winds and huge waves as the gale became a full-blown storm. Krancke, however, was pleased by the turn of events. The howling storm made the prospect of a chance sighting by a British warship a virtual impossibility.

Once around the cape, Krancke altered course and headed the ship north. The storm and bitter cold were left behind. For a week the *Scheer* patrolled southeast of Madagascar without success. Then, in February 12, Krancke noticed the presence of heavy swells. He suspected that a hurricane was brewing and consulted his meteorological officer who disagreed with the captain's conclusion. Nevertheless, Krancke decided to play it safe and ordered an alteration in course. Soon afterward, the wind picked up and huge waves were encountered. Once more Krancke's seaman's instincts had proven correct. A powerful hurricane struck the area where the *Scheer* had been patrolling. By altering course, despite the opinion of his weather expert, the *Scheer* managed to skirt the edge of the hurricane and was spared potential heavy damage.

On February 14 the *Scheer* arrived at a pre-determined position for a rendezvous with the *Atlantis*. Also present was the supply ship *Tannenfels*. From the latter the pocket battleship replenished her fuel supply. While the refuelling operation proceeded, Krancke saw to it that the crews of the *Atlantis* and *Tannenfels* received fresh meat as well as a goodly supply of eggs. To the crews of the two ships, fresh eggs were a delicacy though the *Scheer*'s crew had grown tired of them.

Krancke also held a series of meetings with Captain Rogge of the *Atlantis*. Rogge had been in the Indian Ocean for over a year and had observed a great deal. This information proved useful to the recently arrived *Scheer*. As a result of the intelligence garnered from Rogge's experiences, Krancke decided that the *Atlantis* should patrol an area to the north of the *Scheer*. When the presence of a pocket battleship in the area became known, enemy shipping would naturally detour. Krancke hoped that the detour would take victims right into the hands of the lurking *Atlantis*.

On February 17 the *Scheer* set out on the hunt. At midmorning Krancke ordered the ship's Arado launched. From his vantage point aloft the pilot's field of vision was greatly increased. The Arado could also cover a far greater expanse of ocean than could its mother ship.

Almost immediately the maneuver paid dividends. The Arado's pilot sighted smoke on the horizon and moved in for a closer look. The lone ship made no effort to conceal its location. Its captain said that the scout plane was from a British warship, there having been no reports of enemy ships in the area. En route back to the *Scheer* the Arado's pilot sighted smoke in an entirely different direction. However, as he was running low on fuel he could not verify the sighting. Upon returning to the *Scheer,* the pilot reported both sightings to Krancke.

Krancke now had a decision to make. Two sightings: which one to pursue. Using the bird in the hand better than two in the bush logic, Krancke made the obvious choice. The *Scheer* would seek out the verified target. Besides, there was always the possibility that the other unverified sighting was a British warship. The Arado's pilot had only seen smoke, not the source of the smoke.

At full steam the *Scheer* was able to intercept the hapless merchant ship by midafternoon. As soon as the *Scheer* was in range Krancke ordered the signal, Stop or I'll blow you out of the water. During the chase he had decided to at least investigate the other sighting. Therefore, speed in dealing with the latest victim was of the utmost importance.

The boarding party from the pocket battleship found the stopped merchant ship to be the British *Advocate* with a cargo of eight thousand tons of oil. Because fuel was always a precious commodity for ships far from home, Krancke put a prize crew aboard the enemy ship with orders to make for the next rendezvous point. Then he rang down for full speed ahead and altered course in the direction of the second sighting.

A few hours later the gamble paid off. Steaming leisurely along was the Greek ship *Gregarios*. Once more the *Scheer* ordered the merchant ship to halt and once more the order was obeyed without the doomed ship using her wireless. When the boarding party reached the deck of the *Gregarios* they were informed by the ship's captain that his ship was merely carrying Red Cross supplies and that as a neutral, he should be allowed to proceed. Krancke, however, was skeptical. He was not yet ready to believe that a valuable cargo of medical supplies was sailing unescorted. He ordered a few of the ship's crates opened. If the manifest proved correct, Krancke was perfectly willing to allow the *Gregarios* to proceed on its way.

Once again Krancke's keen instinct proved correct. Inside the crates marked Red Cross was war material destined for North Africa. Krancke immediately ordered scuttling charges placed in the hold of the ship. At 7:20 p.m., the unfortunate Greek freighter plunged to the bottom of the Indian Ocean.

After an uneventful night, daylight dawned bright and clear. Following breakfast Krancke had the Arado launched again. Within the hour word was received from the pilot that another ship had been spotted. This one, however, was some distance away. It would take the *Scheer* some hours to catch up. Undaunted, Krancke altered course.

As the chase would consume the better part of the day, Krancke decided to wait until twilight before intercepting the ship.

Early that evening the *Scheer* positioned itself across the next victim's bow. Krancke had decided to try a ruse once more. The approaching ship was hailed and informed that the warship had secret orders for her. Back came the reply that the ship was an American. Nevertheless, it altered course and headed for the *Scheer*. Just as quickly, the strange ship reversed course and began to run.

Krancke's patience ran out. He ordered the fleeing ship to heave to immediately. When the order was disobeyed, he ordered the *Scheer's* spotlights switched on. The beam from one of the lights pinpointed the American markings on the freighter, yet Krancke was not convinced.

Meanwhile, the fleeing ship began to send out the R-R-R signal. The radio operators on the *Scheer* confirmed that the shore stations at Aden, Zanzibar and Mombassa had acknowledged receipt of the distress signal.

Eventually, the freighter stopped. The *Scheer's* boarding party was met with protestations that the ship was American and that the *Scheer* had no right to stop her. But an examination of the ship's papers disclosed that she was in fact Canadian, the *Canadian Cruiser*. Out of patience and concerned lest the area begin swarming with British warships, Krancke ordered the *Canadian Cruiser* sunk immediately. The scuttling charges did their work to perfection and one more victim sought the depths of the Indian Ocean.

That evening word was received from naval command that Krancke had been awarded the Knight's Cross. Although his officers tried to keep the news a secret until an appropriate ceremony could be arranged, the news soon leaked out and Krancke was handed the official dispatch. Despite the delay in being given a dispatch from naval command, Krancke

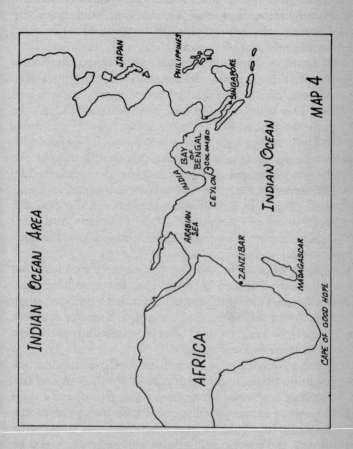

INDIAN OCEAN AREA

JAPAN

PHILIPPINES

SINGAPORE

INDIA

BAY OF BENGAL

COLOMBO

CEYLON

ARABIAN SEA

ZANZIBAR

MADAGASCAR

INDIAN OCEAN

AFRICA

CAPE OF GOOD HOPE

MAP 4

took the entire incident in good humor.

Two days after the capture of the *Canadian Cruiser*, while heading for another rendezvous with the *Atlantis*, the *Scheer*'s lookouts sighted smoke again. Shortly thereafter a small freighter was spotted. Almost immediately she began transmitting the R-R-R signal. The *Scheer* plunged forward after the prey but in the midst of the chase, one of the rain squalls so common in the Indian Ocean suddenly appeared and engulfed both ships. The storm was over in a few minutes and when the *Scheer* emerged from it she found herself within three thousand yards of the hapless freighter.

The latest victim was the small twenty-five hundred-ton Dutch freighter *Rantau Pantjang*, a coal-carrying vessel with a crew of Malaysians. Frightened out of their wits, the crew began to jump overboard. Despite the intense efforts of the *Scheer*'s crew, a few of the pathetic Malaysians were lost. The bulk of them, however, were hauled aboard the warship.

Krancke was in a hurry by now. Thanks to the *Canadian Cruiser*'s warning, he felt that the area would be alive with British warships. Without even considering his latest victim's cargo, Krancke ordered it scuttled. Half an hour after noon the *Scheer*'s latest victim plunged out of sight.

Krancke's instincts served him well. Less than an hour after the scuttling of the *Rantau Pantjang* an observation plane was sighted. The plane could only have come from one source: a British warship. Despite the snooper, Krancke kept the *Scheer* on its present course. If his luck held, there was every chance that the plane's fuel might run out before its mother ship arrived on the scene.

Krancke's gamble paid off. The scout plane did in

fact run short of fuel and was forced to return to its ship. As soon as it was out of sight over the horizon and he was absolutely certain that the snooper was gone, Krancke called for a radical change of course.

Again Krancke's experience proved invaluable. The plane had come from the British cruiser *Glasgow* which, at the time the *Scheer* altered course, was a mere thirty miles away. When the *Glasgow's* plane kept repeating the *Scheer's* course, the British cruiser set out at top speed to intercept the German warship. Fortunately, thanks to Krancke's patience in waiting for the scout plane to break off the reconnaissance before altering course, when the *Glasgow* arrived at the point the British expected the *Scheer* to be, the Germans were in fact miles away and moving in the opposite direction.

Krancke knew that now he would have to call on all his seaman's skill and instincts. He also knew that he needed a measure of good luck as well. The *Glasgow* had shared her intelligence freely with other units of the British fleet. The cruisers *Hawkins* and *Australia* took up the search. The *Emerald* left her convoy escort weakened and also joined in. Out of Mombassa at high speed steamd the *Capetown* and the carrier *Hermes*. From the south the Australian cruisers *Shropshire* and *Canberra* added their weight to the chase. With that many enemy ships in the Indian Ocean the odds were stacked against the *Scheer*. The odds were reduced somewhat when the *Scheer's* radio operators intercepted a message from a merchant ship reporting that it had sighted two cruisers and giving their course and speed. Krancke put this knowledge to good use and altered course to avoid the ships in question for they could only be hostile.

Two days later the *Scheer* made its final rendezvous with the *Atlantis*. The meeting was a brief one for

Krancke was anxious to leave the Indian Ocean behind. Nevertheless, he had more than achieved his objectives. In two weeks the *Scheer* had accounted for four ships, completely disrupted shipping in the Indian Ocean, resupplied the *Atlantis,* and had at least eight British warships searching the area for the elusive raider. Now it was time to return to more familiar surroundings.

After setting a course for the Cape of Good Hope, Krancke ordered all hands assembled on deck and announced that the *Scheer* was leaving the Indian Ocean for good and was headed for home. The crew greeted the news with lusty cheers. They had been at sea for over three months. Krancke, however, was a realist. He knew that the *Scheer* was not out of danger as of yet. The ship had to continue eluding the British units in the Indian Ocean, make its way around the cape where the high seas and violent storms of the "Roarin' Forties" could cause crippling damage, and traverse the entire length of the Atlantic where the potential for stumbling across a British ship existed around the clock.

The homeward voyage began ominously. The *Scheer*'s radar apparatus malfunctioned and the spare part needed to repair it was not aboard ship. Krancke signalled naval command requesting that the part be dispatched aboard a ship leaving Germany for he would need the radar as he threaded his way homeward. The order was quickly filled and the critical device was placed aboard the submarine *U-124.*

During the first week in March the *Admiral Scheer* once again made its way through the perilous waters around the Cape of Good Hope. Once back in the South Atlantic and calmer waters, Krancke astonished the entire crew by ordering the ship stopped. During the course of her time in the warm waters of the South Atlantic and Indian Oceans, a great buildup of barnacles and marine life on the ship's hull had occurred. This growth on the bottom of the ship caused an unreasonable drag thereby reducing the *Scheer*'s maximum speed by a few knots. Krancke knew that if he were to reach Germany safely he would need every knot he could coax out of the ship's engines. Therefore, on March 9, he had the ship careened in midocean so that the bottom might be scraped free of marine life. It was a calculated risk but one that Krancke felt was necessary.

Careening the large ship meant pumping all fuel to one side, thereby exposing a large portion of the ship's bottom. For an entire day virtually the entire crew scraped and repainted first one side then the other. To ensure against being taken by surprise while the ship lay helpless, Krancke used the Arado to fly a constant patrol in a giant circle around the ship. By the end of the day, the operation was concluded and the *Scheer* was completely seaworthy once more.

On the twentieth, the *Scheer* arrived at Point Andalusia for the final time. Waiting there was the faithful *Nordmark*. Under the watchful eye of Krancke the warship was reprovisioned and refuelled. As soon as this vital operation was concluded, the *Scheer* bid farewell to the *Nordmark* for the last time and set off for one final rendezvous before beginning the long and perilous journey homeward.

The final rendezvous was with the auxiliary cruiser *Kormoran* and the *U-124*. Happily, the vital radar part was transferred from the U-boat and quickly installed on the *Scheer*. On the eleventh, Krancke ordered a course set for Germany.

The North Atlantic was a dangerous place for German warships in March of 1941. The British home fleet was searching for the battle cruisers *Scharnhorst* and *Gneisenau* which were at large in the Atlantic. Other British ships were searching for the *Hipper* which had also made its presence known along the shipping lanes.

On the twenty-second, the *Scheer* crossed into the North Atlantic. That day smoke from a ship was sighted on the horizon. Krancke elected not to investigate. One more prize was too high a price to pay for sacrificing the *Sheer*'s location. In the meantime, naval command had informed Krancke that the *Hipper*'s cruise was at an end and that the *Scheer* should allow the former to pass through the Denmark Strait first. It mattered little to Krancke as the Denmark Strait was a long way off. First the *Scheer* had to make its way through the North Atlantic without being discovered.

On the twenty-third, the weather began to remind the men of the *Scheer* that they were back in the North Atlantic. A strong gale began to blow. For two days the *Scheer* was buffeted by heavy winds and high seas. Although the storm made life aboard ship uncomfortable, it was just the type of weather Krancke had hoped to encounter. The heavy seas and poor visibility reduced the chances of discovery to a minimum.

Near the end of the second day the gale began to blow itself out but by that time the *Scheer* was off the southern tip of Greenland. During the day a message was received stating that the *Hipper* had passed safely through the Denmark Straight. Thus the *Scheer* was given the green light for her final run home.

On the twenty-sixth, the *Scheer* approached the entrance to the Denmark Strait. To Krancke's dismay the storm had completely blown itself out and the skies were bright and clear. Visibility could be measured in miles instead of yards. Even this close to home that bit of luck might still spell disaster for the *Scheer*. Nevertheless, Krancke decided to press on. He ordered the helmsman to set a course that would take the ship as close as possible to the edge of the ice pack. It was a wise decision. The contrasting temperature of the sea water and ice produced a thick fog that completely cloaked the *Scheer*, masking her from the probing eyes of enemy lookouts.

That night, Krancke ordered the ship hove to. The entire crew was kept awake and in a total state of readiness. Just before dawn the next morning, a snowstorm began to blow. Krancke decided to use the storm to his advantage and ordered the ship to proceed.

Two hours later, the *Scheer*'s radar began to register a target dead ahead. This could only be a British cruiser patrolling the strait. Krancke had been on the bridge since entering the Denmark Strait and was therefore available to make a decision at a moment's notice. Based on the latest report, he concluded that the enemy ship was looking for the *Scheer* near the edge of the ice. He decided to press on but altered course to pass astern of the British ship, even though the maneuver took him closer to the edge of the fog bank. By this time Krancke was counting on his experience to see the *Scheer* safely home. He knew that his latest move was a gamble for the British cruiser was undoubtedly not alone. There had to be yet another cruiser in the area.

By 11:00 a.m. radar contact with the enemy ship was lost. The *Scheer* had successfully passed astern of the first obstacle. Two hours later, however, the weather cleared again. Not willing to take any chances, Krancke ordered the *Scheer*'s eleven-inch guns aimed at the area of the last contact with the enemy.

Deeper into the Denmark Strait plunged the *Admiral Scheer*. At 4:30 her lookouts sighted masts on the horizon. This could only be the second British cruiser. Once more Krancke ordered a rapid alteration of course and had the ship's guns trained on the new target. Incredibly, the lookouts on the British cruiser failed to spot the *Scheer*.

At 6:30 the radar apparatus broke down again. Krancke had lost his electronic eyes. He resigned himself to relying on the excellent German optical equipment and the experienced eyes of his lookouts.

Around 8:00 one of the lookouts reported the masts of a ship to port. Krancke quickly altered course again and then issued an order that astonished everyone on board. He ordered the *Scheer*'s speed reduced by one half. Turning to his companions on the bridge he explained his maneuver, "At top speed the noise of our screws is very much louder that at half speed, gentlemen, and therefore very much easier to pick up on their asdic apparatus and at a much greater distance. At least we've reduced that danger."[4]

Nevertheless, Krancke kept the ship's guns trained on the target. For a while it appeared as if the British ship had spotted the *Scheer* for she continued to steer the same course. Krancke debated whether to fire on the enemy or not. He had the advantage of being in position to strike the first blow. In addition, the *Scheer* could probably have sunk the British ship, particularly with the element of surprise on her side. But Krancke was anxious to avoid heavy damage this close to home. If he fired, he risked having other units of the home fleet rush to the scene. Accordingly, he resisted the temptation to fire on the unsuspecting enemy ship. Instead, he opted for another change of course so that he could be sure of the enemy's intentions. When the British ship did not alter course as well, Krancke knew that the other ship's similar course had been simply a coincidence.

Just before midnight the *Scheer*'s passage through the narrows of the Denmark Strait was hailed by a magnificent display of the northern lights. Shortly before dawn Krancke stared out over the bridge at the welcome harbor of Bergen, Norway. At 7:00 a.m. the pocket battleship dropped anchor in friendly waters.

The *Scheer* remained at Bergen for just over twelve hours. That evening the anchor was hoisted aboard once more. Escorted by a squadron of destroyers that had trouble matching her speed, the *Scheer* made her final dash for home. In the early morning hours of April 1, the pocket battleship dropped anchor at Kiel, Germany, bringing to a close a voyage of almost four months.

At 10:00 a.m. the same morning, Admiral Raeder arrived to formally welcome the *Admiral Scheer* home. Krancke had a lavish breakfast laid out consisting of steak, vegetables and, naturally, eggs. Raeder jokingly stated that he had heard frequent reports of the *Scheer*'s floating delicatessen, the *Duquesa*, and expressed regrets that it had been impossible to bring the latter home as well.

The voyage of the *Admiral Scheer* had been a tremendous success. Krancke had sunk seventeen enemy vessels totalling one fifty-two thousand tons, damaged seven more, and had completely disrupted shipping from the North Sea to the Indian Ocean. Almost half of the British fleet was deployed in an attempt to run her to ground. In addition, not only had Krancke managed to avoid the fate of the *Scheer*'s sister ship, *Graf Spee*, he had managed to almost double the latter's score.

Krancke had already proven himself as a staff planner during the Norwegian campaign and had now demonstrated that he was equally adept as a commander at sea. Raeder needed someone of that caliber to represent the navy at Hitler's headquarters where Goering and Himmler used every opportunity to belittle the navy while forwarding the prospects of their own branches of the armed services.

Thus, following his promotion to vice admiral, Krancke settled down to the madness of Hitler's headquarters. He took up his new assignment when the navy's fortunes were on the downturn. The mighty *Bismarck* had been run down and sunk by the Royal Navy a few weeks earlier. The *Scharnhorst*, *Gneisenau* and *Prinz Eugene* lay bottled up at Brest. Hitler was preparing to invade Russia and all available resources were being siphoned off by the army. Because of the shortage of critical raw materials, construction of the carrier *Graf Zeppelin* was put on hold. The shortage of raw materials coupled with the army's demands brought new ship construction to a virtual standstill. The navy's meager allotment went primarily for new U-boats, but as the latter was the private domain of Admiral Doenitz, Krancke had little to do with it.

To Krancke, the time he spent at Hitler's headquarters was an ordeal he would rather have been spared. He had no command responsibility and spent most of his time defending the navy against the insinuations of Himmler and Goering. At other times he was used as a whipping boy whenever Hitler felt like venting his wrath against the navy. The Führer was particularly unhappy over the fact that three of his capital ships lay dormant at Brest. Whenever he thought of those three ships, Hitler would summon the only naval representative handy—Krancke—and unleash a tirade regarding the worthlessness of big ships. Even after the ships returned home via the English Channel*, Hitler's attitude changed little.

*See Cilax, chapter five.

Krancke's bitterest experience occurred following the Battle of the Barents Sea at the end of 1942. During that battle five British destroyers, brilliantly handled by Capt. Robert Sherebrooke, kept the *Hipper, Lutzow* and six destroyers from attacking convoy JW-51B, headed for Russia. The two heavy German ships attempted to attack the convoy independently from different angles. Each time they moved in for the kill, two or more of Sherebrooke's destroyers raced out and, using the threat of their torpedoes, barred the way. First the *Hipper* and then the *Lutzow* were driven off. Eventually, the cruisers *Sheffield* and *Jamaica* arrived on the scene, sank the destroyer *Eckholdt*, and forced the German ships to head for home. The German force, however, was powerful enough to stand up to the two British light cruisers as well as Sherebrooke's five destroyers.

The attack on convoy JW-51B had been authorized by Hitler personally after consulting with Krancke. For months, the German heavy fleet units had sat idle in Norwegian fjords while Hitler railed at their inactivity. He was therefore determined to utilize them.

At 10:30 a.m. on New Year's Eve, Krancke informed Hitler that the *Lutzow* and *Hipper* had been in action against the convoy during the night. Hitler was enthusiastic and told Krancke to keep him informed of any developments. At 11:45, Krancke received a signal made during the night by a U-boat that was in the vicinity of the battle: "According to our observation the battle has reached its climax. I see nothing but red."[5]

Krancke passed the message to Hitler at once. The Führer interpreted it as meaning that the merchant ships were burning furiously.

Throughout the day, Krancke waited impatiently

for a report on the battle. None were forthcoming. That evening, a British broadcast was monitored stating that a convoy had been attacked and that one enemy cruiser was damaged and one enemy destroyer sunk. Lacking information to confirm this, Krancke was reluctant to give the bad news to Hitler. Instead, he excused the lack of information on the fact that the German ships had not yet reached harbor and were observing radio silence while at sea. Nevertheless, Krancke phoned Raeder in Berlin and asked him if he would agree to contact the ships at sea. Raeder refused to compromise the ship's positions and denied the request. Therefore, at Hitler's 10:00 p.m. situation conference, Krancke had nothing further to report.

Every half hour Hitler called Krancke asking if there were any news. Each time Krancke had to report that no new information had come in and each time Hitler's mood grew fouler. Finally, after 2:00 a.m. the calls ceased and Krancke retired for the night.

Meanwhile, in Norway, shortly after midnight, Admiral Kunmetz steamed into Altenfjord aboard the *Hipper*. Kunmetz had been the tactical commander of the German battle force. He waited four hours before sending a report, but that report only provided details of damage to his own ship. There was no mention of the convoy. Then, exhausted from the voyage, Kunmetz went to bed.

After a restless night, Krancke aroused around 9:00 a.m. and was incensed that there was still no details of the battle available. At 10:30, Hitler called and Krancke had to relay the news to him.

By the time the noontime conference rolled around, Krancke knew he was in for a bad time of it. There was still no details of the battle available. Sure enough, Hitler went into a tirade against the surface ships. He ordered Krancke to send an immediate wire to naval headquarters demanding a report.

At 5:00 p.m., Krancke received a summons from the Führer. Hitler was seething.

The Führer asked him for news. He then walked up and down the room in great excitement. He said that it was an unheard-of impudence not to inform him; that such behavior and the entire action showed that the ships were utterly useless; that they were nothing but a breeding ground for revolution, idly lying about and lacking any desire to get into action.

"This meant the passing of the High Seas Fleet," he said, adding that it was now his irrevocable decision to do away with these useless ships. He would put the good personnel, the good weapons and the armor plating to better use. "Inform the grand admiral of this immediately."

I tried to point out quietly that, after all, we must wait for the report, but he would not let me get a word in and dismissed me. I then informed the grand admiral.[6]

Two hours later, Raeder called Krancke and gave him the details of the battle. Krancke knew what Hitler's reaction would be. Therefore, as the Führer was taking a nap, Krancke decided to postpone the inevitable.

There was another outburst of anger with special reference to the fact that the action had not been fought out to a finish. This, said the Führer, was typical of German ships, just the opposite of the British, who, true to their tradition, fought to the bitter end.[7]

Krancke argued back. Each time he opened his

mouth he was shouted down by another of Hitler's tyrannical monologues.

The end result of Hitler's wrath was that Raeder resigned, and was replaced by Admiral Doenitz.*

When the U-boat commander took up the baton of grand admiral, he set about revitalizing the navy. Doenitz preferred younger men like himself in responsible commands. Consequently, Krancke was sent to Paris as naval commander in chief, west, with responsibility for all naval operations in France and Belgium, exclusive of U-boats. Doenitz retained a firm hand on those himself.

With no control over U-boat operations and with no surface vessels to speak of in France, Krancke's fancy-sounding title was virtually an empty shell. Other than a handful of torpedo boats, there was no navy left in France.

Krancke got along well with both Field Marshals Rommel and von Rundstedt. He did, however, disagree with Rommel's theory of stopping an invasion on the beaches. Nonetheless, one could not accuse Krancke of being uncooperative. He aided Rommel every way he could as the field marshal set about fortifying potential landing sites. Krancke kept in constant touch with Rommel through his naval advisor, Admiral Ruge. But other than that, the job was a typical bureaucratic desk job. That is until July of 1944.

On the twentieth of that month, as he was poring over the latest situation reports of the Allied advance in Normandy, Krancke was handed a priority dispatch from Berlin stating that Hitler was dead and that Field Marshal Witzleben was the new commander of

*See Raeder, chapter one.

the armed forces. The message went on to state that the SS had been merged with the army.

Krancke was skeptical. He placed an immediate call to Doenitz to confirm Witzleben's message. The commander in chief assured Krancke that Hitler was still alive and that he was not to take orders from anyone but him or Himmler.

After the conversation with Doenitz, Krancke tried for several hours to contact Field Marshal von Kluge, successor of von Rundstedt. Eventually, Krancke got through to Kluge's chief of staff, General Blumentritt. The admiral assured the general of his support and offered the assistance of all naval personnel to put down what was evidently a full-scale revolt. By this act, Krancke had proven his loyalty as far as Hitler was concerned. Virtually every officer of any standing came under suspicion. But Krancke had not been a party to the conspiracy anyway. In fact, very few naval officers were. It was primarily an army show. Nevertheless, by his expression of loyalty, Krancke escaped the bloody retribution that followed the revolt.

A few weeks later, Krancke was out of a job. The Allies broke out from Normandy and overran France, capturing Paris in the bargain. The admiral moved his headquarters to Berlin where he sat out the war, a commander without anything to command.

Krancke's saddest moment came on April 9, 1945. That day the *Admiral Scheer* was attacked by a flight of R.A.F. bombers. The ship lay at her berth in Kiel. Hit repeatedly, the once-proud pocket battleship rolled over and sank. The berth where she was anchored was filled in after the war, burying the *Admiral Sheer* forever.

Krancke was unquestionably one of German's ablest naval officers. His integrity was beyond reproach but, like most senior naval officers, he had ties to the Imperial Navy instead of the Nazi regime. As an administrator in France, a planner for Norway, and a commander at sea with the *Admiral Scheer*, Krancke proved that he was a talented and professional naval officer, equal to any task.

4. ADMIRAL GUNTHER LUTJENS

Gunther Lutjens achieved more during his brief World War II career than any of his colleagues, save Raeder and Doenitz. Lutjens is best remembered for one epic event, the voyage of the *Bismarck*. But few realize that of the seagoing admirals of the Third Reich, Lutjens saw the most action and achieved a remarkable record of accomplishments. With the exception of Doenitz and his U-boats, Lutjens was probably England's single greatest naval antagonist during the war despite a wartime career lasting little over a year and a half.

Even though he had an impressive record as a commander of capital ships, Lutjens was mismatched for the role he played. Most of his career had been spent in smaller vessels, specifically torpedo boats. During the years preceding the war he was considered one of the Kriegsmarine's leading torpedo experts. But Lutjens had decided to make the navy his life and the career of an officer on the rise, even if he was a specialist, required that he be well versed in all aspects.

Gunther Lutjens was born in 1889 in Wiesbaden

where his father was a merchant. As a young boy he remembered being enthralled by stories of the sea. Thus, it came as no surprise to his parents when the young man announced his intention to make the navy his career. In 1907, he joined the Imperial Navy as a cadet and had his first taste of the sea during a cruise on the cruiser *Freya*. In 1909, Lutjens graduated from the naval academy twentieth in a class of 160. His scholastic achievement warranted an assignment to one of the German fleet's heavier units, in this case a battleship.

Lutjens was uncomfortable in large ships. When the opportunity arose he joined a torpedo boat flotilla where he served throughout World War I, eventually rising to command of his own flotilla. When World War I ended and the Treaty of Versailles restricted the size of Germany's armed forces, the navy tapped Lutjens's academic skills. For the next decade, he alternated between training and staff assignments.

Lutjens's most memorable seagoing peacetime command was as captain of the cruiser *Karlsruhe*. With Lutjens at the helm, the cruiser spent the better part of 1935 showing the German flag in South American waters. In addition, while commanding the *Karlsruhe*, he formed a close friendship with his fellow captain, the commander of the cruiser *Emden*, Karl Doenitz.

"I knew Lutjens well and held him in high esteem," Doenitz would later recall. "We were often together both socially and on duty, we held the same views on naval matters and saw eye to eye in most things."[1]

One of the views shared by the two friends was a distinct distaste with Hitler's attitude and actions against the Jews. Lutjens and Doenitz both protested these actions to their superior, Adm. Hermann Bohm but with little effect.

Ludovic Kennedy characterized Lutjens as "a man wholly dedicated to the service, courageous, single-minded, stoical, austere, taciturn as a Cistercian monk. He was not a Nazi, gave Hitler the naval not the party salute, always wore an admiral's dirk of the old Imperial Navy, not one with a swastika. His friend Adm. Conrad Patzig who succeeded him as chief of personnel called him 'one of the ablest officers in the Navy, very logical and shrewd, incorruptible in his opinions and an engaging personality when you got to know him.' "[2]

When the *Karlsruhe* returned home from her South American voyage in July of 1935, Lutjens looked forward to a brief rest followed by a voyage to the Orient. Admiral Raeder, commander in chief of the navy, however, had other plans for Lutjens. At a meeting with Doenitz, Raeder announced that Lutjens was being assigned to head the personnel branch at naval headquarters. A month earlier, Hitler had signed the Anglo-American naval treaty* Thus Raeder needed someone to construct a qualified officer corps to run the suddenly expanded navy. His choice was Lutjens.

Lutjens spent the next few years in Berlin reviewing personnel files, scouring the naval lists and placing as many highly qualified officers as he could into responsible positions. By 1938, however, war clouds had begun to gather over Europe and Raeder wished to install those officers in whom he had confidence in responsible commands. Thus Lutjens was transferred to naval group west as commander, scouting forces.

Naval group west was commanded by Adm. Alfred Saalwachter. In this capacity Saalwachter was

---

*See Raeder, chapter one.

responsible for all naval operations in the North Sea, English Channel and Atlantic excluding U-boats. Immediately below him in the chain of command was the fleet commander, Adm. Hermann Bohm. The latter commanded not only the light cruisers and escort forces, but flew his flag in the battle cruiser *Gneisenau*. At that time the *Gneisenau* and her sister ship, *Scharnhorst,* represented Germany's most powerful warships.

Shortly after the onset of war in September of 1939, German destroyers began making forays into the English Channel where they sowed mines off England's channel ports. Almost immediately Bohm and Saalwachter found themselves at odds over the mining operations. The fleet commander, anxious to exercise his ships, insisted that the fleet go out and escort the destroyers returning from the English Channel, back to Germany. This theory contradicted the traditional naval concept which held that smaller ships provided escort for the heavier units of the fleet, not vice versa. Raeder sided with Saalwachter and Bohm was replaced by Adm. Wilhelm Marschall.

Lutjens was not unhappy to see Bohm go. Ever since his protest regarding treatment of the Jews, relations between Lutjens and his immediate superior had been strained. Their relationship deteriorated even further when Lutjens sided with Saalwachter over the use of capital ships for escort duty. Lutjens respected Marschall and was pleased to serve under him.

Ironically, even after he was fired, the German navy continued to practice Bohm's theory, albeit with cruisers rather than the heavier units. The folly of this tactic was dramatically demonstrated on December 13, 1939. Lutjens had taken the light cruisers *Kiln, Leipzig* and *Nurnberg* out to escort a group of destroyers back to Germany. He was standing on the bridge of the *Nurnberg* when he was suddenly thrown to the deck by the force of a tremendous explosion. The British had positioned submarines along the return route to Germany in hopes of obtaining a crack at the mine-laying force. Lutjens's squadron had sailed directly across the bows of one of the lurking submarines.

Before he could recover his wits the *Leipzig* was also blasted by a torpedo. Lutjens called for an immediate alteration of course and took his crippled squadron back to Germany.

The winter of 1939-40 was one of the severest in recent memory. As a result, the German fleet found itself confined to port by ice and bad weather for the greater part of the season. In the interim, following the *Altmark* affair*, Hitler had decided to invade Norway.

Because the invasion called for major assaults at five separate Norwegian ports, Raeder knew that the entire surface fleet would have to be committed. The *Scharnhorst* and *Gneisenau* would be a prominent part of this commitment.

Marschall was under a cloud for his earlier action against the British armed merchant cruiser, *Rawalpindi*. In the middle of November Raeder had directed Marschall to take the *Scharnhorst* and *Gneisenau* to sea and attack the British ships patrolling the exits to the North Atlantic. In the late afternoon of November 24, the two battle cruisers came across the *Rawalpindi* in the Iceland-Faroes Passage. During the one-sided battle, the *Rawalpindi* was quickly overwhelmed by the eleven-inch guns of

*See Langsdorff, chapter two.

the German ships. After the British ship had sunk, Marschall ordered his ships to search for possible survivors. In the midst of the search, the cruiser *Newcastle* arrived on the scene. Although it was no match for one of the battle cruisers, let alone both, Marschall ordered his ships to leave the scene at high speed. Raeder was unhappy with Marschall's actions but was willing to overlook them. That was not the case, however, with his chief of staff, Admiral Fricke. Fricke continued to agitate and took advantage of every opportunity to discredit Marschall. As a result, the fleet commander began to lose confidence in himself. Just before the Norwegian campaign was scheduled to commence, Marschall reported that he was too ill to take command of the fleet. Raeder quickly appointed Lutjens to fill the void caused by Marschall's sudden illness.

Germany lacked adequate shipping to transport all its troops to Norway. Consequently, those destined for Narvik and Trondheim were slated to be ferried to their destinations by destroyers. Covering this force would be the *Scharnhorst*, *Gneisenau* and the heavier cruiser *Hipper*. The entire force would be commanded by Admiral Lutjens.

England too had designs on Norway. To prevent Germany from establishing bases there the British were prepared to violate Norway's neutrality by occupying the country. In fact, when word came of the German attack on Norway and Denmark, some British invasion units were already at sea. They were hastily recalled but the home fleet was prepared to smash the German invasion.

In the early morning hours of April 7, Lutjens's force began to assemble in the North Sea. The plan called for the fleet to sail along the west coast of Norway towards Narvik. At Trondheim the *Hipper* and four destroyers laden with troops would peel off from the main force and head for that port while the *Scharnhorst* and *Gneisenau* escorted the remaining ten destroyers and their passengers to Narvik. During the attack on Narvik, the two battle cruisers would remain out at sea and provide distant cover against intrusions by the home fleet. Other German landings were scheduled to take place simultaneously at Stavanger, Bergen and Oslo.

To Lutjens's disappointment, the morning dawned bright and clear. He had hoped that the usual gray North Sea weather would serve to mask his movements from the probing eyes of the British. Because the weather was clear, at mid-morning the German force was attacked by a flight of enemy bombers. The evasive tactics and heavy anti-aircraft fire of the German ships prevented the British from scoring any hits but the attack let Lutjens know that the alarm had been sounded and the home fleet would be out in force.

Much to the admiral's relief, that afternoon the weather began to deteriorate. As the seas began to run higher, a man from one of the destroyers was washed overboard. The destroyers signalled the flagship (*Gneisenau*) requesting permission to search for the unfortunate crew member. Lutjens denied the request. Under no circumstances would he allow a deviation from the schedule. Unfortunately, he had no control over the weather. The deteriorating weather caused the fleet to become scattered. In the heavy seas the destroyers found themselves burdened with a load of violently seasick soldiers and unable to maintain pace with the heavier ships. Lutjens had no choice but to allow them to operate independently, but ordered all ships to regroup at daybreak. His troubles were magnified at 10:30 p.m. when he received a signal from naval group west stating that the home fleet had put to sea.

The following morning the presence of British forces in the area became known in dramatic fashion. The destroyer *Berndt von Arnim* was struggling to catch up with the rest of the fleet when it almost collided with the British destroyer *Glowworm*. The latter was part of the battle cruiser *Renown*'s screen and had stopped to search for a crewman who had fallen overboard. Almost at once the *Glowworm* opened fire on the German destroyer. The *von Arnim* put in a frantic call for help. With the ship crammed with troops, her captain could not risk a stand-up fight. Because the *Hipper* was due to leave the formation shortly anyway for the run into Trondheim, Lutjens dispatched the cruiser to the aid of the *Berndt von Arnim*.

Lutjens was not aware that there were heavy enemy units in the area of the besieged destroyer. The *Renown*'s sister ship, *Repulse*, was in fact almost as near to the scene as the *Hipper* but not quite. Had Lutjens known that the *Repulse* was nearby, however, there is no doubt that he would not have risked the *Hipper* but would instead have left the *Berndt von Arnim* to her fate. But the fortunes of war are strange and the unexpected frequently spoils the best laid plans.

Once the *Hipper* arrived on the scene the outcome of the struggle became a foregone conclusion. Her eight-inch guns quickly overwhelmed the hapless British destroyer. Unfortunately, Captain Heye of the *Hipper* failed to reckon with the courage and determination of his opposite number. Lieutenant Commander Roope of the *Glowworm*, intent on exacting as high a price as possible for his sacrifice, pointed his ship directly at the *Hipper* and charged.

The British destroyer tore a huge gash in the *Hipper*'s side, causing the German ship to take on a great deal of water. Then the gallant *Glowworm* slipped beneath the waves taking with her all but thirty-seven men and one officer of her crew. Roope was not one of those rescued. Badly damaged, the *Hipper* limped toward Trondheim at a reduced speed.

Further north, Lutjens's force reached the area off Narvik late in the evening. The ten remaining destroyers raced down Vestfjord and by noon the next day all the troops had been put ashore.

As the assault force headed up the fjord for Narvik, Lutjens took the two battle cruisers away from the coast and out to sea. The admiral knew that his presence in the area would be quickly discovered now that the attack was under way. Therefore, he intended to position his force where it could intercept any British forces seeking to intervene at Narvik and decoy them away from General Dietl's assault force.

Lutjens did not have long to wait for the enemy to make an appearance. Around 3:30 a.m. the next morning the battle cruisers were discovered by the *Renown*. A running gun duel quickly ensued during which the *Renown* had the upper hand. The *Gneisenau* found itself the object of the enemy battle cruiser's attention. A fifteen-inch shell destroyed the flagship's fire control system. A few minutes later one of her turrets was put out of action by a direct hit. The *Renown*'s fire was accurate and heavy.

Lutjens weighed his options. Theoretically his force was superior to the British. However, he dared not risk having one of his own ships disabled to the point where it was an easy target for the torpedoes of the *Renown*'s escorting destroyers. The German admiral decided that he had done his job in keeping the *Renown* from intervening at Narvik. He decided to take advantage of the speed of his force and make a run for port. The *Renown* followed for almost an hour before the murky weather and high seas forced her to call off the chase. By that time Lutjens's force was pulling away to the north.

The storm had hampered both the German and British forces during the fight. Visibility was at a minimum and the two sides caught only an occasional glimpse of each other. The heavy seas pounded the German ships which, because of their design, took on a great deal of water. Lutjens took his force near Jan Mayen Island where he was able to find shelter from the storm.

Once the storm subsided, Lutjens took stock of his condition. The *Gneisenau* was in need of extensive repairs before she could go into battle again. In addition, after the fight with the *Renown*, the *Scharnhorst*'s engines had begun to act up. As a result the ship was unable to steam at full speed. As his objective had been to protect the Narvik landings until all the troops were safely ashore, Lutjens felt it was time to return home. Pausing only long enough to rendezvous with the damaged *Hipper* off Trondheim, the fleet reached Wilhelmshaven on the twelfth.

After his return to Germany, Lutjens's critics began to second guess his actions. Why had he broken off the action with the *Renown* when his force was the superior one? By returning to Germany he had abandoned General Dietl's assault force at Narvik.

Richard Garrett justifies Lutjens's actions adequately:

Gneisenau was virtually incapable of directing the fire of her main armament; and ever present beyond the horizon was the shadow of the battleship H.M.S. *Rodney* with her nine sixteen-inch guns and the rest of the home fleet. Faced by such awesome odds, the outcome was entirely predictable. Germany's only capital ships would have been shot to pieces.[3]

By the time Lutjens returned to Wilhelmshaven, Marschall had recovered from his illness. As a result, he resumed command of the fleet. Lutjens returned to his position as commander of escort forces. A number of months passed before the *Scharnhorst* and *Gneisenau* were ready for sea again. In the interim the situation at Narvik began to turn against the Germans. During the second week in April a force of British destroyers under Captain Warburton-Lee and backed by the battleship *Warspite,* moved up the fjord to Narvik, sank the nine German destroyers defending the area, and landed a force of troops. Dietl was driven back into the hills surrounding the town.

By the end of May, the two German battle cruisers were ready for sea again. Meanwhile, Germany had initiated its attack against France, Holland, Belgium and Luxembourg. As the German streamroller rolled up the Allied front at will, the Allies decided to withdraw their forces from Narvik. On June 4, the *Gneisenau*, *Scharnhorst* and *Hipper* moved out to attack the British ships taking part in the evacuation. The *Hipper* sank a Norwegian tanker and its escorting trawler. The *Gneisenau* accounted for the empty British transport *Orama*. After the *Hipper* was detached, Marschall's battle force came across the British aircraft carrier *Glorious* escorted by two destroyers. The two battle cruisers made short work of the *Glorious* and the destroyer *Ardent* but the captain of the remaining destroyer, *Acasta*, copied a page from *Glowworm*'s saga and rammed the *Scharnhorst* before his ship was sunk. With a huge hole in her side, the *Scharnhorst* limped off to Trondheim for temporary repairs.

Marschall continued to patrol the North Sea with *Hipper* and *Gneisenau* in search of British convoys. On June 20, disaster overtook him again. The submarine *Clyde* fired a torpedo at *Gneisenau* which blew a hole clear through that ship's bow. Both battle cruisers managed to limp back to Germany but they were laid up for another three months. Marschall was severely criticized for allowing his ships to be damaged at such little cost to the enemy. Eventually, his "illness" returned and he requested to be retired. Raeder complied with the request at once and appointed Lutjens to command of the fleet permanently.

The German navy knew that it was incapable of confronting the vastly superior Royal Navy in a head-on clash. Raeder knew that the only way to achieve any measure of success was by resorting to harassing British shipping by using his surface ships as commerce raiders. At the end of October the pocket battleship *Admiral Scheer* set out on a most successful voyage.* The *Scheer* was followed a few weeks later by the *Hipper*. Three days after Christmas, the *Scharnhorst* and *Gneisenau* set out in the teeth of a heavy gale.

Once the two ships left harbor with Lutjens's flag in the *Gneisenau* again, the storm began to increase in intensity. Both battle cruisers were damaged by the pounding seas, causing Lutjens to order a return to base for repairs. They were not ready for sea again until the twenty-second of January.

*See Krancke, chapter three.

Lutjens intended to break out into the Atlantic via the Iceland-Faroes Passage. Unfortunately, his plan was thwarted by a British agent who had watched the German ships sail. This information was quickly relayed to London. Upon receipt of the intelligence report, Adm. John Tovey took the home fleet to sea. The British commander guessed that the German force would attempt to utilize the Iceland-Faroes Passage and deployed his fleet to guard against this eventuality.

As the *Scharnhorst* and *Gneisenau* plunged through the heavy swells of the North Sea, Lutjens received a signal stating that the home fleet had sailed. Shortly afterward, one of the *Gneisenau*'s lookouts sighted a British cruiser. The sighting was confirmed a few minutes later when the German ship's radar indicated that more ships were just over the horizon.

Fortunately for Lutjens, his force had sighted the enemy first. He knew that the number of targets pinpointed by the radar could only mean the presence of the home fleet. Accordingly, he ordered a change of course. But instead of returning to Germany, the admiral set a course for the Denmark Strait between Iceland and Greenland.

After refuelling at sea from a tanker near Jan Mayen Island, Lutjens plunged his force into the Denmark Strait. As a rule, the best the strait has to offer is frequent storms or a heavy mist. To Lutjens's dismay, this time the weather was bright and sunny making it an easy task for patrolling British warships to spot the German ships. Fortunately, once more it was the German force who sighted the enemy first. Sure enough, a lone British cruiser was steaming back and forth dead ahead. Lutjens called for a radical change of course so that his two ships hugged the fog bank at the edge of the ice pack south of Greenland.

Masked by the heavy fog, the *Scharnhorst* and *Gneisenau* slipped by the British patrol and continued on their way undetected. On February 4, the two sisters entered the broad expanse of the Atlantic.

Now Lutjens had his choice of areas to hunt in. One was the convoy route between Canada and England. The other was the England-Gibraltar-Freetown route. As fleet commander, Lutjens exercised operational control of all heavy ships including the *Hipper*, with each ship's captain retaining tactical control. Lutjens ordered the *Hipper*, which was already in the Atlantic, to make for the west coast of North Africa and begin harassing shipping along that route. This left the battle cruisers to ply their craft along the Canada-England route. The admiral felt that if the German ships could make their presence known simultaneously, the British would have to divide their forces if they wished to contend with the dual threat.

Lutjens's operational directive to the captains of both battle cruisers was to avoid contact with superior enemy forces at all costs. With the *Admiral Scheer* and *Hipper* already at large and the *Lutzow* nee *Deutschland* having recently returned to Germany following a disappointing raiding voyage, the British had taken to escorting their convoys with their older battleships. Even though the German ships were more modern and vastly superior in speed, the British R and Queen Elizabeth class battleships mounted eight fifteen-inch guns each and were more heavily armored. Thus Lutjens intended to split his forces and attack the convoy from both sides at once.

Lutjens's force hovered off the southern tip of Greenland waiting for convoy HX-106 to make an appearance. Intelligence reports had confirmed that this convoy had left Halifax on January 31 and was due in the area shortly. A few minutes after breakfast on February 9, the masts of the convoy were sighted by a lookout on the *Gneisenau*. In compliance with Lutjens's battle plan the *Scharnhorst* peeled off and began making for the other side of the convoy.

This time Lutjens was destined to be disappointed. As Captain Hoffmann took the *Scharnhorst* to close on the convoy, the foretop of a heavy ship was sighted. The enemy ship was soon identified as the battleship *Ramilles*. Hoffmann quickly radioed this information to the *Gneisenau* but instead of breaking off as per Lutjens's directions, Hoffmann pressed on thereby incurring his admiral's wrath.

Hoffmann hoped that by deliberately making his presence known, the *Ramilles* would abandon her charges and pursue the *Scharnhorst* thus leaving the *Gneisenau* a clear field. Hoffmann's tactic backfired. The *Ramilles* refused to nibble at the bait. But the presence of at least one of the German battle cruisers in the Atlantic might have been confirmed were it not for a mistaken identification by the *Ramilles*. A lookout insisted that he had seen the *Hipper*. As it was common knowledge that the *Hipper* had sailed recently from Brest while the *Scharnhorst* and *Gneisenau* had moved undetected through the Denmark Strait, Admiral Tovey did not commit the home fleet to the chase. Instead, he felt that his force was needed to guard against a possible breakout by the German battle cruisers which were, of course, already at sea. Thus, Lutjens's force remained safe from pursuit for the time being.

For the next two weeks Lutjens adopted a north-south course off the coast of North America. The lull was broken only by a refuelling operation from two tankers and a typical North Atlantic gale.

On February 22, the admiral's patience was rewarded. That morning *Gneisenau*'s lookouts sighted masts on the horizon. Lutjens quickly ordered a turn toward the position of the sighting. The German force had stumbled across a convoy returning to the United States empty, after having delivered its cargo to England.

As soon as the two battle cruisers hoved into sight, the convoy began to scatter. Consequently, the end result was a disappointment to Lutjens. Chasing targets to all points of the compass was time consuming. The *Gneisenau* accounted for three ships and the *Scharnhorst* one. Later in the day, a fleeing freighter was run down and sunk. Five empty ships of a convoy was a meager total.

Lutjens knew that now his presence on the Halifax-England convoy route would be reported by those ships that had escaped. He therefore decided to find another killing ground. Later that night, for the first time, Lutjens did something that would eventually lead to his downfall. He broke radio silence to make a full report of the day's action to naval group west. At the same time, he ordered his tankers to rendezvous with the battle cruisers near the Azores.

Far to the southwest, astride the Freetown-Gibraltar-England convoy route, the *Hipper* was in dire need of a refit. Lutjens therefore ordered the cruiser back to Germany via Brest. The void left by the departure of the *Hipper* would be backfilled by the *Scharnhorst* and *Gneisenau*.

After refuelling from the tankers *Esso Hamburg* and *Schlellstadt,* the two ships began their patrol back and forth between the Cape Verde Islands and the African coast. The first week in March passed uneventfully until the morning of the seventh when one of the *Scharnhorst*'s lookouts sighted masts. Captain Hoffmann quickly sent off a sighting report to Lutjens and moved closer to investigate. A few moments later the ship below the masts began to take shape. It was the battleship *Malaya*. With his hands tied by Lutjens's battle orders, Hoffmann elected not to investigate further and veered off.

Lutjens, though, was merely echoing Raeder's directives. The grand admiral had no wish to risk the destruction of his capital ships by a superior force. Germany had precious few of them when stacked up against the might of the Royal Navy. Hitler's rush to war before Raeder's "Z" Plan had been completed left the Kriegsmarine unprepared to contest England on an even keel.*

Lutjens thought it strange that the *Malaya* would be steaming alone along the convoy route. Her presence indicated that a convoy was in the area. His instincts were correct. A short time later the masts of a convoy began to take shape. If he could not use his own ships to attack the convoy, Lutjens felt that perhaps there was another method.

Thanks to information from naval group west, Lutjens was aware of the presence of U-boats in the area. Unfortunately, the U-boats and the surface ships were not on the same radio frequency. Thus Lutjens found himself communicating with the U-boats via naval group west.

The admiral maneuvered his ships to the rear of the convoy and assumed a shadowing role. The *Gneisenau* began transmitting data regarding the convoy's route and speed. During the night, the *U-124* and *U-105* managed to sink six ships of the convoy before the escorting destroyers drove them off. Satisfied that there was little else to achieve at that time, Lutjens broke off the chase and made for another rendezvous

*See Raeder, chapter one.

with his tankers.

En route to the latest rendezvous, the *Scharnhorst* ran across the Greek freighter *Marathon*. After determining that the supposedly neutral ship was carrying a load of coal to the British naval base at Alexandria, Captain Hoffman ordered the Marathon sunk. Only, however, after removing her crew.

Lutjens decided that his men needed a rest. Accordingly, he decided that the ships would remain at the rendezvous point for a few days before returning to the Halifax-England convoy route. His intentions were altered on March 11 when he received orders from naval group west directing that the *Scharnhorst* and *Gneisenau* cease operations in mid-Atlantic effective March 18. The *Hipper* and *Admiral Scheer* were due to attempt their return to Germany via the Denmark Strait at any time after that date and Raeder did not want strong enemy units patrolling the Atlantic in search of the two battle cruisers. Instead, they were to act as decoys by heading for Brest.

Lutjens decided to make the return to Brest via a wide detour into the mid-Atlantic. In addition, he elected to take his two tankers, *Ermland* and *Uckermark* along. Four ships could cover a far broader expanse of ocean than could two. This highly irregular tactic paid huge dividends.

By the fifteenth, the small fleet had reached mid-Atlantic and was getting ready to steer a course for Brest. Because the weather was unusually clear, Lutjens positioned his ships thirty miles apart. This allowed him the luxury of being able to cover 120 miles of ocean. The two tankers flanked the battle cruisers.

On that fateful day, four merchant ships fell victim to the German force. Three were captured and sent off as prizes. The fourth was sunk. Unfortunately, only one of the prizes reached home safely. The other two were intercepted by the *Renown*. The German prize crews, however, managed to scuttle the ships before they were made prisoners.

Prior to sending them off as prisoners of war, Lutjens had the captured ships' crews interrogated for information. The information garnered was that four ships were actually the vanguard of a much larger convoy. Lutjens decided to wait in the area. That night the *Scharnhorst* and *Gneisenau* located the rest of the convoy. Twelve more merchantmen were sunk before Lutjens was forced to break off the action by the appearance on the scene of the *Rodney*. The heavily armored *Rodney* mounted nine sixteen-inch guns. The German battle cruisers were no match for the British battleship so Lutjens prudently set a course for Brest.

Thus far, the voyage had resulted in the capture or destruction of twenty-two merchant ships. Thanks to the latest action against the convoy, Lutjens considered the voyage a success. All he had to do now was run the gauntlet of patrolling British warships. If he could manage this, his arrival at Brest would cause the enemy to relax their vigilance thereby leaving the Atlantic less hazardous for the passage of the *Hipper* and *Admiral Scheer* back to Germany.

The voyage to the French port was without incident. On March 22, the *Scharnhorst* and *Gneisenau* dropped anchor at Brest. Raeder sent his congratulations and expressed satisfaction with the way Lutjens had conducted the cruise. "His conduct of operations in the Atlantic were beyond reproach," wrote Richard Garrett. "He invariably judged the situation accurately and he met with deserved success."[4]

An additional bonus of the operation was that the *Scharnhorst* and *Gneisenau* had succeeded in drawing off the British patrols. The *Hipper* returned to

Germany via the Denmark Strait without being sighted. A few days later the *Admiral Scheer* returned in similar fashion.

Lutjens did not have long to savor his achievement. A few days after his arrival in Brest he was handed orders to return to Germany and assume a new command.

The recent successes chalked up by the surface raiders inspired Raeder to begin planning another operation on a grand scale. The new battleships *Bismarck* and *Tirpitz* were completed and conducting working-up exercises in the Baltic. The *Tirpitz* needed at least eight more weeks to iron out her teething problems and train her crew to the peak of efficiency. The *Bismarck*, however, was almost ready. Raeder was anxious to send one of these mighty battleships to sea as soon as possible. Consequently, he allowed his impulsiveness to outweigh strategic sense. The *Bismarck* would be sent on a commerce raiding mission without waiting for the *Tirpitz* to complete her working-up period. Instead of another battleship, the *Bismarck*'s consort would be the heavy cruiser *Prinz Eugen*, sister ship of the *Hipper*.

The *Bismarck* class battleships were the most powerful in the world at the time. The Japanese goliath *Yamato* was as yet incomplete as were the ships of the American Iowa class. England's latest class, the King George V, were inferior as regards weight, size of main armament, and speed.

The *Hipper* class cruisers were probably the finest heavy cruisers of their day. Mounting eight eight-inch guns, these ships displaced almost fourteen thousand tons and were capable of a speed of thirty-two knots. Their relatively limited range was their only shortcoming.

The *Bismarck* and *Prinz Eugen*, however, comprised

only a portion of Raeder's plan. At Brest lay the *Scharnhorst* and *Gneisenau*, poised and ready to move out into the Atlantic at a few hours' notice. Combined in one powerful hunting group, the four ships would represent a force that the British might find impossible to challenge.

Unfortunately, the deployment of the *Scharnhorst* would have to wait temporarily. During the recently concluded operation her boilers had behaved erratically and she was in dire need of a refit. Then Raeder's plan was dealt another severe setback.

Occupied France swarmed with members of the Resistance. No ship or U-boat could enter or leave the Biscay ports without their passage being reported to England. When word was received that the *Scharnhorst* and *Gneisenau* were new arrivals at Brest, the R.A.F. began making plans to sink or immobilize the ships. On April 6, the *Gneisenau* was hit by a torpedo dropped by a low flying British bomber. A few days later, another R.A.F. attack succeeded in planting four bombs directly on the battle cruiser. Repair parties estimated that the *Gneisenau* would require at least six months' repair to make her seaworthy. Repairs to the *Scharnhorst* were scheduled to be completed much sooner but not in time to satisfy the impatient Raeder's ambitious schedule.

On April 26, Lutjens was officially appointed commander of the forthcoming operation, one that he named Rheinubung (Operation Rhine). When the entire operational plan was revealed, though, Lutjens found himself regretting that the two Brest ships would be unavailable. He urged Raeder to postpone the operation until at least the *Scharnhorst* or *Tirpitz* were ready for the sea. "There is a powerful case for waiting at least until the *Scharnhorst* has been repaired . . . if not until the crew of the *Tirpitz* have finished their training."[5] But the commander in chief was in a hurry. Lutjens's recommendation was ignored.

The *Tirpitz* was another matter. She required but a few more weeks of training to work her crew into shape. Because of Raeder's impatience, however, when Captain Topp of the battleship asked Lutjens to postpone Rheinubung for those few weeks, the admiral had no choice but to deny Topp's request.

Another blow to the operation occurred on the twenty-fourth when the *Prinz Eugen* was damaged by a mine that exploded nearby while she was exercising in the Baltic. Although the damage was slight, Raeder's plan suffered a four-week postponement bringing it even closer to the time when the *Tirpitz* would be ready.

On April 27, Lutjens hoisted his flag on the *Bismarck*. Before doing so he took time out to visit Admiral Marschall. Even though Lutjens had replaced Marschall as fleet commander, the two had remained close friends and respected each other's opinions. Marschall was an advocate of allowing the commander at sea freedom of movement instead of restricting him by a predetermined operational directive. He urged Lutjens to do the same. The latter, however, had witnessed Marschall's demise and had his own ideas on the matter.

"No thank you," he told him. "There have already been two fleet commanders who have lost their jobs owing to friction with the admiralty and I don't want to be the third. I know what they want, and shall carry out their orders."[6]

On May 5, the *Bismarck* was honored by a visit from Hitler himself. The Führer was apprehensive regarding the forthcoming operation and made no secret of the fact. He often said that at sea he was a coward. When Lutjens finished conducting Hitler on a grand tour of

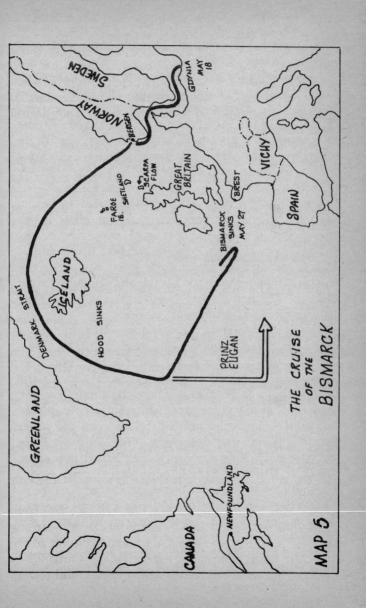

THE CRUISE
OF THE
BISMARCK

MAP 5

the ship, extolling the *Bismarck*'s virtues all the time, Hitler was even more reluctant to risk the magnificent ship. Nevertheless, he decided to allow the operation to proceed as scheduled.

Lutjens used the next few weeks to exercise the ship, conducting gunnery and refuelling drills in the Baltic. Intelligence assessments reporting the current disposition of the British fleet were scrutinized. Tactics were reviewed and rehearsed over and over. Finally, on May 18, the *Bismarck* and *Prinz Eugen* were ready for sea. A few days earlier all leaves had been abruptly cancelled and the crews summoned back aboard.

For a number of weeks the British had suspected that the Germans were planning another major operation. Reconnaissance flights over the Baltic, North Sea and Norway were stepped up. Admiral Tovey, commander of the home fleet, beefed up the patrols in the Denmark Strait and Iceland-Faroes Passage. The home fleet lay at anchor at Scapa Flow waiting to sail at a moment's notice.

The British were not the only ones relying on intelligence gathered from reconnaissance flights. The Germans too placed a heavy reliance on flights over Scapa Flow. The information garnered allowed the German navy to accurately gauge the strength of the home fleet at any given time: which ships were in port and which ones were missing. Along with the usual bevy of cruisers and destroyers, Tovey had available the battleship *King George V,* her brand new sister *Prince of Wales*, and the famous battle cruiser *Hood.* The battle cruiser *Repulse* and the carrier *Victorious* were in the Clyde preparing to escort a troop convoy to the Middle East. The *Rodney* was making ready for a voyage across the Atlantic to Canada where she was scheduled to undergo a much-needed refit. As with all commanders, Tovey wished he had more ships available but resigned himself to the fact that he would have to make do with what was available. Britain's entire fleet was stretched to the limit by the need to protect her empire and the sea lanes vital to her survival.

During the time the *Bismarck* lay at anchor in Gottenhafen, her crew had formed a deep friendship with the crew of a smaller vessel that lay nearby. The submarine *U-556* was dwarfed by the mighty battleship which may have led to the strange bond of comradeship between the two crews. When the *Bismarck* was conducting exercises in the Baltic, *U-556* was practicing in the area as well. Just before departing for an Atlantic patrol, the crew of the U-boat jokingly pledged that if ever the *Bismarck* found herself in trouble, she merely had to call for the tiny U-boat to help out.

On the morning of May 18, Lutjens met with Captains Brinkmann of the *Prinz Eugen* and Lindemann of the *Bismarck* on board the battleship. Final plans were reviewed once more as Lutjens assured himself that everyone thoroughly understood the forthcoming operation. That afternoon, the *Prinz Eugen* put to sea.

At 2:00 a.m. the next morning, the *Bismarck's* massive anchor rattled aboard and the mighty warship set out on her maiden voyage. Lutjens intended to break out into the Atlantic via the Denmark Strait. He selected this route over the Iceland-Faroes Passage because he felt that the latter would be more heavily patrolled and the former was closer to Scapa Flow. Since the *Admiral Scheer* and *Hipper* had recently returned home through the strait without incident and he himself had successfully taken the *Scharnhorst* and *Gneisenau* into the Atlantic using that route, Lutjens felt that this area was the more lightly patrolled and one whose weather could be used to his advantage.

Lutjens erred in his assessment that the British would ignore the Denmark Strait at the expense of the Iceland-Faroes Passage. Tovey did in fact have three cruisers—*Arethusa, Manchester* and *Birmingham*—there on patrol. But two heavy cruisers were also assigned to the Denmark Strait. Admiral Wake-Walker with the *Suffolk* and *Norfolk* stood vigil at either end of the route Lutjens had selected for his breakout into the Atlantic.

After redezvousing with the *Prinz Eugen* at sea, the *Bismarck* and a squadron of destroyers shaped a course for the North Sea. The voyage was without incident until midafternoon of the twentieth when the German formation was sighted moving through the Kattegat by the Swedish cruiser *Gotland*. The neutral ship reported the sighting to its own base. Later that evening, a member of the Norwegian Resistance reported to London that two large German warships had been sighted moving north. This report was passed on to Admiral Tovey as soon as it was deciphered.

Lutjens had decided to make a brief stop at Bergen, Norway to allow the *Prinz Eugen* to refuel instead of attempting to do so at sea even though during the earlier training sessions both ships had become highly proficient at this maneuver. At 9:00 a.m. the German battle force dropped anchor in Grimstadfjord near Bergen. Here Lutjens made his first serious error in judgment. Only the *Prinz Eugen* took on fuel. True, the *Bismarck* had only consumed a small portion of her fuel capacity, nevertheless, a cardinal rule dictated that a warship replenish its supply whenever possible. Lutjens certainly had an opportunity to refuel the *Bismarck* but for some unknown reason elected not to do so.

Around 1:00 p.m. a British reconnaissance plane flew over the fjord. When he saw the two warships at anchor the pilot moved in closer and snapped pictures. When the plane returned to base and the photographs were developed, a close scrutiny left little doubt that the *Bismarck* and a cruiser were now at anchor off Bergen. What the British did not know, however, was the intentions of the two ships. Had they simply stopped off at Bergen during maneuvers before returning to the Baltic or were they en route to the Atlantic?

Upon receipt of the sighting report, Tovey set the home fleet in motion. Late that night Admiral Holland set sail with the *Hood* and *Prince of Wales* with orders to hover southwest of Iceland where he would be in a position to cover either route into the Atlantic. The *Victorious* was ordered to rendezvous with Tovey's flagship, *King George V;* the *Repulse* was directed there as well after turning over her convoy to a force of destroyers.

Another force that was to play a leading role during the subsequent events was Force K based at Gibraltar. This force consisted of the carrier *Ark Royal*; Lutjens's old antagonist, the *Renown*; and the cruiser *Sheffield*, under the command of Adm. Sir James Somerville. Force K was ordered into the Atlantic where it would provide heavy cover for the troop convoy whose escort had been reduced by the reassignment of the *Repulse*.

Once the wheels were in motion Tovey ordered a bombing attack against the enemy ships. Fortunately for Lutjens, shortly after his presence was discovered by the British plane, the weather over Bergen closed down and visibility was reduced to a minimum. Consequently, when the flight of enemy bombers arrived that evening, they were unable to locate their target and dropped their bombs harmlessly.

At 7:00 p.m., Lutjens took advantage of the heavy fog and ordered both ships to sail. Once out of Grimstadfjord, the *Bismarck* and *Prinz Eugen* turned north and set a course for the Denmark Strait.

For most of the next day the area around Bergen remained socked in by a thick blanket of fog. British reconnaissance planes were unable to see through the clouds. Late in the day Tovey ordered one final effort made. When the British plane arrived over the area where the two German ships had been seen, a shifting breeze opened up a small hole in the fog. When he glanced down, the British pilot found that the fjord was empty. Tovey was informed of the latest information as soon as the plane returned and, at 10:00 p.m. that night, took his remaining ships to sea. By that time, Lutjens had almost a twenty-four hour head start.

For the next forty hours the two German ships moved north and west toward the Denmark Strait. Lutjens was confident of success.

The latest intelligence reports indicated that the British battleships were still at Scapa Flow. From this information Lutjens could draw only one conclusion. The home fleet was unaware of his intentions and did not know that the *Bismarck* and her consort were heading for the Atlantic.

Unfortunately, the German intelligence report was in error. Holland had already sailed with the *Hood* and *Prince of Wales*. Tovey had followed with his force after the German plane had flown over the naval base. Seeing the *King George V* and *Victorious*, the German pilot erroneously concluded that all the British ships were present.

Noon of the twenty-third found the German ships approaching the eastern entrance of the strait. A heavy layer of fog blanketed the northern side of the passage and was drifting across the water broken only by prevailing winds. Lutjens did not want to take unnecessary risks and decided to hug the fog bank so as to reduce the chance of discovery. Cautiously the two German ships made their way toward the Atlantic, *Bismarck* in the lead.

At approximately 6:00 p.m. lookouts on the cruiser *Suffolk* were jolted by the sight of a large warship breaking out of the fog dead ahead. A few moments later a second, smaller ship was sighted. Knowing that there were no friendly battleships in those waters, Captain Ellis swung the *Suffolk* around to seek shelter in the fog. When the two enemy ships had passed, Ellis maneuvered his ship into their wake so that he could shadow them from a safe distance using the *Suffolk's* radar. In the meantime, he made a full report to Admiral Wake-Walker aboard the *Norfolk*, further down the strait. Walker passed the *Suffolk's* sighting report to Admiral Holland in the *Hood*. Then curiosity got the best of him. He ordered the *Norfolk* out into open waters in order to get a better view since the flagship had no radar. Almost immediately, the *Bismarck* hove into sight and began firing on the *Norfolk*. Walker swiftly reversed course and sought the safety of the fog bank.

The *Bismarck's* lookout had not only sighted the *Norfolk*, but the *Suffolk* as well. Lutjens now knew that his location had been compromised and that the *Bismarck's* position would soon be known to the home fleet. Frustrated, he had lashed out at the only target in sight, the *Norfolk*, even though he was completely aware that the *Bismarck* had little to fear from the British cruiser. But the only thing the brief action accomplished was that the concussion from the *Bismarck's* guns caused the ship's radar to malfunction. Unwilling to proceed blindly, Lutjens ordered the *Prinz Eugen* to assume the lead position. *Suffolk*'s and *Norfolk*'s sighting reports, however, stated that the *Bismarck* was in the lead. From their position far in the rear of the German force, they had not noticed the change in the German formation.

When the *Suffolk*'s initial sighting report was received on board the *Hood*, Admiral Holland immediately set an intercepting course based on the reported course and speed of the enemy. In that northern latitude, sunset during that time of the year was around 1:50 a.m. Holland planned to intercept the *Bismarck* precisely at that time so that the enemy would be silhouetted against the sunset while his own ships were masked by darkness.

In the interim, Lutjens had altered course slightly to the north. Then the *Suffolk* lost contact and did not regain it for a few hours. Holland's initial plan had gone awry. When the *Suffolk* did regain contact, Holland altered course to intercept the German ships at the earliest possible opportunity.

The battle cruiser *Hood* was the pride of the Royal Navy. Launched in 1918 the ship displaced forty-two thousand tons. With a rated speed of thirty-one knots, the *Hood* mounted eight fifteen-inch guns in four turrets. By modern standards, the *Hood* was outdated. In an effort to concentrate as much speed and firepower in the ship, her designers had been forced to sacrifice armor. Although an effort had been made to correct this fatal flaw in her design during the early 1930's, the measure had been halfhearted. During the ship's career she had represented the might of the British navy and had sailed to virtually every port of call in the world showing the British flag. In the hearts of civilians and seamen alike, the *Hood* was loved and admired.

The *Hood*'s companion on this fateful voyage,

Prince of Wales, was England's latest battleship. She was so new, in fact, that she had not yet completed her trials, and teething problems plagued the ship. Such was the urgency of the situation, however, that the *Prince of Wales* sailed with dockyard workers still on board working feverishly to iron out the ship's mechanical and electrical problems. One of the ship's guns was causing a particular problem, preventing some of her guns from firing.

On board the *Bismarck*, Lutjens was unaware that a powerful enemy battle force was waiting for him. Instead, he seemed buoyant as the *Bismarck* and *Prinz Eugen* broke out of the Denmark Strait. Around 5:30 his mood turned to one of bewilderment as smoke was sighted on the horizon. Taking no chances, the admiral ordered both ship's captains to send their crews to battle stations.

Seven minutes later, lookouts on the *Prince of Wales* sighted the two German ships steaming in line ahead. Captain Leach notified the flagship at once. In his anxiety to decrease the range swiftly, Admiral Holland in the *Hood* ordered a change of course that turned the British ships almost at right angles to the German ships. It was a colossal blunder totally out of character for an experienced naval officer. By turning his ships thus, Holland closed the range rapidly but approached the enemy nearly head-on, thus reducing the number of guns that could fire. From that angle, both British ships could only bring their forward turrets to bear.

As we have already seen, when the two German ships entered the Denmark Strait the *Bismarck* was in the lead. This was the formation reported by the *Suffolk* whose lookouts had actually seen the German ships. Their radar, however, was unable to detect the shift in position caused by the breakdown of the

Bismarck's radar. Therefore, Holland was unaware that the leading ship was now the *Prinz Eugen*. Because the silhouettes of both ships were similar, from a distance the British admiral thought that the leading ship was actually the *Bismarck*. As a result, at 5:49 he gave the order to open fire on the left-hand ship. The *Hood* complied at once. The *Prince of Wales* followed a minute later but just before they fired, the ship's gunners realized their error and quickly shifted their aim to the *Bismarck*.

Lutjens, meanwhile, did not make the same error. He gave the order for both of his ships to concentrate on what he considered the more dangerous threat, the *Hood*. He did, however, mistake the *Prince of Wales* for the *King George V*. At 5:53, both German ships opened up on the *Hood*.

The British fire was fairly accurate as straddles fell near both German ships. A few minutes into the fight Holland realized his error and ordered the *Hood* to shift its fire to the *Bismarck*. Unfortunately, because of the course adopted by the admiral, the *Hood* was able to fire only four of her eight guns, and the *Prince of Wales* only six of ten. Nevertheless, the latter managed to make three fourteen-inch hits on the *Bismarck*.

Shortly after opening fire the *Prinze Eugen* also found the range. As a result of hér accurate gunfire, fires could be seen burning on the *Hood*'s deck.

Then, at 6:00, a fearful eruption rolled across the sea. In a huge flash of fire, smoke, and debris, the *Hood* blew up. As one seaman recollected, "At first we could see nothing, but what we saw moments later could not have been conjured up by even the wildest imagination. Suddenly the *Hood* split in two and thousands of tons of steel were hurled into the air. The fireball that developed where the *Hood* had been seemed near enough to touch. It was like being in a hurricane. Every nerve in my body felt the pressure of the explosion."[7]

The *Prince of Wales* was forced to swerve dramatically to avoid the wreckage. Of the 1,418 men on the *Hood*, only 3 managed to survive the disaster.

Lutjens was awestruck at the untimely and swift demise of the *Hood*. He stood transfixed on the *Bismarck*'s bridge staring at the empty patch of sea where a mighty warship had been moments earlier. He quickly recovered his senses and ordered both German ships to shift their fire to the remaining British battleship.

The *Prince of Wales* now began to feel the full weight of the German guns. She was hit in rapid succession by three fifteen-inch shells and three eight-inchers. One of the fifteen-inch hits exploded on the bridge killing everyone except Captain Leach and one other officer. The ship began to take on water and her speed dropped off. The mechanical problems that had plagued the battleship began to act up again. Accordingly, at 6:13, Leach broke off the action and turned his ship away under cover of smoke.

Lutjens was now faced with a choice. He could finish off the *Prince of Wales* and return home to a hero's welcome after having registered a decisive tactical victory over the world's most famous ship, or he could remain on course as if nothing had happened and carry out his plan for raiding in the Atlantic. The propaganda value of returning to Germany unscathed after the victory was immeasurable but Lutjens chose to continue on into the Atlantic. Captain Lindemann disagreed violently and the two had a heated argument over the decision but Lutjens's mind was made up.

Admiral Wake-Walker in the *Norfolk* suddenly

found himself the senior British officer on the scene. He ordered the *Prince of Wales* to join his two cruisers who now took up a shadowing position astern of the German force albeit at a healthy distance. The *Bismarck*'s speed and course was reported to Admiral Tovey on board the *King George V*.

Now Lutjens took notice of the shadowing British ships. For the rest of the morning he attempted to shake off the British cruisers to no avail. At the same time, he was as yet unaware of the extent of the damage caused by the *Prince of Wales*'s guns.

In the meantime, Tovey, with the *King George V, Repulse, Victorious* and four cruisers and escorting destroyers, was making for the *Bismarck*'s reported position at full speed. At the same time, the British admiralty summoned up every warship available. The *Rodney,* en route to Canada for a refit, was directed to join up with the home fleet. The *Ramilles,* escorting a convoy in mid-Atlantic, was ordered to leave her charges in the hands of destroyers and begin looking for the *Bismarck*. At Halifax, the battleship *Revenge* was ordered to raise steam in the event the *Bismarck* showed up off the North American coast. The cruiser *Edinburgh,* on patrol in mid-Atlantic, was ordered to close on the *Bismarck*'s position to act as a relief shadower.

Around 2:40 p.m., Tovey ordered the *Victorious* to move ahead and launch an air strike if possible. Escorted by the cruiser *Galatea* and three destroyers, the carrier went to full speed and detached itself from the rest of the fleet.

Around the same time, Lutjens asked naval group west to establish a U-boat picket line south of Greenland. If he could, he intended to lead his pursuers across that line thus making them sitting ducks for the submarines. The admiral then began to review the damage reports and concluded that he would have to alter his plans.

One of the *Prince of Wales*'s fifteen-inch shells had punctured a fuel tank. A broad oil slick was clearly visible in the *Bismarck*'s wake but Lutjens had been aware of that for some time. What he did not know until reading the damage reports was that sea water had contaminated the fuel in two other bunkers. As a result, Lutjens now knew that he lacked sufficient fuel for a prolonged voyage, particularly since refuelling at sea was out of the question until the shadowing British ships were shaken off. Thus, Lutjens decided to make for one of the French ports, perhaps Saint-Nazaire, where repairs could be made. Before changing course, though, another operation had to be carried out.

Around 6:30 that evening, the *Suffolk*'s radar operators noticed that the range between their ships and the *Bismarck* was decreasing at an alarming rate of speed. Suddenly, directly ahead, the *Bismarck* appeared heading straight for the *Suffolk*. Captain Ellis quickly swung the wheel hard over and reversed course even as the *Bismarck*'s guns boomed. The *Norfolk* and *Prince of Wales* fired their guns to cover the retreat of the *Suffolk*. Then, just as quickly, the *Bismarck* swung around to her original course. No hits had been scored by either side. The entire tactic had been a decoy to allow the *Prinz Eugen* to slip away into the Atlantic. The *Bismarck* was now alone. Lutjens then sent a wire to Berlin stating his intentions to make for France.

Shortly after 10:00 p.m., the *Victorious* launched nine Swordfish torpedo planes in the direction of the *Bismarck*'s reported position. Almost two hours later, they arrived over their target and dived to attack. The *Bismarck* maneuvered violently in an attempt to avoid the torpedoes and put up a withering anti-aircraft fire. The British pilots claimed one hit but this was never confirmed.

As soon as it was dark, the *Bismarck* began zig-zagging to confuse the British, at the same time making herself a more difficult target for any lurking submarines. The *Suffolk*'s radar was a relatively primitive device mounted on the fore part of the mast in a fixed position unable to rotate. On the outward leg of the *Bismarck*'s zigzag the *Suffolk* would lose contact only to regain it on the inward leg. Shortly after 3:00 a.m. the next morning, however the *Suffolk* failed to regain contact. The *Bismarck* had not turned inward again. Instead, on the outward leg, Lutjens had straightened out the course temporarily before taking them in a great circle around the rear of the British ships. The admiral then set a course directly for France while the *Suffolk* continued to search in vain.

Around 6:30 on the morning of the twenty-fifth, Tovey was informed that the *Bismarck* had slipped away. He ordered the *Prince of Wales* to join the main body of the fleet and the *Victorious* to launch an aerial search. The carrier's planes combed the sea but found nothing but water. Shortly afterward the *Repulse,* low on fuel, was detached.

Lutjens was unaware that he had given the British the slip. The *Bismarck* continued to receive radar impulses but they were not originating from any enemy ship in the area. Still under the impression he was being followed, at 8:00 a.m., the admiral made the decision that eventually led to his doom. He sent a long message to Berlin detailing the battle with the *Hood:*

Presence of radar on enemy ships, with range of at

least 35,000 meters has a strong adverse effect on operations in Atlantic. Ships were located in Denmark Strait in thick fog and could never again break contact. Attempts to break contact unsuccessful despite most favorable weather conditions. Refueling in general no longer possible, unless high speed enables me to disengage. Running fight between 20,800 and 18,000 meters . . . *Hood* destroyed by explosion after five minutes, then changed target to *King George V*, which after clearly observed hit turned away making smoke and was out of sight for several hours. Own ammunition expenditure: 93 shells. Thereafter *King George* accepted action only at extreme range. *Bismarck* hit twice by *King George V*. One of them below side armor compartments XIII-XIV. Hit in compartments XX-XXI, reduced speed and caused ship to settle a degree and effective loss of oil compartments. Detachment of *Prinz Eugen* made possible by battleship engaging cruiser and battleship in fog. Own radar subject to disturbance, especially from firing.[8]

The length of the transmission allowed British radio direction stations to home on the *Bismarck*'s position. At 10:30, Tovey was given the *Bismarck*'s coordinates. Unfortunately, the plotters miscalculated and reported that the *Bismarck* was two miles north of her actual position. Based on this latest information, Tovey could only conclude that the *Bismarck* had elected to return to Germany after all. He ordered the *Prince of Wales* to head for the Iceland-Faroes Passage while he took the flagship off in pursuit. The *Rodney*, which had yet to join up, was directed to guard the approaches to France just in case.

May 25 was Lutjens's birthday. He was fifty-two years old. Just before noon a congratulatory wire was received from Admiral Raeder:

"Hearty congratulations on your birthday. After the last great feat of arms, may more such successes be granted to you in your new year."[9]

Lutjens was jubilant. If the *Bismarck* could steer clear of trouble for another forty-eight hours, she would be in range of Luftwaffe air bases in France. The Luftwaffe could throw up a powerful aerial blanket and cover the battleship's final run to harbor.

At 2:30, the admiralty redirected the *Rodney* and ordered Captain Dalrymple-Hamilton to join up with the home fleet. The *Rodney*'s speed, however, made this virtually impossible but she nevertheless altered course. Force K, coming up from Gibraltar, was ordered to cover the approaches to the Bay of Biscay. The *Rodney*'s orders were changed again four hours later and she was ordered back in the direction of France.

Just before 7:30 p.m. British direction finders, after rechecking their calculations, realized that they had made a drastic error. Tovey was quickly informed of the error and told that in their estimation, the *Bismarck* was indeed making for France. Regrettably, by that time the *Bismarck* was over 150 miles ahead of the *King George V*. Nonetheless, Tovey ordered the home fleet to change course and take up the chase once more.

As darkness began to descend on the sea, the weather began to deteriorate. Heavy seas broke over German and British ships alike, reducing their speed. The home fleet destroyers, low on fuel, were detached and ordered to head for Iceland to refuel. Tovey radioed the admiralty requesting more destroyers to act as escorts. The admiralty ordered Captain Philip Vian, commanding nine destroyers that were escorting a convoy, to take five of his ships and join up with the home fleet. Vian took the *Zulu, Sikh, Maori, Polish*

Piourin, and his own ship, *Cossack,* and set off at high speed for the home fleet's reported position.

As already related, Force K was steaming at high speed north from Gibraltar towards the Bay of Biscay. With Tovey 150 miles behind the *Bismarck,* Admiral Somerville's ships were the only thing standing between the *Bismarck* and safety. At her present speed and course, by the morning of the twenty-seventh, the *Bismarck* would be close enough to France for the Luftwaffe to throw an aerial umbrella over her. If the Bismarck were to be stopped at all, it had to be on the twenty-sixth.

Somerville's only major warship was the *Renown.* This ship was almost as old as the *Hood* and certainly no match for the *Bismarck.* In fact, the admiralty had already given Somerville direct orders not to allow the *Renown* to engage the enemy. Thus, Somerville's only hope was the torpedo aircraft on board the *Ark Royal.*

Despite the stormy seas, at dawn on the twenty-sixth, Somerville decided to launch an air search from the *Ark Royal.* The *Bismarck* had still not been located. Around 10:30 a.m., a patrolling Catalina flying boat spotted a lone warship heading in the direction of France. A closer look revealed the ship to be the *Bismarck.* Finaly, her exact position was known.

The Catalina's sighting report was received by the final ship to join the hunt. The cruiser *Dorsetshire* was escorting a convoy from Sierra Leone to England. Her captain turned over the escorting duties to an auxiliary cruiser and made off in the direction of the *Bismarck.*

The *Ark Royal's* aircraft, using the Catalina's report, now began to shadow the *Bismarck.* The drone of enemy planes nearby infuriated Lutjens. He had the battleship's anti-aircraft guns fire at the planes but the only thing accomplished was the soothing of the admiral's temper.

Meanwhile, Somerville had directed the *Ark Royal* to prepare a full strike of torpedo planes. Just before 3:00 p.m. fifteen Swordfish began to roar down the ship's flight deck. They had not, however, been informed that an hour and a half earlier, Somerville had detached the *Sheffield* with orders to gain visual contact with the *Bismarck*.

Ark Royal's aircraft were armed with torpedoes using a new magnetic warhead which were designed to explode when the torpedo came within the magnetic field of a ship's hull. This was in contrast to contact warheads that only exploded after hitting a solid target. Forty minutes after the Swordfish had lifted off from the *Ark Royal*, the British realized their mistake. A radio message in the clear was sent to the planes: Watch out for Sheffield. It was too late.

Just before 4:00, the *Sheffield*'s lookouts heard the drone of airplane engines overhead. Then, to their amazement, the British planes began to swoop in for the attack. The British pilots had not received the warning. The new magnetic warheads proved the *Sheffield*'s salvation. Most exploded on contact with the water. The others were evaded by Captain Larcom's skillful maneuvering of his ship. Red-faced, the British pilots returned to the *Ark Royal*.

After having spent the day in a rather pessimistic mood, Lutjens's spirits began to lift. Thus far, no enemy ships were in sight and darkness was but a few hours away. Under cover of night, the *Bismarck* could slip away from the shadowing aircraft and by morning be under the protection of the Luftwaffe. If all went well, by the next evening the *Bismarck* would be safely anchored at Saint Nazaire. At 5:40 his hopes were dealt a blow when the *Bismarck*'s lookouts sighted the

Sheffield. Lutjens ordered a few salvos fired in the *Sheffield*'s direction, but except for a few splinter hits which wounded half a dozen men, the *Sheffield* was unharmed. After thirty-seven hours, a British warship had finally regained visual contact with the *Bismarck*.

There was still time for one more torpedo attack before nightfall. Somerville wasted no time in ordering the attack as it represented the last chance to stop the *Bismarck*. This time, however, the torpedoes were armed with contact warheads. In addition, the British pilots were told to make visual contact with the *Sheffield* before attacking the *Bismarck*. At 7:10 p.m. fifteen more Swordfish roared down the deck of the carrier. At 8:45, after having been given the exact direction by the *Sheffield*, the Swordfish dropped out of the skies close to the *Bismarck*.

B.B. Schofield described what happened next this way:

> One torpedo which hit amidships caused no damage, but the second affected the rudders disastrously by jamming the portside rudder at a fifteen-degree angle. Immediately the *Bismarck* became no longer maneuverable. Plates were thrown in the air and the hull vibrated violently . . . The stern compartments in the ship were now flooding. . . . Eventually it was found possible to connect the hand rudder. But the old rudder would not budge and to attempt to cut it away with underwater saws was quite impossible because of the heavy swell. A proposal to force the rudder out from below with the help of explosives was rejected because of the proximity to the propellers.[10]

The hit had occurred while the *Bismarck* was

heading north. Captain Lindemann had maneuvered the ship in a twisting, turning effort to avoid the torpedo planes. All the while, the battleship put out a withering stream of anti-aircraft fire but the British pilots had pressed the attack home. The rudder was virtually the only part of the ship vulnerable to torpedo attack. The *Bismarck*'s thick armor hide was capable of absorbing a tremendous amount of punishment anywhere else.

Unable to steer, the *Bismarck* sailed north at a reduced speed. When Admiral Tovey received a report from one of the aircraft that the *Bismarck* was heading north he thought that the pilot had made a mistake or, at best, the course was only temporary. Thirty minutes later, the *Sheffield* confirmed that the *Bismarck* was indeed steaming north, directly toward the home fleet. Tovey could not believe his luck. The last chance had paid off.

Aboard the *Bismarck*, every effort was made to free the damaged rudder. When this proved futile, Lindemann attempted to maneuver the ship by running the screws at different revolutions. This also failed. Lutjens now knew that he was in for a fight, one that there was little hope of surviving. But the *Bismarck* was a mighty warship; perhaps there was still hope. Just before 11:00 p.m., he sent a signal stating that the *Bismarck* was unable to maneuver. He closed by saying that the battleship would fight to the last and ended with the traditional, Long Live the Führer!

Vian's destroyers had been steaming full out for the *Bismarck*'s reported position. Around 10:00 the ships sighted the *King George V* which flashed a message ordering the destroyers to continue on toward the *Bismarck*. At 10:30 the destroyers made contact.

Vian placed his ships in a circle around the

Bismarck but at a safe distance. Lutjens was made aware of the destroyers' presence at once and directed Lindemann to be on the alert for possible torpedo attacks. Consequently, the entire crew spent the night at action stations.

Vian did in fact attempt to torpedo the *Bismarck*. Throughout the long night the five destroyers raced in independently to unleash their deadly fish. The *Bismarck*'s heavy guns made the effort perilous but no British casualties were incurred. Reports from survivors vary whether any hits were made but unless it was as very lucky shot, it is highly improbable that any of the British destroyers managed a hit. None of the torpedoes were fired from under eight thousand yards, most were fired at a greater distance. Nevertheless, Vian's action had the effect of keeping the *Bismarck*'s crew awake and tense throughout the night.

Just before 8:00 a.m. the next morning, the wolves began to assemble. The *King George V* and the *Rodney*, which had finally joined Tovey, sighted the *Bismarck* just over nine miles away. Half an hour later the *Norfolk*, after a long stern chase, arrived on the scene. Wake-Walker was determined to be in at the finish. Ten minutes after that, the *Dorsetshire* sighted the *Bismarck*.

That morning, Lutjens and his staff were encountered on the *Bismarck*'s deck heading for their battle station on the bridge. Lutjens was strangely quiet and did not return the salutes of the crew. That was the last anyone saw of the admiral.

Tovey positioned the *Rodney* and *King George V* on the port side of the crippled *Bismarck*. Instead of insisting on a rigid battle formation, he signalled the *Rodney* that she had freedom of action and movement. The *Norfolk* was off the starboard bow and the

Dorsetshire moved in from astern. At 8:47, the *Rodney*'s sixteen-inch guns shattered the stillness. The flagship followed a few moments later. Two minutes after that, the *Bismarck* replied.

Anyone in a position to observe the entire battle failed to survive the action. Those that did were only aware what occurred near their own action stations.

"Shortly after the battle commenced, a shell hit the combat mast and the fire-control post in the foremast broke away," wrote Schofield. "At 0902 both forward heavy gun turrets were put out of action. A further hit wrecked the forward control post, the rear control post was wrecked soon after . . . and that was the end of the fighting instruments."[11]

With the *Bismarck*'s firing sporadic and inaccurate, the British battleships moved closer and continued to pound the helpless enemy warship. Meanwhile, the *Norfolk* and *Dorsetshire* had also joined in. No one knows at what point in the battle Lutjens perished but survivors stated that halfway through the battle a terrible fire broke out in the vicinity of the bridge. There was little chance that he could have survived the inferno.

Around 9:30, the *Bismarck* fired her last salvo from her rear turrets. Then the guns ran down to maximum depression and ceased for good.

With her other guns pointing in all angles and on fire from stem to stern, the *Bismarck* drifted forlornly but refused to sink. Tovey moved his ships even closer and continued to fire at the drifting inferno but the *Bismarck* remained defiantly afloat. At 10:15 Tovey broke off the action. The *Rodney, King George V* and *Norfolk* were desperately short of fuel. The *Dorsetshire* was ordered to finish off the *Bismarck* with torpedoes.

Around the same time, one of the few surviving

officers aboard the *Bismarck* gave the order to set the scuttling charges. At 10:20, the *Dorsetshire* fired two torpedoes into the *Bismarck*'s starboard side. The cruiser then circled around to the other side and fired one more. All three torpedoes struck home. At 10:40 the mighty *Bismarck* slipped beneath the waves.

Out of a crew of 2,400, only 119 lived to tell the tale. The *Dorsetshire* and the destroyer *Maori*, aided by aircraft from the *Ark Royal*, remained in the area and plucked the survivors out of the water.

During the *Bismarck*'s final hours, the submarine mentioned earlier, *U-556*, was returning from a patrol in the Atlantic. The tiny U-boat had pledged to aid the *Bismarck* in her time of peril. In fact, before sailing for their Atlantic patrol, the U-boat's crew had given their friends in the *Bismarck* a cartoon-type picture depicting the *Bismarck* being towed by the *U-556*. Now, across the submarine's bows streamed the *Renown* and *Ark Royal*. In their haste to catch up to the *Bismarck*, neither ship was zigzagging. They were perfect targets for the u-boat. Lieutenant Wohlfarth brought his boat up to periscope depth and could only sigh as the two enemy capital ships steamed by. He had used his entire load of torpedoes during the recently concluded voyage and was powerless to intervene.

Admiral Lutjens has been severely criticized for his actions during the pursuit and chase of the *Bismarck*. Should he have continued the first battle, sunk the *Prince of Wales*, and returned to Germany the victor of a magnificent battle? His decision at the time was probably the correct one. He was unaware of the extent of the *Bismarck*'s damage until hours after the battle was over. His primary mission was to break out into the Atlantic and attack merchant shipping, not risk major damage to his ship in a battle against heavy enemy units. He was confident that, eventually, the *Bismarck* could shake off her shadowers. Lutjens made the decision to head for France only after the shortage of fuel was discovered.

Then, of course, there was the *Prinz Eugen* to consider. Could she have survived a battle against the *Prince of Wales, Norfolk* and *Suffolk?* Lutjens was responsible for seeing to it that the *Prince Eugen* was able to break away on a commerce-raiding voyage of its own. Unfortunately, mechanical problems plagued the *Prinz Eugen* and, on June 1, she arrived at Brest after an uneventful voyage. She eventually reached Germany in company with the *Scharnhorst* and *Gneisenau.**

Admiral Lutjens had made the British dance to his tune for almost eighteen months. With the *Scharnhorst, Gneisenau* and *Hipper* he had safely escorted the invasion force to Narvik and Trondheim. In command of the two battle cruisers, Lutjens managed to sink twenty-two merchant ships while the home fleet searched the North Atlantic for him. Finally, with the *Bismarck,* he had sunk the "Mighty Hood," England's most famous warship. For seven days he had kept no less than fifty-six British warships tied down hunting him, a remarkable feat in itself. Surely, he must rate with Germany's finest naval commanders.

*See Cilax, chapter five.

5. ADMIRAL OTTO CILAX

In 1588 Philip II of Spain assembled the greatest number of ships the world had yet seen, placed them under command of the Duke of Medinia-Sadonia, and sent them into the English Channel for the purpose of destroying Elizabeth I's empire. The Spanish Armada suffered a devastating defeat at the hands of Drake and Hawkins. Another 350 years passed before anyone else dared challenge the might of the Royal Navy in its own backyard. In 1942, Vice Adm. Otto Cilax of the German navy led the battle cruisers *Scharnhorst* and *Gneisenau* and the cruiser *Prinz Eugen* up the Channel, defied the Royal Navy, and brought his force safely home to Germany. It was one of the truly remarkable achievements of WWII. The reverberations shook the very foundations of Whitehall and the British admiralty. Churchill and King George VI demanded explanations. There were none. Cilax had thumbed his nose at the British navy and had gotten away with it.

The "Black Czar," as Cilax was known in navy circles, was a veteran navy officer accustomed to challenging the Royal navy. In WWI he had fought at the great battle of Jutland. Following that war, the Treaty of Versailles severely limited the size of the Germany navy. Consequently, Germany had to be highly selective in choosing which officers to retain. Only those with exceptional potential and ability were considered. Cilax was one of those retained.

Of all the leading German admirals of World War II, Cilax probably had the most seagoing experience. During the between-war period there had naturally been periods of staff assignments ashore designed to make an up-and-coming career officer a well-rounded commander. In Cilax's case, however, these periods ashore were brief. He much preferred the feel of a deck under his feet to a chair behind a desk.

Cilax gained valuable experience in virtually every seagoing branch of the navy. He served in U-boats, destroyers and in the mid-1930s commanded the pocket battleship *Admiral Scheer*. In January of 1939, he became the first captain of the battle cruiser *Scharnhorst*. Along the way, Cilax earned a reputation as a short-tempered martinet who insisted on strict compliance with the navy code of conduct. He was a spit and polish officer in the true sense of the phrase, thus his nickname, the Black Czar.

Late in 1939, Cilax left the *Scharnhorst* to become chief of staff, naval group west under Adm. Alfred Saalwachter. He chafed at being bound to a desk but his seniority precluded his being in command of a single ship and there were few fleet commands. The fleet commander in the West was Admiral Marschall, later succeeded by Admiral Lutjens. Both were senior to Cilax who did not gain an active seagoing assignment until July 1, 1941 when he was named fleet commander to succeed Lutjens who had gone down with the *Bismarck* some weeks earlier.*

*See Lutjens, chapter four.

Cilax's new command consisted of the battle cruisers *Scharnhorst* and *Gneisenau* and the cruiser *Prinz Eugen*. All three ships lay bottled up at the French port of Brest. There, the ships were convenient targets for the Royal Air Force. Shortly after her arrival, the *Gneisenau* was heavily damaged by a torpedo and a few days later, three bombs. The mighty ship was laid up for six months.

The *Scharnhorst* was also immobilized. During her raiding cruise, the battle cruiser's boiler tubes had malfunctioned. When the ship reached Brest, a thorough inspection concluded that the troublesome tubes would have to be replaced. The *Scharnhorst* too required months of repairs.

On June 1, the *Prinz Eugen*, recent consort of the ill-fated *Bismarck*, arrived at Brest from an unsuccessful raiding voyage during which that ship's engines had acted up. The *Prinz Eugen* was also in dire need of dockyard work although the cruiser's requirements were not as extensive as those of the battle cruisers.

For months Cilax watched in frustration as his ships lay idle, virtual sitting ducks for the almost daily raids by the R.A.F. Elaborate camouflage, huge nets over the ships, beefed-up anti-aircraft defenses and machines that produced artificial fog over the anchorage reduced the chances of hitting the ships. Nevertheless, British bombs managed to take their toll. Shore installations were hit as were barracks, the town of Brest itself and dockyard facilities. Even though they could not actually see the German ships, British bombardiers released their bombs at random. Under those circumstances, a few bombs could not help but fall on and near the ships.

That autumn, Hitler began to espouse another one

of his strategic theories. He was convinced that the Allies intended to invade Norway in the near future. Occupied Norway was unusually lightly defended. German troops were fighting in North Africa and Russia, and a large occupation army was required for France, the Balkans and the Lowlands. Thus there were few troops left for the defense of Norway which had become a backwater of the war.

Hitler wanted to use the ships of the German fleet, including those at Brest, to bolster the Norwegian defensive positions. He railed at Admiral Raeder and ordered him to bring the Brest fleet home as early as possible. The ships were of absolutely no use sitting idle at Brest.

There were but two routes that the German ships could use to reach home. One was via the Denmark Strait, the other, up the English Channel. The former route had been successfully utilized by virtually every heavy ship in the German navy. *Scharnhorst* and *Gneisenau* used this route to break out into the Atlantic on the first leg of the voyage that saw them wind up in Brest. The *Bismarck* and *Prinz Eugen* began their fateful voyage through the same body of water. The pocket battleships *Lutzow** and *Admiral Scheer* returned home via the Denmark Strait as did the cruiser *Hipper*. By now, however, if the ship left Brest intent on breaking home by this route, their absence would be noted by the enemy and the fleet would find itself having to slip around the rear of the British home fleet based at Scapa Flow. The chances of accomplishing this were remote at best.

The other route, up the English Channel, was equally perilous. The channel was narrow, laced with

*Formerly *Deutschland*

mine fields, in close proximity to enemy airfields and, at its narrowest point, the Straits of Dover, ships were in range of coastal artillery. In addition, with enough advance notice, the home fleet could move south and plug the northern end of the channel.

The British did not consider the possibility of the German ships using the channel to be remote. As early as May of 1941, the admiralty began drafting plans, code-named Fuller, in the event the Brest ships did break up the channel. The channel itself was divided into three sectors which were constantly patrolled by British aircraft. In addition, daily reconnaissance flights observed the activity at Brest. If the German ships did leave port, it would be reported almost immediately. As insurance, the British sent submarines to patrol the vicinity of the harbor. If the reconnaissance planes missed the German ships, the submarines were ideally positioned to report their sailing.

Many of the high-ranking officers of the German navy were lukewarm to the idea of bringing the Brest fleet home via the English Channel. The rest opposed the idea totally. The route was simply too fraught with potential hazards. On the other hand, as the Denmark Strait alternative was equally as dangerous, the admirals had no answer to the problem.

Hitler was not averse to using the English Channel. In October, he suggested to Raeder that the *Prinz Eugen* be brought home via that route. Raeder was willing to concede bringing one cruiser up the channel but not the entire fleet including battle cruisers. Admiral Saalwachter added his endorsement to Raeder's vehement objections, as did Cilax. Hitler was unmoved. He wanted the large guns of the *Scharnhorst* and *Gneisenau* stationed in Norway. The Führer told Raeder in no uncertain terms that if the admiral insisted on the ships remaining in Brest, he would have the guns removed from them and shipped to Norway where they could be put to use as coastal batteries. Unwilling to see his precious ships dismantled, Raeder caved in.

On New Year's Day, 1942, Cilax met with Saalwachter in Paris and was informed that Hitler had ordered the three ships back to Germany via the English Channel. Cilax returned to his flagship, *Scharnhorst*, with orders from Saalwachter to develop a plan. He summoned the fleet navigator and ordered him to obtain as many charts of the channel as he could lay his hands on. So as not to compromise the operation, Cilax also ordered the navigator to secure charts of other areas as well. Then Cilax began making plans to take his fleet home.

Previous German plans had called for the ships to traverse the narrow Straits of Dover in darkness. This meant that the ships would have to leave Brest in broad daylight. Cilax disagreed with this plan of action. He felt that if the ships left port in daylight, they would be quickly discovered by enemy reconnaissance planes. This would give the British ample time to prepare their defenses and make the voyage one that none of the ships would be likely to survive. Cilax proposed sailing at night when British planes were hindered by darkness. Then, taking advantage of the element of surprise, they would have a huge head start on British countermeasures. The drawback to this plan was that the fleet would find itself in the Straits of Dover in broad daylight. Cilax was not as impressed with the British coastal batteries as his superiors were, thus he was willing to risk it. He did, however, have reservations about the ability to maneuver in the narrow straits in the event of an attack from sea or air.

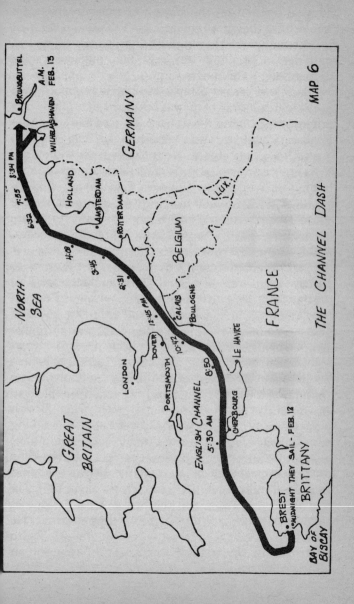

BRUNSBÜTTEL
A.M. FEB. 15
WILHELMSHAVEN

8:34 PM
7:55
6:32
4:08
3:45
2:31
12:45 PM
10:42
8:50
5:30 AM

GERMANY

Holland
AMSTERDAM
ROTTERDAM

BELGIUM

CALAIS
BOULOGNE

NORTH SEA

DOVER
PORTSMOUTH

LONDON

LUX.

GREAT BRITAIN

ENGLISH CHANNEL

LE HAVRE

CHERBOURG

FRANCE

BREST
MIDNIGHT THEY SAIL — FEB. 12

BRITTANY

BAY OF BISCAY

THE CHANNEL DASH

MAP 6

Cilax's plan was an elaborate one. The capital ships would be escorted by a squadron of destroyers and a large flotilla of U-boats. Ahead of the ships, the channel would be swept free of mines before the ships approached. Finally, the Lutftwaffe would have to cooperate by covering the ships with an impenetrable aerial umbrella.

Up to that point, the Luftwaffe had been loath to cooperate with the navy. Raeder and Goering, the Luftwaffe head, were bitter rivals. Intraservice rivalry for Hitler's favor was bitter and intense.

On January 12, a meeting was held at Hitler's headquarters. Present were Admirals Raeder, Saalwachter and Cilax. Also in attendance were General Jeschonnek, chief of staff of the Luftwaffe, and Col. Adolf Galland, commander of fighters in France. Raeder raised the same old objections but these were swiftly swept aside by Hitler. Then Jeschonnek voiced doubts that the Lutftwaffe had enough planes readily available to carry out its phase of the operation. Hitler, intent on carrying out the plan, was not about to let jealousies stand in the way this time. He coldly informed the general that the Luftwaffe would cooperate to the fullest extent or find itself answerable to him personally. Reluctantly, Jeschonnek pledged his support.

Galland too was skeptical. Nevertheless, there were few challenges Adolf Galland would not accept and he cast his lot with the plan's supporters. He later wrote, "The technical coordination of this typical combined operation was planned in such a way that the Luftwaffe was not under the navy but had to rely on teamwork. I must say that this coordination worked without friction."[1]

Hitler also endorsed Cilax's recommendation that the ships leave port in darkness. The element of surprise was something the Führer always appreciated. "In view of past experience," he said, "I do not believe the British capable of making and carrying out lightning decisions."[2]

Thus Operation Cerebus received official blessing. Because of the favorable tides during that period, the operation was scheduled for the second week in February.

Secrecy was paramount if Cerebus were to be a success. The Brest anchorage swarmed with French Resistance agents and the slightest deviation from the norm was reported to the British immediately. Outside of Hitler's headquarters, the only ones party to the secret were Raeder, Saalwachter, Cilax, Galland and his chief navigator, Geisler, Commodore Ruge, commander of the mine-sweeping forces, and the captains of the three ships, Hoffmann of *Scharnhorst*, Geneisenau's *Fein* and Brinkmann of the *Prinz Eugen*.

Cilax was determined not to allow the secret to slip out. Stringent security measures were instituted. Every effort was made to deceive the numerous enemy agents in Brest. Tropical uniforms were loaded aboard the ships and the rumor was deliberately spread that the ships were preparing for an extensive voyage in the South. Plans for a fancy costume ball celebrating Fasching* went ahead. Saalwachter sent printed invitations to a handful of officers stationed at Brest inviting them to a party in Paris on February 11, the very date selected for Cerebus's kickoff.

There were numerous problems still to be over-

---

*German pre-lenten festival.

come. Besides the need for secrecy, there was the ever-watchful eyes of the British reconnaissance planes. Along the coast, the British had an entire string of radar stations. Unless these could be jammed, the ships would be quickly discovered as they entered the channel. General Martini, the Luftwaffe signals expert, devised a method of jamming the radar stations intermittently so that the British would assume the problem was the result of atmospheric interference instead of deliberate jamming. However, if the stations were jammed constantly, the British would be sure to suspect something. Therefore, Martini planned to jam only those stations in range of the ships at any particular time.

Then there was the ship's crews themselves. Because they had laid idle for so long, the veteran crewmen had been transferred elsewhere and were replaced by inexperienced sailors. Cilax worried that the inexperienced and greatly reduced crews would not be able to react efficiently.

During the week preceding the operation all three ships began making final preparations. Camouflage nets were removed and one by one they made brief forays to conduct gunnery practice. Fuel bunkers were topped off. Six destroyers arrived at Brest to act as escort.

Meanwhile, Colonel Galland had assembled 280 fighters at airfields all along the route. Thirty of these were night fighters responsible for covering the ships during the predawn hours.

Galland was hard pressed not to reveal the purpose of the concentration of fighters to the pilots. He covered it by telling the pilots that they were scheduled to take part in a joint navy-Luftwaffe exercise. At all times, Galland planned to have at least sixteen fighters over the fleet. With each patrol's schedule overlapping its predecessor's by ten minutes, for twenty minutes of each hour the ships would be covered by thirty-two fighters. Added to the anti-aircraft fire of the fleet itself, the escorting destroyers and U-boats, the aerial defense was formidable indeed.

By the eleventh, all preparations were complete. Cilax held a noontime conference with his three captains. Charts were reviewed, final orders pored over and a toast drunk to the operation's success. The admiral reminded the captains that none of the heavy ships was to stop to aid another. If one of them were disabled, the others were to steam on without slowing down. He then voiced one last opinion:

It is a bold unheard of operation for the German navy. It will succeed if these orders are strictly obeyed. There is no margin for interpretation. They must be adhered to at all times. Ships will sail in the following order . . . *Scharnhorst, Gneisenau* and *Prinz Eugen*.

Do not seek combat, but only engage the enemy if the operation cannot otherwise be carried out.[3]

By 6:00 p.m., darkness had begun to descend over Brest. The fleet was scheduled to sail at 7:30. A few minutes before that, however, the port's air-raid sirens began to wail. The ships were particularly vulnerable to attack at that moment. Their camouflage had been stripped and steam was up. The artificial fog machines quickly laid a thick blanket over the anchorage. The raid lasted for forty-five minutes. Fortunately, although the enemy bombs had fallen on Brest and the dockyards, the ships were unhurt.

In one respect the British raid proved fortunate.

Through holes in the fog caused by shifting winds, reconnaissance planes were able to snap photos showing all three ships in port. Had the raid arrived half an hour later, the fleet's sailing would have been discovered.

Another stroke of luck for Cilax was the impatience of the commander of the British submarine patrolling the entrance to Brest. Around 8:00 p.m. the *Sealion* moved out to sea so that it could surface and recharge its batteries. No one on the British side actually expected the Germans to risk moving through the Straits of Dover in daylight. If the Brest squadron sailed, the British expected it to do so during daylight hours thus allowing them to sail through the narrowest part of the channel under cover of darkness. Consequently, after dark, vigilance was relaxed.

At 9:00 p.m., the British air raid had been over for nearly half an hour. Despite this, the all clear had not been sounded. On the *Scharnhorst* Cilax paced nervously back and forth. The ships had to sail by 9:30 at the very latest if they were to adhere to the rigid timetable. At 9:15 Cilax was ready to postpone the operation for another day. At that moment, the all clear sounded and the admiral gave the order to proceed.

By 10:00, *Scharnhorst, Gneisenau* and *Prinz Eugen* had cleared the harbor and were headed up the channel. The operation had been such a well-guarded secret that not even the crews were aware of their ultimate destination. A few minutes after midnight their speculation came to an end. Aboard the three ships an announcement from Cilax was read:

Warriors of the Brest forces. Our next task, to the execution of which we were called upon last night, lies ahead of us. It is: Sail through the channel eastward into the German night.

This task imposes on men, weapons and machines the highest demands.

I lead the squadron conscious that every man at his post will do his duty to the utmost.[4]

The first obstacle to contend with where the British aerial reconnaissance patrols. The aircraft were fitted with radar that allowed them to detect shipping activity despite the darkness. On this particular night, Cilax was extremely lucky. The radar apparatus on both reconnaissance aircraft assigned to the area between Brest and Ushant malfunctioned. As the German fleet sailed up the channel almost directly beneath them, both British planes returned to base unaware that the breakout was in progress.

The same problem bedeviled the patrol plane responsible for the area between Ushant and Brittany. A third patrol, covering the area between Le Havre and Boulogne ended an hour early when fog began to settle in on the plane's home airfield. The station commander thus ordered the patrol cut short so that the pilot could land safely before the field was closed down. Thus, the German squadron was able to elude an enemy submarine and moved safely through three reconnaissance areas without being discovered. Cilax's luck was in.

As dawn approached the ships were approaching the Straits of Dover. Incredibly, even though they had been at sea for over ten hours and had covered almost three hundred miles, the German fleet remain undetected. Cilax's decision to leave port under cover of darkness was unquestionably the correct one. Overhead, Galland's fighters hovered vigilantly over the fleet. The arrival of the aircraft, however, gave the British the first indication that something was amiss.

There were a few radar stations that the Germans did not know existed. Obviously, Martini's jamming efforts did not affect them. One of these stations began monitoring the German aircraft activity over the channel. The radar blips seemed to be moving slowly up the channel as if covering something. At first it was thought that the Germans were carrying out an air-sea rescue mission. Nevertheless, the radar contact was tracked until three larger blips appeared on the radar screen. Two flights of Spitfires were dispatched to investigate.

Around 10:30 the Spitfires were intercepted by Galland's fighters. Attempting to outmaneuver and elude the German planes, the British pilots dove seaward and found themselves directly over the German fleet. The four Spitfires quickly turned tail and headed for home.

Three of the British pilots elected to follow orders and maintain radio silence. The last one radioed its observations to its home base. But Cilax's luck had still not run out. Through a breakdown in communications and the unwillingness of some high-ranking British officers to believe that the German ships were actually at large in the channel, the alarm was not sounded for another hour. By that time Cilax's squadron was in the approaches to the Straits of Dover.

On the bridge of the *Scharnhorst* Cilax peered over the side at the British Spitfires. He turned to Captain Hoffmann and said that an attack could be expected at any moment, just where he had feared it would happen, at the narrowest point in the voyage.

Commodore Ruge's mine sweepers had cleared a narrow channel along the route. On both sides of the channel, however, there remained a number of mines. In the Dover Straits the path through the mine fields was rather small. This left the German ships little room to maneuver in the event of an attack. Cilax was acutely aware of this.

Fortunately, Hitler's pronouncements proved prophetic. The British did not react quickly. The only thing that barred the German ships from sailing through the straits with impunity were the enemy coastal batteries.

Originally, the batteries were intended as defensive positions designed to hinder an invasion. In the case of the larger guns, they were designed to fire clear across the straits at targets in France. The gunners were not accustomed to fire at moving targets at relatively short range. Consequently they were unequal to the task.

As they moved through the straits, huge shell splashes could be easily observed from the decks of the German ships. In the van, *Scharnhorst* had almost passed out of range before the guns began firing. The *Gneisenau* and *Prinz Eugen*, though, remained in range for some time but the British firing was sporadic and far off target.

The British missed a golden opportunity for attacking Cilax's squadron when it was most vulnerable. Not until the fleet had passed Calais and were leaving the Straits of Dover did the first serious attack occur.

At 11:45, the six torpedo boats stationed at Dover received word that the German squadron was moving through the straits. Lieutenant Commander Pumphrey's MTBs* set out at once. Half an hour later the tiny, wooden boats sighted the German fleet. Pumphrey attempted to maneuver his boats close enough for them to launch their torpedoes. Every attempt

*Motor torpedo boat

211

proved futile. The German U-Boats and destroyers laid down a withering fire and prevented the MTBs from getting close. Galland's fighters chipped in, harassing the small boats with machine gunfire every foot of the way. Frustrating and thwarted at every turn, Pumphrey aimed his boats at the fleeing German capital ships and launched his torpedoes from long range. Every one ran wide, the range was simply too great. With their stingers pulled, the British boats turned for home.

The next attack was the most pathetic of the day, but perhaps one of the most heroic of the war. Stationed at Manston airfield was a squadron of six Fairey Swordfish torpedo planes of 825 Squadron. The squadron commander was Lt. Cmdr. Eugene Esmonde who had led the *Victorious*'s air attack against the *Bismarck*.* Early that morning the squadron had been "stood down" after being on stand-by all night in the event the German ships attempted to move through the straits. Shortly after breakfast, the air crews were put on stand-by again when word was received that the German ships had been sighted. At 11:40 the sighting was confirmed: it was the Brest squadron all right. Six grim-faced pilots and twelve equally apprehensive crewmen climbed aboard their planes.

The Fairey Swordfish had no business even being in combat in 1942. A bi-winged relic of the 1920s, the Swordfish resembled the ancient World War I planes as opposed to the sleek fighters of the 1940s. The plane's body was covered with fabric and the crew flew in open cockpits. Top speed was ninety knots with a torpedo suspended beneath the fusilage. Esmonde had been promised a heavy fighter escort of some fifty

*See Lutjens, chapter four.

planes but as he hovered over Manston, only one of the five promised Spitfire squadrons arrived. Ten fighters out of fifty. Finally, Esmonde could wait no longer. He set a course for the position of the German squadron.

By this time Cilax was beginning to relax a bit. He had brought his fleet through the Straits of Dover contested only by the ineffective fire of coastal batteries and a puny attack by a handful of torpedo boats. He was puzzled. The R.A.F. and the Royal Navy thus far had not lifted a finger in opposition. The admiral had no way of knowing that Admiral Pound, the British naval chief, refused to risk his heavy ships in the narrow confines of the English Channel. The home fleet would not intervene. But that was a moot point. By the time Cilax's force was discovered, it was too late for them to lend a hand anyway.

The R.A.F. was also caught by surprise. Virtually all of its fighters were committed to the defense of England while its bombers attacked Germany. A pitiful handful of bombers were allotted to prevent the Brest ships from breaking up the channel. Of course, the British had always assumed that there would be plenty of time to muster an attack once the ships were discovered leaving port. Cilax had crossed them up by sailing at night thereby gaining almost half a day's head start.

Cilax's bewilderment with the lack of R.A.F. interference came to an abrupt end just before 1:00 p.m. As he watched from his position on the flagship where he was sipping coffee with Captain Hoffmann, the ancient Swordfish appeared to port. Esmonde's planes were quickly jumped by the German fighters. A few moments later the anti-aircraft guns of every ship within range opened up. 825 Squadron was shot to pieces. Only five members of the squadron survived the ordeal. Esmonde was not one of them.

Cilax was amazed at the bravery of the British air crews. He referred to it as, "The mothball attack of a handful of ancient planes piloted by men whose bravery surpasses any other action by either side that day."[5]

Still, the Royal Navy's absence was conspicuous and this continued to puzzle Cilax. The admiral's usual foul mood was beginning to modify somewhat, however, once the fleet had passed safely through the Straits of Dover and into open water with more room to maneuver.

Around 1:30, the German ships were nearing an extensive mine field off the hook of Holland. Although a narrow path had already been cleared by the mine sweepers, the fleet approached the area with caution. Cilax was handed a dispatch stating that a flotilla of enemy destroyers was approaching at high speed. Six British destroyers had set out from Harwich a few hours earlier and made straight for Cilax's squadron.

The destroyers shortly became the least of Cilax's worries. At 2:30, virtually every man standing on the *Scharnhorst* was thrown to the deck as the great ship lurched to a sudden halt. The flagship had struck a mine. The *Scharnhorst* quickly began to take on water and all power was temporarily knocked out. Obeying Cilax's orders that none of the heavy ships was to stop to aid cripples, the *Gneisenau* and *Prinz Eugen* swept by and continued on their way.

With all radio communications lost Cilax now found himself unable to control Cerebus. He quickly ordered a command made by signal lamp to the destroyer Z-29. The Z-29 was directed to move close to the flagship to pick up passengers. As soon as the destroyer moved alongside, Cilax and his staff, including the Luftwaffe advisor, jumped from the *Scharnhorst* to the deck of the *Z-29*. As soon as her passengers were secured, the destroyer set out in pursuit of the rest of the squadron while a handful of smaller ships hovered around the *Scharnhorst*.

Captain Hoffmann's crew worked miracles. In less than an hour the *Scharnhorst* was under way again. Despite the damage and the urgings of officers, Hoffmann worked the ship up to full speed.

Just after 3:30 the six British destroyers located the main body of the fleet. Almost immediately they opened fire on the larger German ships. The main target of the destroyers appeared to be the *Prinz Eugen*. All German ships opened up on the approaching destroyers. The heavy guns of the *Gneisenau* and *Prinz Eugen* began to tell quickly. The British ships were hit repeatedly by shells from the German destroyers and large caliber shells from the two heavy ships. Those German fighters not engaged in dogfights with the destroyers' aerial screen strafed the tenacious little British ships. The *Worcester* was heavily damaged and in danger of sinking. The remaining destroyers were driven off after launching their torpedoes from long range. Just as in the attack of the MTBs, all torpedoes missed.

Aboard the *Z-29*, Cilax watched the action with dismay. Thanks to the excitement of the attack his chronic stomach trouble was acting up and his foul mood returned. In addition, he had no word of the fate of the *Scharnhorst*. Was the flagship under attack by other British ships? If so, in her helpless state the *Scharnhorst* would be hard pressed.

The admiral need not have worried. The *Scharnhorst* was well under way. Cilax's immediate concern was for the fate of his current flagship, *Z-29*. One of the destroyer's own shells had exploded in the barrel of a gun during the British attack, resulting in enough damage to cause the *Z-29* to loose headway. Therefore, Cilax decided to transfer ships once again. He selected the destroyer *Hermann Schoemann*. The admiral boarded *Z-29*'s cutter and began to move off towards the *Schoemann* when, suddenly, out of the mist that had settled over the channel, the huge bulk of the *Scharnhorst* loomed up bearing directly for the tiny cutter. Quick reflexes by the cutter's helmsman prevented the cutter from being run down by the huge bulk of the *Scharnhorst* as it sped by. Nevertheless, it had been a narrow escape. A few minutes later, a shaken Cilax boarded the *Schoemann*.

Now that their destroyer attack had been beaten off, there was only one weapon left in the British arsenal. That was a few squadrons of medium bombers. Every available plane was dispatched in a last-ditch effort to stop the German fleet. To Cilax's joy, however, the weather was beginning to deteriorate. Thus, only a handful of the British planes managed to locate his ships. As soon as the bombers approached, they were quickly jumped by Galland's fighters and forced to drop their bombs ineffectually. One man on the *Prinz Eugen* was killed by a bomb splinter and a few of the thin-skinned U-Boats holed, but for all intents and purposes, the British effort was a halfhearted failure. A few other British planes did, however, manage to drop mines in the channel, directly in the path of Cilax's squadron. Assuming that a path through the mine fields was completely clear, the Brest squadron continued along at high speed.

The last British air attack ended shortly after 6:00 p.m. By then darkness was beginning to set in and the temperature was dropping. An hour later, the

Hermann Schoemann passed the *Scharnhorst* and moved into formation ahead of the battle cruiser. Further ahead were the *Gneisenau* and *Prinz Eugen*. Even though the last enemy attacker had turned for home, Cilax's problems were far from over. They were, in fact, just beginning.

Thanks to the ineffective opposition of the British, by evening the squadron had made up the two-hour delay caused by the air raid at Brest just prior to sailing. Even the *Scharnhorst*, despite being stopped for nearly half an hour to repair damage, was on schedule. To Cilax's acute dismay snow began falling at dark. This close to home the snowstorm could only hinder operations for the blackness of nighttime was more than adequate for protection. In the blinding snow squalls, the *Scharnhorst* and *Schoemann* lost contact with each other. Because of the need to maintain radio silence, Cilax found himself out of touch with the rest of the squadron.

Miles ahead of the admiral's ship, Captain Fein of the *Gneisenau*, as senior officer, found himself directing the operations of the main body of the fleet. At 7:55 disaster struck. The *Gneisenau* struck one of the mines dropped by the R.A.F. earlier in the day. The battle cruiser lost all power and began drifting toward the shallow Terschalling shoals. Like her sister ship, the *Gneisenau*'s damage-control party performed magnificently and thirty minutes later the ship was under way again although her speed was reduced to almost one-half and she was forced to proceed cautiously through the shallow waters into which she had drifted. Nevertheless, the *Prinz Eugen* and *Gneisenau* continued on toward their destination, Brunsbuttel, at the mouth of the River Elbe.

Meanwhile, Cilax was searching for the *Scharnhorst*. Just after 9:00 the flagship passed the site where

Gneisenau was mined though by then she was underway and miles ahead. At 9:35 the unfortunate *Scharnhorst* shuddered to a dead stop as another explosion rent her frame. The force of the explosion was far heavier than the earlier one. All power was lost, the engines stopped abruptly and the ship went black. A survey of the damage revealed that the starboard shaft was jammed and the ship was taking on tons of water. The blast destroyed or jammed all the sophisticated instrumentation including the fire control. Dead in the water, the *Scharnhorst* began to drift toward the shallow coastal shoals.

Those on board the *Schoemann* heard the explosion that shook the *Scharnhorst*. Although he was in his cabin, Cilax could also hear the report of the mine, so great was the bang. He rushed to the bridge and ordered the destroyer to attempt to make contact by signal lamp. Ten minutes later the *Scharnhorst*'s signal lamp reported back: Have hit mine. Then contact was lost again.

The brief message from the flagship only served to increase the admiral's anxiety. Through the snow the *Schoemann* began circling, searching for the battle cruiser or at least a sign of wreckage that might indicate the fate of the flagship. Thirty minutes after the explosion, Captain Hoffmann's intrepid crew had the *Scharnhorst* underway once again, although only two of the ship's three screws were operable.

In the interim, the *Schoemann* was circling the area vainly searching for the *Scharnhorst*. The destroyer sailed through a heavy film of oil on the water's surface. When he saw this, Cilax feared the worst. At 11:13, the two ships again made contact. Cilax decided to break radio silence and sent off a message stating that the *Scharnhorst* was in dire need of assistance. A few minutes later, Captain Hoffmann reported that the ship was under way under its own power. The admiral immediately cancelled the request for help and returned to his cabin to worry about the fate of the rest of the squadron. There was no word from the other two ships and, as far as Cilax knew, they might well have been sunk.

In London, Admiral Pound, unaware of the damage caused by the mines, found himself faced with the unenviable task of reporting the apparent success of Cilax's voyage to an unhappy prime minister. At 1:00 a.m., Churchill was summoned to the phone.

"I'm afraid, sir," said Pound, "I must report that the enemy battle cruisers should by now have reached the safety of their home waters."[6]

Churchill, usually so eloquent, was so taken aback that he merely answered, "Why?" Then he hung up the phone. Churchill could not comprehend the fact that the Germans could sail up the English Channel with impunity.

Meanwhile, the *Gneisenau* and *Prinz Eugen* were approaching the Elbe. Captain Fein was astounded to find that no arrangements had been made for tugs or pilots to see the heavy ships safely to their berths. The cooperation of the Luftwaffe naval group west had been superb, but because of the need for secrecy, naval group north had been left out of the planning. Consequently, they were not aware that the fleet was due to arrive and had made no plans to accommodate the ships.

Fein was incensed. He demanded help to no avail. The ships would have to lay outside the harbor until tugs arrived to guide them safely in. Fearing that there might be further mines in the area, Fein dropped anchor and elected to wait until assistance was forthcoming. On the other hand, Captain Brink-

219

mann of the *Prinz Eugen* was more concerned with attacks by enemy aircraft. He kept his ship steaming slowly back and forth all night.

As the *Gneisenau* and *Prinz Eugen* waited outside Brunsbuttel, the *Scharnhorst* received orders to proceed instead to Wilhelmshaven. Just after 6:30, the great battle cruiser approached the port and was met by a lone tugboat. One tug was totally insufficient for guiding the *Scharnhorst*. As at Brunsbuttel, group north had made no arrangements for the battle cruiser's arrival. *Scharnhorst* lay in the outer harbor, vulnerable to air attack.

Around 9:30, a second tug arrived carrying Admiral Cilax. The admiral reboarded the flagship a few minutes later. Until his ship was safely at its berth, however, Captain Hoffmann would not rest. The longer he remained in his present position, the greater the potential of air attack. Shortly afterward a message was received from group north stating that no tugs were available. The weary Hoffmann decided to take the huge ship into its berth on its own. With a masterful demonstration of seamanship, Hoffmann guided the battle cruiser into its slip with inches to spare.

In the meantime, at Brunsbuttel, shortly after dawn, tugs arrived to guide the *Gneisenau* and *Prinz Eugen* to their berths. Camouflage nets were quickly placed over the ships. Thus, at midmorning, when the *Scharnhorst*'s anchor splashed into the harbor at Wilhelmshaven, it marked the end of the Channel Dash. Cilax radioed Admiral Saalwachter at naval group west headquarters in Paris, "It is my duty to inform you that Operation Cerberus has been successfully completed. Lists of damages and casualties follow."[7]

In England, the furor over the Channel Dash had

just begun. The *London Times*'s editorial shouted:

Vice Admiral Cilax has succeeded where the Duke of Medina-Sidonia failed. Nothing more mortifying to the pride of our sea power has happened since the seventeenth century.[8]

A board of inquiry was set up to establish blame for the failure to mount a decent challenge to the German force. After weeks of haggling and testimony, the board was disbanded. Everyone connected with the fiasco shared some measure of blame.

In his own official report, Cilax stated, "The enemy betrayed his surprise to the advantage of our formation, by throwing his air forces precipitously and without plan."[9]

In a letter to Raeder and Hitler, Cilax further explained:

Now that the three ships have put into German estuaries, the operation "Cerbus" is ended. With it closes one day of the war at sea, a day which will probably go down as one of the most daring in the naval history of this war. In spite of the damage sustained by *Scharnhorst* and *Gneisenau*, it can be said that the success achieved was above all expectations.[10]

Hitler's goal of transferring the ships from Brest to Norway never was completely fulfilled, though. Both battle cruisers required months of repair. It was six months before the *Scharnhorst* was ready for sea again. By late 1943 the battle cruiser was finally repaired and, in keeping with the Führer's demands, was transferred to Norway. On Christmas Day the *Scharnhorst* sailed from Altenfjord to intercept convoy JW-51B, heading for Russia. The next day Adm. Bruce Fraser with the battleship *Duke of York* and the cruisers *Sheffield, Jamaica, Belfast* and *Norfolk* located the German ship. In the ensuing Battle of North Cape, the *Scharnhorst* was overwhelmed and sunk with all but thirty-six members of her crew.

The *Prinz Euean* set out for Norway eight days after her safe arrival at Brunsbuttel. Off Trondheim she was torpedoed by the British submarine *Trident*. The torpedo destroyed much of the cruiser's stern but, despite the heavy damage, the ship managed to reach port. However, she was not operational again for over a year, until the final months of the war. After the war, the *Prinz Eugen* was handed over to the United States. In 1948 the *Prinz Eugen* was sunk during the atom bomb tests at Bikini Atoll in the Pacific.

Gneisenau suffered perhaps the most ignominious fate. Two weeks after the Channel Dash the humiliated R.A.F. exacted revenge by attacking the dry dock where the ship was undergoing repairs. For three days straight, large bomber formations attempted to hit the ship. On the third day, February 27, the bombers found the range. The entire front of the *Gneisenau* was smashed beyond repair. The battle cruiser never went to sea again. A few months later her guns were dismantled and relocated ashore as coastal batteries. Eventually, the battle cruiser's hull was filled with concrete and sunk as a blockship at Gdynia, Poland.

As for Cilax, he never again approached the notoriety of his Channel Dash. He was transferred to Norway as commander in chief, battleships. In December he took the *Tirpitz* to sea in search of an allied convoy. For five days he searched without success for the convoy. Finally, after receiving a report that the home fleet was out, he took the *Bismarck*'s sister ship back to port. For the rest of the war he remained ashore in Norway waiting for the invasion that never came.

Admiral Cilax accomplished something that no other admiral in modern history managed to achieve. He took an enemy battle fleet up the English Channel in plain sight of the English shore. Although he was aided by the ineptitude of the British reaction to his move, it was Cilax who disrupted the enemy's dispositions by utilizing the element of surprise. That the Channel Dash was a remarkable feat of arms remains undisputed to this day.

6. GRAND ADMIRAL KARL DOENITZ

With Germany in ruins, her SS and Luftwaffe chiefs, Himmler and Goering, both disgraced and automatically disqualified as successors, Hitler turned his office over to Grand Adm. Karl Doenitz. From 1935 until he was named commander in chief of the German navy in 1943, Doenitz had led the feared U-boat arm. His theories on submarine warfare nearly brought the Allies to bay. By 1943, the gross shipping tonnage lost was so excessive that at the Casablanca Conference, the Allies declared the destruction of Germany's U-boats a major priority. Only Karl Doenitz could take credit for this superior achievement. Furthermore, he was a loyal officer and never once strayed from that loyalty. Only after the war was over did he modify his opinion of National Socialism but it took the revelations of the Nuremberg Trials to convince him of the evils of Nazism. However, he was no mere toady to Hitler. The fact that he became Germany's second Führer was merely dramatic testimony to the fact that Doenitz produced results.

The Doenitz family trace their lineage to

Westphalia. Though originally farmers, by the nineteenth century they had left the soil for the professional world, some into the schools, the church, the business world and even the military. Karl's father, Emil Doenitz, was an engineer. His wife, Anna, gave birth to a son, Karl, on September 16, 1891, in Berlin. The young boy attended the Realgymnasium in Weimar. On April 1, 1910, Karl, having demonstrated an aptitude for military life, entered the training school of the Imperial Navy. In 1912 he was assigned to the light cruiser *Breslau* which at the beginning of World War I, together with the cruiser *Goeben,* broke through the British Mediterranean fleet and reached the Dardanelles where they joined the Turkish forces fighting against the Russian Black Sea fleet. He remained in the Near East until October of 1916 when he was ordered to join the submarine fleet.

After undergoing initial training Doenitz was appointed watch-keeping lieutenant on the *U-39.* By 1918 he had his own command, *U-68,* which was based in the Mediterranean. His command brought him into contact with the adventurous U-boat captain, Steinbauer. The youthful Doenitz learned the tactic of night submarine attacks on the surface. The U-boat, taking advantage of the small silhouette of its conning tower, could slip past an enemy destroyer screen and penetrate the merchant ship convoy where it would discharge its deadly missiles.

Early in October, successfully utilizing this tactic, Doenitz torpedoed a British ship near Malta. Unfortunately, following the attack, his boat became a target for searching British destroyers. Though submerged, the submarine was forced to the surface where Doenitz was forced to scuttle his boat. He was then picked up by an enemy destroyer and spent the next ten months in a British prisoner-of-war camp at Yorkshire.

While in prison, Doenitz found plenty of time to dwell on the principles of U-boat tactics and their use against convoys. He understood that the British employment of convoy tactics in 1917 had seriously weakened the effectiveness of the U-boats. He therefore gave careful consideration to methods whereby submarines could successfully penetrate convoys. He concluded that "the traditional submarine attack, delivered in daylight with the submarine submerged, no longer had any validity against ships escorted in convoy."[1]

Unfortunately, he was captured too soon to fully develop this theory.

In 1919 he returned to Germany from the prisoner-of-war camp. Restricted to a one hundred thousand man army, Germany had little room for its millions of servicemen. Doenitz, however, was asked to remain in the German navy. But that force was a mere shell of its former self. Its capital ships no longer existed and the Versailles Treaty had denied Germany the right to have submarines. Nevertheless, the navy revamped for its reduced role in the republic.

Secretly, the Versailles Treaty was circumvented. In Spain, Finland, and even as far away as Japan, covert submarine development continued beyond the eyes of the watchdogs of Versailles. For Doenitz, submarine service seemed in the past at this time even though the potential was there for Germany to again have a U-boat arm in the future.

Upon his return to active duty, Doenitz was assigned commander of a torpedo boat. In 1923 he was transferred to the staff of the torpedo boat *Inspectorate* in Kiel and later the naval headquarters in Berlin. In 1927 he returned to sea duty as a navigation officer and in 1930 was given command of a destroyer flotilla. From 1930 to 1934 he was head of the admiralty staff division of the high command of the North Sea. In 1934 he was promoted to the rank of captain and given command of the new cruiser *Emden*.

In 1933, with Hitler's assumption of the chancellorship of Germany, Doenitz found renewed hope that naval rearmament would commence. The navy commander in chief, Adm. Erich Raeder, had received assurance from Hitler that naval construction would be put into effect immediately. This construction plan was later termed the "Z" Plan and an integral part of it was the submarine force.

Doenitz's hopes soared. Quickly he became a supporter of Hitler. Though he did not join the Nazi party, it was not because he did not want to. It was because Raeder insisted that naval personnel take no active part in politics. Though loyal to Hitler, Raeder refused to support Nazi ideology.

In 1935 Doenitz's hopes came true. He was named the head of Germany's fledgling submarine fleet with the all-important task of rebuilding that arm. His appointment coincided with Germany's signing of the Anglo-German naval agreement with Great Britain. This agreement legitimized Germany's return to U-boat development. Under the terms of the treaty, Germany's naval strength was to be thirty-five percent of the British in gross tonnage for capital ships. But in the case of submarines, Germany was allowed forty-five percent. This percentage could be raised to one hundred percent upon mutual consent.

Because Germany had been covertly building submarines even before the naval agreement, it was not long before the first operational flotilla came into existence. As commander of this flotilla, Captain Doenitz was free to develop further those submarine theories that had occupied him during the final months of the Great War.

Doenitz approached his new job with great enthusiasm. There were no instruction manuals for the crews to follow. It was Doenitz himself who provided the manuals. He worked out and explored his theories and ideas. He based his philosophy on two precepts. First, he said, the primary target of the submarine was not the enemy's warships, but rather their merchant fleet. The main job of the U-boats was to sever the enemy's supply routes. The sinking of warships would merely be an added dividend. He said, "The war against trade was to be prosecuted with complete ruthlessness and disregard for the loss of civilian lives."[2]

This concept was important but Doenitz found that the Hague Convention had tied his hands. This convention stated that merchant ships were first to be stopped and then searched with every provision made for the safety of the crew before being sunk. He spent many hours searching for loopholes in this restriction. Eventually, he put forward the proposal that a merchant ship warning a warship of the presence of a submarine was in effect acting as an intelligence source and was thus not protected by the terms of the Hague Convention.

His second precept was that a submarine was basically a surface vessel which had the capability to submerge. It should, however, fight as a surface vessel. He viewed the submarine role differently than the traditional manner which held that the submarine should remain submerged and wait for enemy vessels to cross its path and then attack while submerged. Instead, Doenitz believed, and had previously attempted before his capture in 1918, that because of its tiny silhouette, the submarine was virtually invisible at night. Therefore, using this near invisibility and rapid speed, the U-boat should attack on the surface in groups at night.

Tirelessly he worked his submarines in exercises in the Baltic. Day after day his theories were put into practice. Doenitz put his crews through rigid training designed to instill, in both officers and men, confidence in their submarines and their ability to handle them despite adverse conditions. Using the surface fleet in the role of merchant ships, he tested his theory of night surface attacks. The U-boats managed to penetrate the destroyer screen with ease thereby proving the correctness of his tactics.

Continuing to improve upon his attack theories, Doenitz developed the idea of using a pack of U-boats against a convoy. This idea called for the U-boats to be spread across the path that a convoy would most likely use. When sighted, the convoy's position would be transmitted to other boats lurking in the area and then shadowed until such time as the group could form.

Once assembled, the group of submarines, later called wolf packs, would position itself ahead of the convoy in order to be in a position to attack at night.

Doenitz also pondered how to control operations. Should he maintain his command in a submarine at sea or from a shore-based headquarters? Trying both, he concluded that a central shore-based headquarters would be more efficient in light of the size of the submarine fleet he envisioned. He did forsee one problem, however: the danger of the enemy being able to plot U-boat positions by intercepting radio signals. He was willing to risk this for the needs of efficiency. Besides, he had confidence in the German Enigma code which he was sure the British would not be able to read. As for the radio signals, it was possible that the British did not possess an efficient system of high-frequency direction finding.

Another important aspect of his job was U-boat design. Between 1936 and 1939 he concentrated on a more efficient design. Doenitz strived for smallness but also demanded the greatest practicable endurance in terms of fuel use.

The smaller the submarine, the greater would be its ability to maneuver, dive quickly in an emergency, and cloak itself at night. He concluded that 500 tons was the optimum size for the majority of the fleet. This design was commonly known as the Type VII. It had four torpedo tubes in the bow and one in the stern with a load of from twelve to fourteen torpedoes. The boat could travel sixteen knots on the surface and become totally submerged within twenty seconds. Its design, however, was eventually enlarged to 517 tons so that extra fuel tanks could be added. This improvement gave the submarine an effective radius of eighty-seven hundred miles whereas the 500 ton boats had a radius of sixty-two hundred miles.

Naval command wanted a larger U-boat developed. This was the Type IX, displacing 740 tons with an endurance ability of 13,450 miles. Later on, a much larger submarine was developed weighing 1,688 tons. This boat would serve the fleet as a tanker and be known as "Milch Cows." The Milch Cows did not become available until 1941.

Doenitz was convinced that in another war Britain would once more be the enemy. He also realized that war would come soon. He believed that if Germany was to be ready to fight such a war, a massive submarine fleet was necessary, at least three hundred boats. According to the existing "Z" Plan, however, that number of submarines would not be available until 1948. This bothered Doenitz for he was positive that the U-boat was the weapon that could play the most vital role in isolating Britain. Unfortunately, his opinion was in the minority. Raeder gave construction priority to capital ships. The "Z" plan favored that branch of the navy.

Doenitz vehemently disagreed with the "Z" plan for a number of reasons. First, it would take from six to eight years to complete. Secondly, if battleships, cruisers and aircraft carriers were produced in large numbers, Germany's adversaries would most probably follow suit thereby initiating an expensive arms race. Third, a surface fleet could be decimated by air attacks. Lastly, Germany's geographical position made it difficult for her to utililze a large surface fleet. World War I had proven that. Moving the fleet into the Atlantic from Baltic bases was a monumental task. Only the U-boat could pass unseen into the Atlantic where it could attack enemy vessels. Doenitz used World War I as evidence to substantiate the fact that submarines were Germany's most important offensive. weapon.

Between 1936 and 1939, besides arguing for an increase in the size of the U-boat arm and working towards improving the style of submarines, Doenitz spent time instilling an *esprit de corps* among the submariners. He made it a policy to meet his captains, instilling in them his enthusiasm for submarines and his own theories. After each exercise, a U-boat captain could expect to see Doenitz at the quay waiting to greet him. As a result, Doenitz quickly endeared himself to all submariners.

During the training exercises, Doenitz theorized England as the enemy. Because of this he pushed for training exercises to be extended into the Atlantic in addition to the Baltic and North Sea. When Germany repudiated the Anglo-German navel treaty on April 26, 1939, Doenitz's forecast of enemies proved correct. In late August of 1939, with the prospect of war imminent, Doenitz wrote:

> With the number of U-boats at present available and the additions that can later be expected on the basis of the current building programme, it does not appear that we shall be in a position, within the forseeable future, either to exercise any materially appreciable pressure on Britain or to strike any decisive blow at her vital lines of supply, but shall have to content ourselves merely with a series of pin-pricks against her merchant navy.[3]

When Britain and France declared war on Germany on September 3, 1939, there were only fifty six U-boats, forty six of which were operational. Only twenty two of these were suitable for Atlantic duty. The remaining twenty four were the smaller 250-ton displacement submarines, suitable only for the North Sea and other confined areas.

Though Doenitz had twenty two boats which were suitable for the Atlantic, only seven could be actively deployed at any one time. The others were either replenishing or en route to or from their destination. Basically, as he stated above, all he could hope to do was to become a nuisance. His dream of strangling England seemed remote at this stage.

Being restricted by numbers was one thing, but being restricted by rules of military conduct hampered his strategy in the beginning. From the outset of the war, Doenitz desired to place an unrestricted submarine blockade around the British Isles, one that would allow the submarine commanders the right to sink on sight any ship found in these waters. The German admiralty's orders, however, forbade outright sinkings of ships unless they were zigzagging, were blacked out, or radioed the position of the U-boat to a warship. Otherwise the submarine would have to surface before it could halt a ship. Then the crew would have to board the stopped ship and determine whether or not it was carrying contraband. If it was, then the submarine was required to see to the safety of the merchant crew, if necessary even taking them aboard their own boat. However, merchant ships escorted by destroyers were not entitled to prior inspection. Doenitz decried these regulations and stated that not only were they time consuming, they exposed the U-boats to attacks.

The sinking of the liner *Athenia* within a few days of the beginning of hostilities was not a sign that Doenitz had repudiated the regulations. It was actually an error on the part of the captain of *U-30* who mistook the *Athenia* for a troop carrier. The ship was blacked out and was following a zigzag course. When he heard of the sinking, Doenitz immediately dispatched other boats to aid in the rescue of the *Athenia*'s passengers and crews.

The British immediately accused the Germans of waging unrestricted warfare in defiance of international law. The German government quickly denied the allegation but when the full story was known by Doenitz, he ordered the *U-30* commander, Lemp, to destroy any record of the sinking. In fact, German propaganda went so far as to accuse the British first lord of the admiralty, Winston Churchill, of sabotage in order to throw the blame onto Germany.

The upshot of the *Athenia* affair, however, was to cause Hitler to restrict the U-boats even further. They were now ordered not to sink any passenger ship even if it was in enemy service. Hitler still hoped not to broaden the war. He also ordered that French ships were not to be attacked except as a defensive measure, in hopes of avoiding a deeper rift with that country.

As the war progressed and hardened, many of these rules were ignored. By the end of September, Admiral Raeder had convinced Hitler to approve the sinking of all merchant ships that made use of their radios when stopped. On the twenty-fourth of that month, Raeder also recommended that the order protecting French ships be rescinded. Hitler concurred. Little by little the U-boats were freed from their shackles.

On October 29, a new order was issued when the Germans discovered that British troops were being ferried to France in passenger liners: "Passenger liners in enemy convoys may be subjected to immediate, unrestricted armed attack by U-boats."[4]

On November 7, still another restriction was lifted: "U-boats are permitted to attack immediately with all weapons at their command all passenger ships which can be identified with certainty as enemy ships and whose armament is detected or already known."[5]

Military targets, of course, were not restricted. On September 17, *U-29* sunk the British aircraft carrier *Courageous* with a loss of 518 British sailors. This event caused great rejoicing in Germany. Hitler himself came to review the captain and crew of the U-boat.

Doenitz's most daring early operation was a plan to penetrate the enemy naval base at Scapa Flow in order to attack the British fleet while it lay at anchor. For this task he chose Lt. Cmdr. Gunther Prien, captain of the *U-47*. Before selecting Prien, Doenitz interviewed him and asked if he would be willing to undertake this highly dangerous mission. He layed out the many possible dangers for Prien. Doenitz then gave the U-boat captain fourty-eight hours to decide before reporting back with his answer. Prien accepted immediately.

On October 13, in strict secrecy, Prien's *U-47* moved toward Scapa Flow which is situated in the Orkney Islands north of Scotland. The crew of the *U-47* were as enthusiastic as its commander for at the conclusion of World War I, the German fleet was impounded at Scapa Flow and scuttled itself rather than be subjected to the humiliation of British domination. Now was Germany's chance to exact some long-overdue retribution.

At nightfall on the thirteenth, the U-boat surfaced and made for Kirk Sound. There, directly in front of *U-47*, lay the battleship *Royal Oak*, swinging lazily at anchor. A prime target ripe for the plucking. From a distance of four thousand yards, Prien fired three torpedoes. Only one managed to hit and this caused little damage. Having caught the British entirely by surprise, however, Prien had enough time to reload his bow torpedo tubes. The second salvo mortally wounded the *Royal Oak* which rolled over and sank within thirteen minutes of being hit with a loss of 833 men.

Prien's boat now became the object of an intense search. He knew that he would have to leave Scapa Flow immediately. Miraculously, the *U-47* made good its escape. The action netted Prien the Knight's Cross. His superior, the genius behind the operation, was promoted from commodore to rear admiral. The jubilant crew of the *U-47* were flown to Berlin where the Führer and the city honored them for their daring feat. Doenitz was highly gratified.

These feats, however, were the exception. The real meat and potatoes for the U-boats were the destruction of merchant ships. In this, the submarines, though small in number, managed to wreak havoc on the British. In the month of September, 1939, they sunk forty-one ships with a gross tonnage of 153 thousand and the following month twenty-seven more ships with a gross tonnage of 135 thousand. November and December saw a decrease in these numbers with twenty-one ships of 52 thousand tons and twenty-five ships of 81 thousand tons being sunk respectively. Not until the beginning of the new year did the number of sinkings begin to rise again. In January, forty ships were sunk with a tonnage of 111 thousand followed by February's total of forty-five more ships with 170 thousand tons.

In March, however, the U-boats were ordered away from commerce raiding and positioned off the coasts of Norway and Denmark to aid in the planned German invasion of those countries. Their job was to cover the landings and protect them from any possible Allied moves. When the invasion began on April 9, the U-boats' role was almost exclusively confined to reconnaissance, transport and protection. Doenitz protested that this was not the proper use of the submarines but his pleas fell on deaf ears.

One sour note was interjected at this time. The torpedoes used by the U-boats were performing very erratically. Often they failed to explode, at other times they ran off course. Gunther Prien, the hero of Scapa Flow, had fired his torpedoes three times at targets only to have the erratic fish spoil his attack. Luckily he escaped what could easily have been destruction.

Doenitz ordered a formal inquiry into the torpedo problem. On April 20, 1940, the torpedo commission began their investigation. They found that in some torpedoes the striker failed to fire the charge. In others, the initial charge exploded when hitting the target but failed to detonate the main charge. As a result of their investigation, in June the commission recommended that only contact percussion torpedoes be used and the use of magnetic torpedoes discontinued. It would be some time, however, before that could happen. In the interim, the U-boats would have to rely on the magnetic torpedoes. This required them to fire more than one torpedo at a target so as to ensure success. It also caused them to needlessly expend their complement of torpedoes necessitating an earlier return to base with a reduced kill ratio. Often, frustrated U-boat captains watched helplessly as a vast array of ships passed with impunity because the submarines had spent all of their torpedoes.

In June, with the Norwegian campaign over, the U-boats were allowed to resume their primary function, commerce raiding. The fall of France, also in June, made French bases available to the German navy at Lorient, Saint-Nazaire and Brest. No longer did the U-boats have to return to Germany for refitting. Instead, they now had ports right on the Atlantic which allowed them to range further into the ocean thereby increasing their operational radius.

By the summer of 1940, Doenitz was able to put into practice his tactic of night attacks on the surface. Asdic (sonar) was powerless to locate boats on the surface. In addition, the submarine's speed under diesel engines made them more than a match for the enemy's escort vessels which during 1940 were few. Furthermore, thanks to their low silhouette, the U-boats were able to sneak into the heart of a convoy.

The summer of 1940 was indeed a "happy time" for Doenitz's U-boats. On August 17, Hitler ordered a total blockade of the British Isles giving the submarines authority to sink any vessel sighted, neutral or belligerent, military or otherwise. In one two-day period in October 325 thousand tons of shipping were sunk. Gunther Prien alone accounted for 200 thousand tons of that total.

From July through October, 216 ships were sunk with a gross weight of over 1,111,000 tons. This was accomplished with the loss of only 6 U-boats. Doenitz could be very proud of the achievement of his sub-mariners. They had vindicated his theory of attacking at night in groups. These groups were designated wolf packs.

The wolf packs operated in an efficient manner. The entire operation was controlled by Doenitz from his headquarters. There, all enemy ship movements were plotted on large wall charts. Once intelligence sources determined the dates and times of an Allied convoy, individual U-boats were spread in a line at right angles to the estimated course of the convoy. Each boat would patrol from twenty-five to thirty miles apart depending on the visibility. Once the convoy was sighted the sighting boat would send off a report to Doenitz while it trailed the convoy at a distance. The U-boat would continue to report any changes in speed and direction together with weather information.

Upon receiving the sighting reports, Doenitz would then signal the other U-boats in the area. Then the wolf pack would begin to form. the U-boats were under strict orders not to attack until the entire pack was formed. They then took station ahead of the convoy at a point to ensure interception when night-fall arrived. Then, using their low profile, they would penetrate the destroyer screen, maneuver into the convoy and close their target to a distance of six hundred yards before firing their torpedoes. Once daylight dawned, they would break off the attack and, still surfaced, use their speed to move ahead of the lumbering convoy. The following night the ritual would be repeated.

From his headquarters Doenitz monitored the entire operation. It was his job to decide when to attack, when to call the attack off, and what speed to maintain during daylight hours so that his boats would be properly positioned by nightfall.

The British suffered huge losses at the hands of the wolf packs. Their detecting device, Asdic, was useless against the surfaced U-boats. Radar was as yet unavailable to the escort vessels and air patrols were limited to two hundred miles from the nearest coast. The fact that German naval intelligence, B-Dienst, had broken the British convoy cipher also contributed to the U-boats' effectiveness.

By November of 1940, U-boat kills had, however, begun to decrease. A number of factors contributed to the reduction. First, many of the U-boats required refitting thereby necessitating them to spend time in dry dock. Secondly, fierce late autumn storms hindered their activity. Finally, with the threat of invasion of Britain over, more escort ships were freed for convoy duty. The latter made convoy penetration increasingly difficult. The result, of course, was lower shipping losses. In the last two months of the year, sixty-nine ships of 360 thousand tons were lost.

For an increased success in his effort Doenitz required cooperation from the Luftwaffe. But that was a difficult proposition. Before the war Raeder had had many long and bitter battles with the Luftwaffe chief, Hermann Goering, trying to convince him of the need for an independent naval air arm. Raeder's arguments were in vain. Goering was not about to relinquish a portion of his empire.

Doenitz was acutely aware that his U-boats were

incapable of carrying out their own reconnaissance. With air support, the navy could seek out convoys and direct the wolf packs to them, thereby making the submarine arm more efficient. In addition, aircraft could provide an air carpet for U-boats returning to and leaving their bases.

In December, Doenitz sent a memorandum to naval high command detailing the need for an organized air reconnaissance. Meeting with Raeder in Berlin on January 2, he elaborated further. Raeder agreed and arranged for Doenitz to have an interview with Gen. Alfred Jodl, chief of the staff at Supreme Head-quarters. Jodl was also convinced by the admiral's arguments and passed the memorandum on to Hitler. The Führer, recognizing the wisdom of the recom-mendation, ordered a group of Focke-Wulf long-range aircraft stationed at Bordeaux to place them-selves at the disposal of the U-boat service. Goering, who was away on a hunting trip at the time, was notified of the move.

When the Luftwaffe chief found out what Hitler had done, he was angered and demanded that the order be cancelled immediately. He invited Doenitz to dine with him at his mobile headquarters aboard a train. Goering, always jealous of his prerogatives, sought to enlist the admiral's backing to have the Führer order rescinded. When he found out what Goering actually wanted, Doenitz became furious, refused dinner, and stormed out on the Luftwaffe chief.

Unfortunately, the aircraft did not immediately prove as useful as Doenitz had hoped. Their range was inadequate and there were not enough of them to cover large areas in any organized search pattern. In addition, when the pilots did locate a convoy, their navigating ability proved so poor that they usually failed to provide accurate data. This resulted in U-boats wandering aimlessly to spots where the pilots erroneously reported convoys to be. In time, cooperation between the planes and submarines improved but it took many months.

In 1941, British scientists developed a more effective radar set. In January of that year, a new, smaller set was fitted into the aircraft of coastal command and in a handful of escort vessels. The U-boats, however, still managed to destroy a number of enemy ships. Thirty-nine went down in February.

Early in March Doenitz ordered his U-boat packs to congregate just south of Iceland. From intelligence garnered, he estimated that an Allied convoy would be passing there. He was correct. Initially the wolf packs earned some successes but then the escorts tore into them. *U-47* was depth charged and fatally hit. Doenitz was extremely upset with this loss. He personally wrote the obituary for his friend Gunther Prien, the hero of Scapa Flow.

Later in the month, *U-100*, under another of Germany's aces, Lieutenant Commander Schepke, was rammed and sunk. Half an hour later, Otto Kretschmer's *U-99* was hit by depth charges and forced to the surface. Kretschmer, another leading ace, and his crew were forced to surrender.

The shock of losing his three top aces in the space of a few days hit Doenitz hard. The losses convinced him that the day of the aces was numbered. Now more than ever group tactics, i.e. the wolf pack, would totally dominate his philosophy. No longer did the submarine force herald the exploits of individual captains but emphasized the exploits of the pack itself.

During the summer of 1941, Doenitz found his U-boat strength dissipated by peripheral duties. For example, the Luftwaffe was in constant need of long-distance weather information. In order to gather this data, the services of two U-boats were enlisted to report weather conditions. In June, with the war now extended into Russia, Doenitz was ordered to dispatch six of his boats from the Atlantic fleet for operations in the arctic. Other U-boats found themselves escorting auxiliary cruisers and supply ships.

Doenitz decried this misuse of the U-boats for as a defensive weapon, submarines were less effective. Then, in September of 1941, another six boats were dispatched to the Mediterranean in order to provide support for Rommel in his North African campaign. In November four more boats were dispatched to this station. The U-boats were desperately needed in the Mediterranean for the British navy was wreaking havoc in the Italian fleet. The submarines quickly made their presence felt. On November 13, *U-81* torpedoed and sunk a British aircraft carrier, the legendary *Ark Royal*. A few days later the battleship *Barham* disintegrated in a massive ball of fire after being hit by a torpedo fired by *U-331*. On December 14, *U-557* sunk the cruiser *Galatea*.

The end of 1941 found ten U-boats permanently stationed in the Eastern Meditteranean. Fifteen more were on patrol around Gibraltar. The loss of twenty-five U-boats from the Atlantic weakened Doenitz's effectiveness. He railed at the loss for he felt that commerce raiding in the Atlantic had to be given first priority. U-boats in the Mediterranean, he said, were simply put "in a mousetrap."[6]

The results, then, for the second half of 1941 were greatly reduced. July and August showed the loss of only forty-five Allied ships. During September the U-boats again began to increase their effectiveness as Doenitz sent them to northern waters where on September 10, they located a convoy. Later in the same month another convoy was savaged by a wolf pack. By the end of the month, fifty-three ships had fallen victim to marauding U-boats. Then the results began to deteriorate once more. October and November saw the loss of forty-three Allied ships.

One major contributor to the low total of sinkings was the British installation of flight decks on some of their merchant ships. This provided convoys with some measure of air cover in the "gap."* The results were telling. In December, there were only fifteen U-boats covering the entire Atlantic. As a result of this and the newly provided air protection, only nine Allied ships were lost. The cost was four U-boats, a ratio that the Germans could ill afford.

As the end of the year approached, Doenitz, despite his losses, was still convinced that attacks on convoys were still the most important objective of his U-boat campaign. He also remained firmly committed to the technique of the wolf pack and continued to plan for the deployment of more of them.

The end of 1941 presented him with an entirely new situation, however, and many more opportunities. After Japan's attack on Pearl Harbor on December 7, Germany, in keeping with the provisions of the Tripartite Pact, declared war on the United States on December 11.

Though officially at war on December 11, the United States Navy and Germany U-boats had been existing in a state of undeclared war since September. During that month the American destroyer *Greer* traded shots with *U-652*. On October 10, the destroyer *Kearney* was torpedoed and heavily damaged by a U-boat while escorting a convoy. On October 31, the

---

*The "gap" was the area in the Atlantic where the convoys could not be reached by land-based air cover. Another name for the gap was the "black pit."

destroyer *Reuben James* was sunk by another U-boat. Two days before Germany declared war, Hitler lifted all restriction on U-boat attacks against American ships.

Doenitz looked with enthusiasm upon the opportunity to send his forces to a new hunting ground. He quickly dispatched twelve U-boats to the American coast. At this time Germany possessed ninety-one submarines, sixteen in the Mediterranean, eight off Gibraltar, and four off Norway. The remainder were in dockyards either being overhauled or waiting to be repaired. Others were either heading for or returning from operations.

The U-boats which arrived off the United States found easy pickings. The Americans had virtually no anti-submarine defense. Ships sailed with their normal peacetime lighting; cities and towns along the coast were not blacked out, making it relatively easy for the U-boats to spot their intended victims.

The U-boats easily adapted themselves to their routine. By day they lay on bottom. At night they approached the coast submerged. When they reached the middle of the shipping routes they surfaced and attacked. Another "happy time" was encountered by the submariners.

In the month of January alone, a mere five U-boats accounted for the sinking of sixty-two ships in American waters.

Doenitz naturally ordered all available U-boats to proceed to the happy hunting grounds. Unfortunately, he was foiled somewhat by Allied deception techniques which had convinced Hitler that Norway was in constant danger of being invaded. Throughout the war, that fear caused Hitler to keep more than a hundred thousand occupation troops stationed in Norway. For Doenitz it was a catastrophe. Hitler,

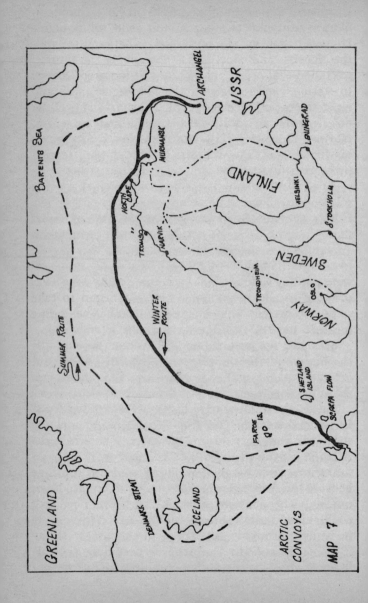

convinced that the Allies would make a move on Norway, ordered the admiral to send all available U-boats to concentrate in the waters between Iceland, the Faroes and Scotland. Though he eventually rescinded that order, the Führer still required Doenitz to station twelve boats in the Norwegian area and eight more off Iceland. On February 15, Hitler directed that an additional twenty U-boats be sent to Norway. Doenitz greatly lamented this dissipation of his forces at a time when the U-boats were scoring such amazing successes off the American coast.

As a result, only twelve U-boats were left to operate off America. That so much carnage was produced is a tribute to the skill of the submarine crews. Despite their relatively small number, the tremendous American losses continued to mount. In the first six months of 1942, 585 ships weighing 3,081,000 tons were lost. By summer, however, the "happy time" was drawing to a close as the Americans began to take steps to protect the merchant ships. The prime measure was the establishment of coastal convoys.

This did not mean that the U-boats were totally thwarted. On the contrary. The wolf packs were deadlier than ever as they left the U.S. coast and again resumed their attacks in the central Atlantic. In addition, the number of U-boats was increasing daily. By June there were 140 boats in operation and the shipyards were busy turning out more. The war in the Atlantic continued to hang in the balance.

Doenitz knew that the killing had to continue because the Americans had the ability to replace losses quickly. The question he soon faced was how long could his U-boats continue killing before the enemy had more sustaining power.

Throughout 1942 Doenitz was becoming increasingly troubled by the ability of Allied aircraft to spot his U-boats. He was convinced that the British had developed a new and highly efficient long-distance surface location device. When he took this problem to the technical department of the naval high command, they could add no insight to this problem.

What the British had actually invented was a one-and-a-half meter radar set small enough to be carried in an aircraft. It was this device that gave them the ability to home in on the U-boats.

Realizing that some sort of airborne was causing his woes, Doenitz called a meeting in Paris with his technical experts in order to develop some method of overcoming that radar. What they discovered was a device which could easily be installed in all U-boats and had the capability of picking up the approach of an enemy aircraft, thus allowing the U-boat to submerge before being spotted. What this device, called Metox, did was to pick up the signal from the enemy radar. The signal was in turn deflected back to the aircraft. In addition to Metox, Doenitz initiated measures for all U-boats to be equipped with radar sets of their own. The effects of Metox became immediately apparent. By October of 1942, the Allied air offensive against the U-boats had literally been stifled.

In September, Doenitz issued the controversial Laconia Order. The *Laconia* was a British liner which was sunk by *U-156*. In addition to her crew, the *Laconia* carried British civilians including women and children as well as eighteen hundred Italian prisoners of war. When Doenitz discovered who the passengers were, he ordered the captain of the *U-156*, Lieutenant Commander Hartenstein, to pick up survivors. During the rescue attempt, American planes circled over the submarine and dropped bombs. To save his boat, Hartenstein was forced to transfer the survivors to life-boats and submerge. Doenitz subsequently sent a signal ordering Hartenstein to take all precautions to preserve the safety of his ship even if it meant abandoning rescue operations. Other submarines which were also involved in the rescue attempt quickly found themselves under attack. As a result, Doenitz issued the Laconia Order which "stipulated that all attempts to rescue the crews of sunken ships would cease, including picking up men from the sea, righting capsized lifeboats, and supplying food and water."[7]

These activities, Doenitz said, stood in the way of the main objective of a U-boat at war, the destruction of enemy ships and their crews.

It was this order which eventually blew up in Doenitz's face at the Nuremberg trials after the war. He was accused of giving his U-boat commanders a license to murder survivors. A statement he made in 1943 was used in evidence: "In view of the desired destruction of ships' crews, their sinking is of great value."[8] At the trial, however, he was cleared of this charge because of its vagueness.

In November of 1942, the Allies landed in Northwest Africa. Doenitz received the news of the landing on November 8 as soon as it happened. He quickly ordered all U-boats operating between the Cape Verde Islands and Gibraltar to proceed immediately to the Moroccan coast. Those boats in the Mediterranean were also diverted to the Gibraltar area. When they arrived in the area on the eleventh they found that the landings were covered by large concentrations of destroyers and aircraft. Dauntlessly, the U-boats maneuvered closer toward the Allied ships. Doenitz feared for his boats in these murderous waters and appealed to naval high command for permission to reduce the number of submarines in the danger area off the Straits of Gibraltar. The admiral reasoned that the Allied invasion involved a heavy concentration of ships which would leave the Atlantic convoys devoid of many escort vessels. He was anxious to get the U-boats back to the Atlantic doing what he still felt was their primary function, commerce raiding.

The last six months of 1942 proved to be lucrative ones for the U-boats. In September, 98 Allied ships were sent to Davy Jones's locker. October witnessed the destruction of 94 more and November saw a whopping 109 ships sunk. All told, during 1942, U-boats had sunk 1,160 ships of 6,266,215 gross tons. All in all it was a satisfying year. 87 U-boats were lost during this period.

In January of 1943, the Allies held a major conference at Casablanca, Morocco. At this converence the U-boat menace was discussed at great length. The Allied leaders realized the importance of eliminating that dangerous threat. As the official United States history put it, "The defeat of the U-boat menace was accepted by the delegates as a primary charge on the resources of the associated powers."[9] Thus, the Allies placed a high priority on the defeat of the U-boats.

While the Allies were determining strategy, Germany was changing their naval commander in chief. Grand Admiral Raeder and Hitler had never seen eye to eye. On January 6, 1943, during a conference, the Führer raged over the inept performance of the pocket battleship *Lutzow* and the cruiser *Hipper* during an attack against the British convoy. The battle was known as the Battle of the Barents Sea. For ninety minutes Raeder was subjected to the Führer's mad ravings. In anger, Hitler gave Raeder instructions to dismantle the capital ships of the navy and farm out their crews to the U-boats or turn them into infantry. Raeder did everything in his power to dissuade Hitler but to no avail.

In the middle of the month Raeder telephoned Doenitz at his Paris headquarters and informed him that he intended to tender his resignation and that he would propose Admiral Carls or himself as successor. Raeder needed to know whether Doenitz felt that he was physically well enough to assume the appointment. He needed Doenitz's answer in twenty-four hours.

In his memoirs, Doenitz stated that the announcement came as a complete surprise:

> I had no idea that Grand Admiral Raeder was contemplating retirement. Nor did I know that at the end of the December, 1942 he had had differences of opinion with Hitler on the subject of the operations of heavy ships against British convoys to Russia. These latter had not achieved the success which Hitler had felt justified in expecting of them, and he had forthwind issued an order that they were to be paid off as being of no value to our war effort.[10]

Doenitz telephoned Raeder the next day with word that he was in perfect health and would be fit enough to assume command. The ball was now in Hitler's court.

Over the previous few years Doenitz's star had been rising. In May of 1942, Hitler had asked for his presence at all regular Führer conferences. Doenitz realized that his position and the success of the U-boats were ingratiating him to Hitler. The Führer came to rely on his judgment. If it came down to a choice between himself and Carls, Doenitz felt that undoubtedly Hitler would select him.

On January 30, 1943, Doenitz officially took up the

position of commander in chief of the navy. He still retained his position as head of the U-boats, however. From his new place he hoped to further promote the importance of the U-boat arm in the prosecution of the war.

One of the first things he realized upon taking up the supreme command was that the surface fleet could not be sacrificed. The Führer, however, was adamant on that point and bluntly told Doenitz so on the very day that he assumed his new command. Doenitz replied that he needed time to study in detail the tasks that lay before him. On February 8, he submitted a detailed plan for paying off the big ships. In it he refrained from raising any objections to Hitler's decision.

After more study, Doenitz reached the same conclusion as had his predecessor. Accordingly, on February 26 he reported to Hitler and stated that he would not be able to give his support to the order to pay off the surface fleet. Hitler gave ground grudgingly. From that time on, Doenitz said, "he treated me with exceptional civility, and he continued to do so until the end of April, 1945."[11]

Doenitz had many problems to face as commander in chief. One of the main problems was Goering who always loved to poke jibes at the navy. Doenitz said, "I, too, very soon became aware of Goering's tactics, which were to hasten to Hitler and be the first to report, often in quiet inaccurate form, the failures of the other services. As a result there were not a few collisions between us."[12]

Being responsible now for both the surface fleet and the U-boat arm, Doenitz sought to streamline the cumbersome chain of command which linked the German admiralty to his fleet commanders. To him, however, the major responsibility of the navy remained commerce raiding. Therefore, all his structural changes were geared to improve, enhance and facilitate the promotion of that goal.

Meanwhile, the U-boats were still registering tremendous successes against the convoys. In January of 1943, thirty-nine ships were sunk. The following month U-boats accounted for sixty-three more ships. The carnage continued well into March. As the British admiralty tallied up the losses they concluded, "The Germans never came so near to disrupting communications between the New World and the Old as in the first twenty days of March, 1943,"[13] Had the U-boats finally brought the Allies to their knees? Were the convoys helpless as evidence by the tremendous losses?

Unfortunately for Doenitz, the weeks following his great March victories did not match the successes of the previous weeks. Late in the month a U-boat captain reported to him that an aircraft carrier had been seen sailing with a convoy. This was the first time a carrier was used in the trans-Atlantic convoys.

The British had mounted flight decks on the hulls of unfinished merchant ships and created small escort carriers which were then used to escort convoys. The air gap which provided the U-boats with their happy hunting grounds no longer existed. In April, U-boat losses began to mount. May was a horrible month. Over forty-one U-boats were destroyed in less than three weeks.

Faced with the ability of enemy aircraft to locate his U-boats by radar and the increased skill of the surface vessels in following up the sightings, Doenitz decided to withdraw his submarines from combat temporarily. On May 24 he painfully ordered his U-boats to abandon the convoy routes.

Why was Doenitz forced to withdraw his submarines

in May when victory seemed so close only two months previously?

Stronger convoys definitely contributed to the German losses. In addition, British aircraft had been fitted with a new type of location device, a ten-centimeter radar. Realizing that the Allies had acquired this radar had caused Doenitz as early as March to order all U-boats to remain submerged as soon as they became aware of radar transmissions. In addition, the Allies were using the broken German naval code to pinpoint the location of U-boats. Then of course there was the introduction of the escort carrier. Taking all this into consideration, Doenitz found himself bested.

Doenitz was now faced with the immense problem of how to regain the initiative. In the late summer he turned his attention to the possibilities of a counter-offensive made possible by developments in the technical field. On July 30 he told Hitler of some of the latest scientific breakthroughs which might change Germany's fortunes. Such items as a new method of jamming Allied radar, new types of torpedoes, a new style of submarine which could operate at faster speeds underwater, and a new Walther U-boat which used a hydrogen peroxide fuel were just a few of the amazing things the scientists were working on. Meanwhile, a Type XXI and Type XXIII U-boat with a faster underwater speed were being produced though they would not be ready for many months.

In the interim, until the new, faster submarines became available, Doenitz pondered the present situation and felt depressed over the tremendous losses. His usual confidence was greatly shaken. All the Allied advances "led him to the conclusion that if he continued to operate the U-boat arm in its present condition, before the new designs and improved weapons were available, he would only be sending hundreds of young men to their death, and throwing dozens of U-boats into an uneven battle from which large numbers would not return."[14]

Even so, the Allies could not be made to think that the waters of the Atlantic were free for them to roam at will. Something had to be done. With all those U-boats ready to be used, Doenitz, knowing that it would be suicide to send them against the strong Atlantic convoys, sent them instead to Africa and into the Indian Ocean. These were the Allies' weakest spots. By the end of the year the U-boats had sunk over fifty-seven ships in the Indian Ocean. But it was a hollow victory for it was in the Atlantic that the war would be either won or lost and here, unfortunately, his U-boats had come up second best.

Another problem was that of aiding the Italian navy in the Mediterranean. The Italians were vainly attempting to keep the Allies from building up their strength in North Africa.

On March 17, 1943, Doenitz went to Rome where he had a face-to-face meeting with Mussolini in the Palazzo Venezia. Il Duce agreed to allow the German navy full participation in the protection of convoys to Tunisia. But by May the Allies were victorious. Doenitz now had to assume that the Italian mainland was next. On May 12 he again flew to Rome to discuss the strategic situation with the Italian high command. He felt frustrated and disappointed with the lack of energy and determination demonstrated by the Italians. When the Allies did land in Sicily on July 10, it became apparent that the Italian armed forces were no longer willing to fight. When Mussolini was overthrown on July 25, Doenitz felt that the new Badoglio government would probably seek an armistice with the Allies. When the Italians did finally surrender in

September, the weak German naval forces were incapable of preventing the Italian fleet from sailing to Malta in mass surrender.

Still another debacle facing Doenitz was that of the capital ships. Rather than scrap the fleet as Hitler desired, he recommended that the battleships *Tirpitz* and *Scharnhorst* be sent to Norwegian waters and given the opportunity to attack arctic convoys. The cruisers *Prinz Eugen, Hipper, Nurnberg* and the pocket battleships *Admiral Scheer* and *Lutzow* would be stationed in the Baltic for training purposes. In February he submitted this plan to Hitler which, as already seen, was grudgingly accepted. The plan proved beneficial for the very presence of these ships in northern waters was enough to cause fear to reign in many of the Allied convoys.

On September 8, 1943, there occurred the last sortie of Germany's battle squadron in World War II. The *Tirpitz, Scharnhorst* and ten destroyers sailed out of Atlen Fjord to destroy shore installations on Spitzbergen. This was the only time the massive *Tirpitz,* sister ship to the *Bismarck,* had fired her fifteen-inch main armament in anger. The German ships accomplished very little in the way of material damage. The sortie did, however, make the Allies sit up and take notice.

On September 22, having just returned to its berth, the *Tirpitz* was damaged by British midget submarines. The huge battleship was forced to undergo extensive repairs.

Meanwhile, the Russians requested that the convoys, which had been temporarily halted, be resumed. The Allies were concerned about the presence of German heavy ships in Norwegian waters and were taking no chances. When the convoys were resumed, Doenitz decided to use the *Scharnhorst* against them. On December 19 he informed Hitler that he *Scharnhorst* would attack the next Allied convoy to Russia. The British, however, were certain that the *Scharnhorst* would strike and were prepared to meet it. On the twentieth a British convoy sailed; on Christmas Day came the order for the *Scharnhorst* to sortie. The commander in chief, battle group, Adm. Erich Bey flew his flag in the *Scharnhorst*.

Unknown to the Germans, two groups of British warships were covering the convoy at a distance. One consisted of the cruisers *Sheffield*, *Belfast* and *Norfolk*. The other was comprised of the cruiser *Jamaica* and Adm. Sir Bruce Fraser's flagship, the new battleship *Duke of York*. The resulting battle was known as the Battle of North Cape. The unwitting Germans sailed into a beautifully laid trap. At the end of the battle the *Scharnhorst* was gone. Richard Humble said, "The last fight of the *Scharnhorst* was not only the last time that Hitler's High Seas Fleet challenged the Royal Navy. It was the last time that battleships engaged in a running fight in the style of Jutland with aircraft taking no part in the battle apart from preliminary scouting."[15]

That left only the *Tirpitz*. To the British she represented a major threat. She had already caused a great deal of harm a year earlier simply by being a deterrent.* The British were therefore determined to destroy her. The midget submarine attack in September had damaged the mighty ship extensively but by the spring of 1944 the *Tirpitz*'s repairs were nearing completion. The R.A.F. attacked her at her berth in

---

*On June 27, 1942, Convoy PQ17 scattered for fear of the *Tirpitz*. The convoy subsequently lost twenty-four merchant ships to U-boats and German aircraft. This disaster led to the temporary suspension of all arctic convoys.

Alton Fjord but the damaged inflicted was superficial. Three more months of repair, however, were required. During the next few months she became a major preoccupation of the British who expended valuable energy on her destruction. Energy that might have been put to better use in other theaters.

On September 15 the *Tirpitz* received more damage, enough to destroy her seaworthiness. Her guns, however, were still useful so it was decided to make her a coastal defense battery to support the Norwegian garrison. At a reduced speed, which was all she was capable of, the ship was sent to Haakoy Island near Tromsö Fjord. There Doenitz ordered sandbanks to be constructed for her. Shortly thereafter, Lancaster bombers of 617 Squadron, the famous Dam Busters, located the ship and began to pound her. After many attempts, she met her doom on November 12, 1944, taking with her over a thousand crewmen. With the *Tirpitz* gone, so too was the effectiveness of the German navy.

Doenitz had never given up on halting the Atlantic convoys with his U-boats. In the fall of 1943 he again sent his submarines into the Atlantic but with little success. The powerful Allied convoys were simply too deadly and U-boat losses mounted.

By the end of November, Doenitz was forced to suspend his wolf pack tactics. He had to disperse his forces because their concentration, which had earlier proved so deadly to the convoys, now worked in the opposite way. During the entire month of November the U-boats managed to sink only six ships. Seven more were sunk in December. However, the cost for these thirteen sinkings was the loss of sixteen U-boats.

Doenitz still maintained that the convoys had to be stopped. With the dawn of 1944 he decided to concentrate his submarines in the western approaches to the British Isles. By the middle of January he had positioned twenty-four U-boats from the Faroes to Brest, each one approximately thirty miles from the other. Every attempt to attack an approaching convoy, however, resulted in negative results for the Germans. U-boat losses continued to mount.

Doenitz then ordered the U-boats further westward but that only led to even further destruction of the submarines. By May, U-boat activity in the Atlantic had virtually ground to a halt.

In June of 1944, Doenitz came to the conclusion that the only task left to the U-boats was that of tying down enemy forces. David Mason has written:

> So that was it. After the years of aggressive, spirited sinking of merchant ships by the eager men of the U-boat arm, after all Doenitz's bitter battles with his superiors to allow him to wage his war against the enemy's supply lines . . . After his magnificent convoy duels . . . the U-boat arm now became resigned to the secondary task of tying down enemy forces.[16]

U-boats were now to be used as bait to keep away Allied air and sea forces, drawing their fire to allow other German forces a greater chance to defeat the enemy.

While Doenitz pondered this new defensive role, a glimmer of hope began to shine on the horizon. The dockyards began turning out new revolutionary U-boats.*

When the Allies invaded Normandy on June 6, 1944, Doenitz issued orders to his captains to sink any

---

*These U-boats were fitted with the schnorkel device which allowed them to travel at great speeds completely submerged.

Allied ship possible. He ordered them to risk everything in the attempt. For the good of Germany, every sacrifice, even one's own life, had to be made to halt the Allies.

Doenitz ordered every U-boat available to proceed to the invasion area where they faced some of the fiercest opposition of the war. The new submarines fitted with the schnorkel proved their worth.

Those without it, however, were quickly recalled when thier losses began to mount. Though the U-boats managed to sink a few ships, by the middle of June the U-boats had ground to a halt in light of their heavy losses. Through July the losses continued to mount as Allied anti-submarine forces struck back with deadly accuracy.

On the whole the achievement of the U-boats during the invasion period was disappointing. Only twelve merchant ships, four landing craft and five escort vessels were sunk with an additional five merchant ships, one escort vessel and one landing craft damaged. Doenitz, however, praised his forces for at least hampering the buildup but the cost in U-boats had been tremendous. The only bright spot was the success of the submarines fitted with the schnorkel. The admiral discovered that because of the schnorkel the U-boat had proven itself almost immune from airborne radar. The radar was unable to pick up an echo from the small head of the schnorkel. Doenitz therefore continued to hold out hope that when more U-boats equipped with this device that allowed them to travel faster underwater became available, there was still a slight chance to inflict some damage in the Atlantic.

In August, United States forces broke into Brittany thereby threatening the U-boat bases at Lorient, Brest and Saint-Nazaire. Doenitz ordered his U-boats to make for Norway and safety. Despite the Allies being aware of this move, twenty-two submarines managed to escape from their bases under the probing eyes of Allied aircraft. It was only because of the schnorkel that they were able to evade destruction.

For the balance of 1944 the U-boat war remained heavily weighted in the Allies' favor. During the final four months of the year only twenty-four Allied ships were sunk at a cost of fifty-five U-boats. Doenitz's only remaining hope was that more of the newer submarines would soon be ready for action. He continued to cling to the hope that these could snatch the initiative from the enemy.

In January of 1945, the first of the Type XXIII boats were finally ready. The *U-2324* left its Norwegian base for action. Others soon followed. Travelling in silence, the U-boats evaded detection by Allied tracking stations. Only when they made their attack could the search for them begin. By the end of the month six more U-boats were lost but so were seven Allied ships. Doenitz sent more boats to British coastal waters determined to prey on the shipping there. In February alone, forty-one U-boats sailed for the English Channel.

Unfortunately, all they could accomplish was the sinking of fourteen Allied ships at a cost to themselves of twelve submarines. In March thirty-seven more U-boats left Norway but fifteen of these were quickly destroyed after sinking only thirteen Allied ships.

Allied technical development had managed to produce a new type of radar set capable of picking up an echo from the schnorkel. Other inventions were soon added to the Allied arsenal, spelling doom for the U-boats. Doenitz's hopes were dashed. Still, he persisted in sending more boats into the fray, particularly the newer type submarines. Thus far most of the losses had been the older types.

By the spring of 1945 the Western Allies had reached the Rhine and the hated Russians were on the Oder. Hitler was in his bunker in Berlin still issuing orders as if Germany still had a chance. When the Führer issued his Scorched Earth order on March 19, Doenitz's primary concern became to see that control of any measures which the navy might be called upon to take remained in his own hands.

The admiral felt one of his primary duties was the evacuation of as many Germans as possible from the eastern provinces to prevent them from falling into Russian hands. Thanks to his initiative, between January and May, two million people were evacuated. This was largely due to the determined efforts of the fleet. In the words of Richard Humble, "It was a performance which, all in all, certainly ranks with the miracle of Dunkirk as a successful use of sea power in the teeth of enemy opposition."[17]

Doenitz assumed direct responsibility for directing the evacuations. At times he even provided naval personnel to fight alongside army units in an effort to shore up crumbling fronts.

On April 22, just before the Russians entered Berlin, Doenitz went to Ploen in Holstein where he was given command of the defense of northern Germany. The next day he invited the Gauleiters of Mecklenberg, Schleswig-Holstein and Hamburg to come to Ploen to discuss plans. Only two of them came. The admiral knew that it was vitally important to hold Hamburg. In that port were a number of U-boat crews which had been put into field gray uniforms and placed at the disposal of Major General Wolz, commanding the Hamburg district. Wolz turned the sailors into an anti-aircraft battalion.

On April 28, Doenitz left Ploen for Supreme Headquarters in Rheinsberg where he met with Himmler who was already styling himself as the new head of the government. The two discussed the question of whom would succeed in the event of Hitler's death. Himmler asked Doenitz if he would place his services at his disposal. Doenitz replied that "the only thing that now mattered was to prevent a reign of chaos which would inevitably lead to further bloodshed, and that I was therefore prepared to serve under any legally constituted government."[18]

Doenitz felt that his greatest service to the Reich at this time was the rescue of as many Germans as possible from the Russians.

On April 30, Doenitz again met with Himmler. This took place after Hitler had ordered Himmler's arrest for allegedly opening up negotiations with the West through the mediation of Count Bernadotte of Sweden. Doenitz asked the SS leader point-blank if he was in contact with the West. Himmler lied, replying that he was not. Even if Himmler was sending out peace feelers, Doenitz reasoned, he was in no position to order the arrest of Germany's most powerful person.

After returning to his headquarters in Ploen, Doenitz received an important message from Berlin:

Grand Admiral Doenitz:
  The Führer has appointed you, Herr Admiral, as his successor in place of Reichmarshal Goering.* Confirmation in writing follows. You are hereby authorized to take any measures

---

*Goering attempted to take over the leadership of the Reich saying that Hitler was incapacitated. This action infuriated Hitler who ordered Goering's arrest.

which the situation demands.

Doenitz was taken completely by surprise. Yet, he was Hitler's obvious choice. Doenitz was devoted, he produced, and most importantly, he was loyal.

On April 30, Hitler committed suicide in his Berlin bunker. Doenitz was now the Führer. At the time he thought that he had been nominated because Hitler had wished to clear the way for an officer of the armed forces to put an end to the war. It was only after the war that he found out that Hitler had wished for him to continue the struggle.

After assuming the leadership of the government, Doenitz decided that his policy should be to try and save as many lives as possible and to prevent chaos. He feared that Himmler would pose a problem so he invited the latter to Ploen for a conference. Shortly after midnight on May 1, the SS chief arrived. Doenitz kept a pistol on his desk just in case. He handed Himmler the telegram confirming his appointment. The astonished Himmler asked if he could be considered for the number two position. Doenitz refused and, to his great relief, Himmler left quickly and quietly.

That same night, Doenitz summoned Field Marshal Keital and General Jodl to Ploen to discuss the military situation. Then in the morning he broadcast an announcement of his succession to the German nation. Doenitz stated that his primary task was to save the German people from destruction at the hands of the Bolshevists.

Meanwhile, the military situation continued to disintegrate.

On May 3 Doenitz received a message from Field Marshal Kesselring in southern Germany. Kesselring informed the admiral of the surrender of the German forces in Italy which had transpired the previous day. The field marshal then asked for permission to negotiate independently with the Western Allies with regard to his own sector in the southeast. Doenitz agreed.

At the same time, Doenitz sanctioned negotiations with Field Marshal Montgomery in the north. He dispatched Admiral von Friedburg as head of a German delegation to initiate talks with the British. On May 4, Montgomery informed Doenitz that he was prepared to accept the separate surrender of North Germany but that Holland and Denmark would also have to be included. Montgomery also insisted that all ships be surrendered and that none of them be scuttled. This last demand disturbed Doenitz for it meant the end of the evacuation of troops and refugees from Eastern Europe by sea. Not only that, it was against the tradition of the German navy to hand over their ships. Anxious to save lives, however, Doenitz accepted the terms.

On the morning of the fourth, after receiving Montgomery's demands, Doenitz sent Friedburg back to British headquarters. After relaying Doenitz's decision, Friedburg went on to see Eisenhower at Rheims.

Eisenhower proved difficult in contrast to Montgomery. He would not compromise and absolutely refused to consider any separate surrender. Instead, he insisted on immediate and unconditional surrender on all fronts, including the Russian. Eisenhower also demanded that all German troops stay where they were, hand over their arms intact, and surrender on the spot. German Supreme Headquarters would be responsible for seeing the conditions of the unconditional surrender were followed.

This was precisely what Doenitz had feared would happen. He did not want to abandon the struggle in the east against the hated Russians. The admiral truly believed that Eisenhower was doing a great disservice not only to the Germans, but to the Western Allies as well, and that "the British and Americans in that case will not be fighting in the interests of their own people but solely for the expansion of Bolshevism in Europe."[20]

Doenitz would not accept these conditions and once more attempted to convince Eisenhower that he could not allow German troops and the civilian population of the eastern provinces to fall into Soviet hands. Jodl was sent to Rheims in an effort to reason with the Allied supreme commander but Eisenhower was unmovable. Doenitz now had to make a quick decision. He had no choice but to authorize Jodl to sign the instrument of surrender, which he did on May 7 in Rheims. The next day, Keitel repeated this act at the headquarters of Marshal Zhukov in Berlin. As a result, thousands of German soldiers and civilians fell into the hands of the Russians.

With the war at an end, Doenitz continued to function as Germany's legitimate ruler but the Allies refused to recognize him. The Russians demanded his removal as did Eisenhower. Churchill opposed his removal initially but eventually he too agreed. On May 22, the Allied Control Commission demanded Doenitz's presence at their headquarters aboard the steamship *Patria*. There, the admiral was taken into custody. A few months later, he was placed on trial at Nuremberg as a major war criminal.

The charges against Doenitz were that of waging aggressive warfare, the so-called Laconia Order, and the waging of war against hundreds of noncombatants, including women and children who had been passengers on merchant ships.

As for the first charge, that of waging aggressive warfare, the written testimony of American Admiral Nimitz and the British admiralty helped in his defense. Both sources admitted that their submarines had orders to sink any ship on sight without regard to visit and search. Nimitz also testified that it was not the practice of American submarines to rescue survivors if such an effort constituted an undue or additional hazard to the submarine.

As the trial wound down, the case against Doenitz boiled down to the ambiguity of his orders concerning treatment of shipwrecked crews, orders which in effect were similiar to what the Allies themselves had done. It was his pro-Nazism, his blind obedience to Hitler, his anti-Semitism and the fact that he had been named Hitler's successor that condemned him.

The court found him guilty of having committed crimes against peace but not having conspired to commit them. He was therefore guilty of war crimes. As for Hitler's Commando Order,* i.e. the order to kill any captured commandos, the court agreed that it was not Doenitz's order. They did, however, state that he intended to breach the Geneva Convention via the advice that he had given to Hitler during the war. Thus, despite an excellent defense, Doenitz was sentenced to ten years in prison for waging aggressive warfare.

The next ten years of his life spent behind the walls of Spandau prison in Berlin. On October 1, 1956, Doenitz was released. He immediately went to work writing his memoirs which were published in 1958. Doenitz lived a good long life before passing away on

*See Raeder, chapter one.

December 24, 1980 at Hamburg, West Germany, in his eighty-ninth year.

As a submariner, Doenitz was without peer. He will forever be known as the head of the German U-boat arm more than as commander in chief of the navy or as the second Führer of the Third Reich. As a politician, Doenitz was a failure. His political opinions were not enlightened but were simply no more than the stale party rot. He was a Nazi and believed in National Socialism and all that it stood for. As a patriot he believed in Hitler's dreams of a new Germany. Only at his war crimes trial did he gradually learn of the dark side of Nazism and therefore modified his position.

Doenitz was a better submariner than he was a commander in chief. One of his beloved U-boat captains, Lt. Cmdr. Peter Kemp has said, "He had neither the grasp of strategy nor the breadth of vision necessary to survive in the rarefied atmosphere of top naval command."[21]

Therefore, when we evaluate Doenitz, it is his record as head of the U-boat arm that must be scrutinized. During the war, the U-boats managed to sink 2,603 merchant ships of 13.5 million tons, not to mention 175 enemy naval vessels. At one point, the U-boats had all but severed Britian's life line.

Scientific advances eventually doomed the U-boats to inevitable defeat. Of the 1,162 U-boats possessed by Germany during the course of the war, 784 were sunk with a loss of twenty-eight thousand lives. Nevertheless, Doenitz was the architect of a theory that nearly proved successful. Whenever wolf packs are mentioned, the name of Grand Adm. Karl Doenitz will be mentioned in the same breath.

7. ADMIRAL WILHELM CANARIS

Adm. Wilhelm Canaris presents the historian with a dilemma. Was the inscrutable Admiral a German patriot or a cosmopolitan intriguer, a double agent or a traitor? His enigmatic actions caused many to wonder. Gen. Louis Rivet, the one-time head of the French secret service called him a "trapeze artist."[1] Gen. Efisio Marias, Italian military attache in Berlin described him as an "extraordinarily intelligent man who is quite without scruple."[2]

Otto Skorzeny, Hitler's master commando asserted, "Canaris betrayed his country's military secrets directly and wittingly from the beginning of his career to its end."[3]

Gen. Alfred Jodl stated that Canaris "served the enemy for years."[4]

The American head of the O.S.S.*, Alan Dulles described Canaris thusly: "One of the bravest men of modern history, gentleman, patriot, visionary of a United States of Europe led by England, France and Germany."[5]

Canaris's principal British counterpart, Sir Stewart Menzies referred to him as "damned brave and damned unlucky."[6]

But Canaris's wife had this to say of her husband: "He used his powers to oppose as much as possible the grow-

*Office of Strategic Services, forerunner of the C.I.A.

ing lawlessness. . . . Many people who were persecuted by the Gestapo came to him, such as Jews, pastors, members of the Christian organizations. . . . He and his friends suffered so terribly because they had to fight on the German side and loved their fatherland, and yet their sympathies were not on that side and could not be because their philosophical attitude was so different."[7]

Adm. Wilhelm Franz Canaris was head of the German military secret service, the Abwehr. From that position he used all his powers for the good of his homeland and was indeed a patriot. This patriotism, however, caused him to do things that could brand him a traitor. Because of this, his actions have been open to boundless interpretation. He could be viewed as the man responsible for the Third Reich's heinous crimes. On the other hand, many see him as the spiritual leader of most of the opposition movements against Hitler and a martyr in the cause of the resistance against Nazism, actions which are viewed as traitorous.

The authors will attempt to unravel the various threads and establish what they feel is a balanced interpretation of this inscrutable officer.

As far back as he could remember, young Wilhelm had been fascinated by the sea. He thirsted for the strange and unknown, seeming to share the restless spirit of his ancestors, the Canarisi. The family boasted that Canarisi blood flowed in Napoleon and Constantine Kanaris, the co-founder of modern Greece.

Since the Industrial Revolution the Canaris family had been deeply involved in mining and industry. Wilhelm Franz Canaris first saw the light of day on January 1, 1887 at Aplerbeck, a small mining town in the Ruhr. Born into wealth the future admiral enjoyed all the luxuries life had to offer to the upper middle class of that era. Influenced by his environment, he developed a dreamy nature that inwardly concealed an inscrutable personality. Although outwardly he appeared calm, his enigmatic character was developing within.

His father, Carl Canaris, took notice of his son's interest in military matters and accordingly sought the boy's admittance to one of the army academies. But, to the chagrin of his father, who utilized all his arts of persuasion in an effort to change his son's mind, young Wilhelm insisted on joining the navy. The father argued that Germany's heros were virtually all army men.

Nevertheless, the turn of the century was an exciting time for Germany's budding navy. The kaiser himself took a great personal interest in creating a navy that could rival England's. As a result attractive offers were made to entice young men to enlist in the Imperial Navy. Kaiser Wilhelm expounded the theory that the future is on the sea. His naval secretary, Adm. Alfred von Tirpitz convinced his imperial majesty that Germany's future went hand in hand with a dependency on its fleet.

To the young Canaris, the prospect of being part of this great expansion was most appealing. Pro-navy pamphlets and articles were readily available at his schools. He wanted to be a part of that growth for he felt that the navy could satisfy his desire for adventure.

On September 26, 1904, Carl Canaris died of a stroke. Though a tragic occurrence for the Canaris family, the event opened the door for Wilhelm to pursue a naval career. Thus his name was presented to the naval cadets' admission board at Kiel. He was quickly accepted and set off for Kiel where, on April 1, 1905, Canaris presented himself to the warrant officers' school.

The initial weeks were ones of severity and discipline with obedience and physical fitnes stressed. The exhausting days passed slowly. After four weeks the cadets were assigned to one of three sail-training ships. Canaris was posted to the *Stein*, reputed to be the toughest training ship in the entire navy. The budding officers soon learned what it meant to be the lowest of the low. Drill, work, followed by more drill filled every hour of the day. However, for the first time in his life, Canaris found himself on the high seas. The *Stein* sailed first to the North Atlantic and subsequently to the Mediterranean. Though the grind aboard ship was difficult, Cadet Canaris was determined to succeed. Upon completion of the cruise, an eighteen-month course at the naval academy lay ahead. Being intellectually miles above his classmates, Canaris finished at the head of his class.

In October of 1907, Midshipman Canaris passed his final exams and swore his oath of loyalty to the kaiser. As a passed midshipman, Canaris was posted to the cruiser *Bremen*, which held station in the Southwest Atlantic off the coast of Central and South America. He held many, varied jobs from training seamen to delivering lectures to the crew. Thanks to his ability to speak four languages, Canaris also was assigned one other important position. That was to place his linguistic skills at the disposal of the ship's captain in the event the ship became involved in any international complications.

On September 28, 1908, Canaris was commissioned a sublieutenant. His superiors came to appreciate the talents of the young officer and his fitness reports usually glowed with high praise.

In January of 1910, Canaris was transferred to a torpedo boat patrolling the North Sea. By December of 1911, he was a full lieutenant and to his delight was once more posted to the Southern Hemisphere, this time with the cruiser *Dresden*. With the outbreak of hostilities in the Balkans, the *Dresden* was temporarily moved to the Eastern Mediterranean but by the end of the year was back in familiar waters off the western coast of civil-war-torn Mexico. The *Dresden* helped carry those foreign nationals whose lives were in jeopardy to safety. The ship's adjutant, Canaris, who spoke perfect Spanish, aided in the negotiations with the Mexican government.

In July of 1914, just as the *Dresden* was making preparations to return to Germany, word was received of the assassination of the Austrian archduke and the subsequent Austrian ultimatum to Serbia. War seemed imminent. Just as the *Dresden* was about to leave for home it received new orders telling it not to return home but to instead conduct cruiser warfare (Kreuzerkrieg).*

The *Dresden* was in an unenviable position. It had orders to conduct warfare thousands of miles from home with little or no friendly help. Among the many essentials lacking was current information. The *Dresden*'s captain instructed Lieutenant Canaris to establish a network of informants on the South American mainland who could accurately report enemy dispositions and intentions. As the mysterious had always fascinated Canaris, he was in his element and more than eager to assume the role of spy.

At the end of July the *Dresden* sailed south to rendezvous with Admiral von Spee's Far East squadron of cruisers off the west coast of Chile. En route to the rendezvous, the *Dresden* managed to capture five British merchant ships. Finally, on October 14, after a voyage around Cape Horn, the *Dresden* joined up with von Spee's squadron. Thanks to information supplied by Canaris, the admiral was alerted to the presence of British ships in the area. On November 1, the German force inflicted a decisive defeat on a force of British warships at the Battle of Coronel. Two British cruisers were lost along with their commander, Adm. Christopher Craddock.

*To disrupt, if possible paralyze, the enemy's overseas trade.

With the ability to obtain supplies becoming more difficult each day, von Spee decided to return to Germany via the South Atlantic. Once more the *Dresden* found itself rounding Cape Horn. Off the Falkland Islands the German squadron was ambushed by a superior British force. The cruisers *Leipzig*, *Nurnberg*, *Scharnhorst* and *Gneisenau* were lost as was von Spee. Of the German formation, only the *Dresden* managed to make good her escape.

For the third time in a few weeks, the *Dresden* made its way through the dangerous waters south of Tierra del Fuego at the southern tip of South America. Once more the ship began commerce raiding in the Pacific. On February 27, 1915, one more British ship fell victim to the raider. Canaris was elated. He had received the Iron Cross Second Class for his intelligence work, had been involved in a major naval battle, and had seen his ship escape imminent disaster.

On March 8, however, the *Dresden*'s luck ran out. The British cruiser *Kent* located the elusive German raider. The *Dresden* quickly made for the Más Atierra and, on March 9, dropped anchor in Cumberland Bay. The Chilean harbor master quickly came aboard and told the Germans that their ship had to conform to international law. This meant that the ship would be required to leave the bay within twenty-four hours.

Since the ship was critically short of coal, the *Dresden*'s captain, Ludecke, asked the Chilean representative if the crew could be interned. The harbor master replied that he was in no position to protect the *Dresden* from the British.

Meanwhile, the British had discovered where the *Dresden* lay and showed up to finish her off. Disregarding Chilean neutrality, the British pounded the German cruiser until it was doomed.

Canaris was given the task of parleying with the enemy

while the *Dresden*'s crew prepared their vessel for scuttling. The British captain proved difficult to deal with. His orders were to destroy the *Dresden*. Canaris argued that the British were in violation of international law because the German vessel had sought the protection of Chilean neutrality. The British turned a deaf ear to all of Canaris's points.

However, Canaris was performing a vital task, he was buying time needed to prepare his ship for scuttling. When he returned to the *Dresden*, Ludecke was ready to sink the cruiser. With the completion of this sad chore, the crew was interned on the island of Quiriquina. Canaris found life there boring and itched to leave the internment center and get back into the war. He plotted an escape.

With permission from his commander, Canaris managed to break out and work his way across Chile's mountains to pro-German Argentina. Hiding by day and travelling by night, he made his way across the treacherous wilderness. The journey consumed months but the young officer finally made it across the vast Andes Mountains.

Arriving in Argentina, the sickly and emaciated young lieutenant was nevertheless anxious to return to Germany and the war. Armed with false papers, he booked passage on a neutral Dutch ship, the S.S. *Frisia*, bound for Rotterdam.

Taking the name of Reed Rosas, son of a Chilean father and a British mother, Canaris began the dangerous passage across the ocean. Off England, the ship was ordered into Plymouth harbor despite the Dutch captain's loud protests. There the passengers and crew were interrogated. Reed Rosas completely fooled the famed British naval intelligence service. The *Frisia* was allowed to leave and continue on to Rotterdam. A few days later, on October 4, 1915, Canaris was in Hamburg, Germany.

Upon his return to Germany, Canaris was promoted to senior lieutenant. His talents as an agent were now utilized by the German admiralty and he was sent to Madrid with instructions to develop a supply system for U-boats operating in the Western Mediterranean. He was also directed to create an improved reconnaissance service capable of providing information on enemy ship movements.

Using the name Reed Rosas once more, Canaris went to Spain and there began life as a secret agent while taking a clandestine name, Kika.

Canaris excelled at his work and quickly gained the confidence of his superiors who reported to Berlin on his activities. His reputation began to grow. Eventually the Allies became aware of his activities and sought to stop his efforts.

In the fall of 1917 Canaris was asked to return to Germany for reassignment. However, in order to make the trip to Germany he was forced to run the Allied blockade. This time he decided to travel by train. When he reached the French border, police came on board the train and began a lengthy border check. They were specifically looking for German spies.

Still using the passport of the Chilean, Reed Rosas, Canaris was asked his destination by the border guard. "Switzerland," he told the policeman, saying he was going there for a cure for tuberculosis. That was enough to make the guard validate the passport.

The same trick was successful on the Italian frontier. Unfortunately for the spy, just as he was about to enter Switzerland his luck ran out and French intelligence, having finally realized who Reed Rosas really was, caught up with him and convinced the Italians to arrest him. After lengthy interrogation, Canaris was sentenced to be hung as a spy.

Fortunately, friends in Madrid applied pressure on

Rome and successfully argued that Reed Rosas was not a spy but a Chilean citizen. The Italians buckled under the pressure and put Canaris aboard a Spanish freighter bound for Marseilles, France. En route Canaris confided in the Spanish captain and revealed his actual identity. Realizing what would happen to the spy if he landed in France, the Spaniard altered course and brought Canaris to neutral Spain.

Canaris finally managed to reach Germany later in the year and was assigned to a U-boat. By May of 1918, he had risen to command of a submarine of his own. It was in this capacity that he received the sad news of Germany's surrender on November 11, 1918.

The Germany Canaris returned to was not the prewar nation of pomp and circumstance. Instead, Germany's defeat opened up a floodgate of discontent and revolution. November, 1918 brought chaos to the country. Canaris was particularly shocked by the conduct of numerous sailors who mutinied against their officers and left behind a trail of blood and destruction. Who was responsible for this chaos?

It did not take the naval elite or Canaris long to pinpoint the cause of the mutinous actions of the sailors. It was the Marxist Communists who had infiltrated the fleet and subverted the ideas of the sailors. Canaris sought law and order and gravitated to those who offered stability. He joined a unit of like-minded officers under Lt. Cmdr. Wilfred von Lowenfeld who followed the ideals of prewar Germany and dedicated themselves to the task of eliminating the "Red Terror." Gradually, Canaris came to realize that any hope for law and order and the end of the Communist threat lay with Gustav Noske, the Social Democratic champion of law and order.

Canaris was present when Noske led his army, comprised of former soldiers (the Freikorps), against the hated Communists. Ruthlessly the men of the Freikorps raided Communist outposts, gunning down anyone suspected of Communist sympathies.

As a member of the new Republican Navy, on May 1, 1919, Lieutenant Commander Canaris was chosen to serve on a court of inquiry to investigate the slaying of two Communist leaders, Karl Liebknecht and Rosa Luxemburg. It was a strange choice indeed for Canaris was a noted hater of the Communists and Socialists and at that very time was secretly preparing a fake passport for one of the accused murderers.

When the murderer fled, the left-wing press protested and demanded Canaris's jailing. He was arrested but did not remain incarcerated for long. The naval command raised a loud ruckus and because of the threat of revolution in Bavaria, Canaris was released.

Soon afterward Canaris was involved in the attempted right-wing national revolution of 1920. The aftermath of that aborted attempt found him once more behind bars. He was released after a few days. This was followed by days of intensive interrogation in an attempt to elucidate his role in the abortive Kapp Putsch. Although he was acquitted of any traitorous activity, his reputation as a schemer was growing.

The "rehabilitated" Canaris was now transferred to the Baltic Station Headquarters at Kiel as a naval staff officer, grade 1, with the job of helping to build the new German Baltic Fleet, a mammoth task in light of the rigid restrictions of the Treaty of Versailles.

Canaris quickly set to work on the herculean task. The major problem facing the German navy was, of course, the restrictions of the treaty. Canaris utilized all his expertise to help reconstruct the navy by circumventing the harsh treaty restrictions. Never having abandoned the utopian dream of Germany's world power status, Canaris and similar-minded naval officers sought ways of circumventing Versailles.

One method of doing this was the development of a personnel reserve. Another was the illegal stockpiling of arms and equipment which were stored beyond the eyes of the inquisitive Versailles watchdogs.

Utilizing his numerous contacts, Canaris managed to obtain the needed financing and arms. He then began to tap the available human reservoir from which he hoped to recruit his secret reserve. The Freikorps, that aimless bunch of former soldiers, were a willing group.

After a few years in that role, Canaris was relieved of his duties and appointed executive officer of the training cruiser *Berlin,* based in Kiel. In this capacity he encountered a young cadet, handsome in appearance, who eventually would cause the future admiral many a sleepless night: Cadet Reinhard Heydrich. The two formed a close friendship for they both shared many ideas, hobbies and tastes.

By 1924, Lieutenant Commander Canaris, feeling depressed, began to ponder his future. He contemplated resigning from the navy but was persuaded to stay by the offer of an attractive assignment. Once more he returned to the world of espionage.

Canaris's new assignment took him to Japan for secret discussions with the Japanese on the possibility of collaborating on submarine development. Upon making contacts in Osaka, the German officer found that the Japanese were eager to collaborate.

Returning to Berlin upon completion of his Japanese assignment, Canaris was once more assigned to a desk job. Desk work hardly suited the free-spirited naval officer. As one of his fitness reports recorded, "He is a restless soul who is stimulated by difficult and out-of-the-ordinary assignments."[8]

Though tied to a desk, Canaris continued to work covertly on submarine development. He sought permission to travel to Spain in hopes of enlisting that country as a would-be collaborator in submarine construction. When permission was finally granted, Kika, as he once again called himself, reopened his World War I Spanish contacts. It was said of Canaris that, "Better than any German officer of his day, Canaris knew the rules of Spanish politics and could manipulate the Spanish mentality and love of tradition."[9]

His superiors observed that he was highly sensitive to the psychology of foreigners and this, coupled with his faculty for foreign languages, made him ideally suited for a career in espionage. While in Spain, Canaris truly demonstrated his ability. The many Spanish contacts he forged would, within a decade, become high officials of the Franco government.

Canaris was a whirlwind, constantly on the move: Berlin, Spain, Argentina and the Mediterranean. He was unquestionably a man on the rise, intriguing and scheming all the way. A report written by his superiors in the late 1920s described him as a "restless spirit, provoked to great performance by extraordinary and difficult challenges in the handling of confidential military political assignments on his frequent missions abroad."[10]

On June 22, 1928, Canaris was appointed executive officer of the old battleship *Schlesien*. His sudden transfer from the world of espionage was considered by his naval superiors to be vital because of various antipolitical views against covert naval activities. It was therefore deemed necessary to give Canaris an active command to save him from further criticism by left-wing politicians and newspapers.

Canaris's contacts in Spain, however, were too important for the naval authorities to throw off completely. Thus he was still allowed to continue his covert activities even in his present assignment.

As 1928 continued, his reputation suffered another setback as the left-wing political machine defamed his abilities. The new chief of the navy, Admiral Raeder, found Canaris congenial and decided it was best to keep him remote from any political wranglings. There was strong pressure on Raeder to keep Canaris away from Spain despite his invaluable contacts.

Denied his espionage activities, Canaris immersed himself in his job on the *Schlesien*. On September 29, 1930, Canaris was promoted to chief of staff, North Sea station. However, he continued to secretly long for a recall to Berlin and the world of espionage. Unfortunately, his prior role in the escape of the murderer of Karl Liebknecht and Rosa Luxemburg came back to haunt him and barred him from Berlin. Even his promotion to captain on October 1, 1931 failed to satisfy him, for he felt that his career was at a dead end.

One hope remained for the exiled captain: the demise of the republic. A monarchist at heart, Canaris was not adverse to turning to another form of government, one which could provide many of the same benefits as a monarchical government.

The National Socialists seemed such a political force. Adolf Hitler was just the man to revive Germany and put an end to the dismal republic. If Germany's navy was to achieve the greatness Canaris dreamed of, then perhaps Hitler could do it. Because of this, Canaris was receptive to the slogans of the National Socialist movement which professed to build such a Germany and a navy commensurate with his dream. In addition, the Nazi program was vehemently anti-Communist, which of course was appealing.

In this frame of mind, on September 29, 1932, Captain Canaris was named commander of the battleship *Schlesien*. Hitler became chancellor on January 30 of the following year. Canaris was caught up in the anticipation of a dawn of a new era. Though he heard stories of Nazi brutality, Canaris chose to shunt the rumors aside. Being a patriot he found himself caught up in the enthusiasm of the time. Though he would later become an avowed opponent of the regime, during those early days he was an ardent supporter.

Nevertheless, even with the Nazis in power, Canaris continued to languish in his command. Indeed, it went from bad to worse. On September 29, 1934, he was appointed commanding officer at Fort Swinemunde. For all intents and purposes he could now assume that his career was virtually at an end. For a forty-five-year-old captain, the job of fortress commander was usually the end of the road. Little did he realize that his career was in fact just beginning.

No sooner had Canaris settled into his job at Swinemunde than news broke out that the Reich war ministry was in dispute over who should head the military intelligence service, the Abwehr. The present head of the Abwehr, Capt. Conrad Patzig had been forced to resign because of his inability to work with the rival SS organization headed by Heinrich Himmler. Patzig specifically could not go along with Himmler's main security office headed by a former naval officer who had been cashiered for misconduct, Canaris's former friend Reinhard Heydrich. In addition, Patzig had also alienated Admiral Raeder.

Raeder wanted to retain the Abwehr leadership in naval hands. What he required for this was someone with the ability to work with the SS but a person also skilled in the field of espionage. Though not an admirer of Canaris, Raeder knew that there was no one else with Canaris's experience and qualifications. Therefore, the German naval chief rescued Canaris from the backwater of Swinemunde.

Just before Christmas of 1934, Canaris received orders to report to Berlin and assume the position as head of the German military intelligence organization on January 1.

Early on New Year's Day, the new Abwehr chief entered the Fox Lair (the colloquial name used by the inner circle for main headquarters) for the first time. Captain Patzig was waiting for him and frankly explained the difficulties he would have with Himmler and particularly with Heydrich. Patzig was obviously relieved to be going and told his successor, "I am sorry for you, Captain, because you don't seem to realize what a mess you're getting into. . . . I am sorry to say that this day is the beginning of your end."[11] Canaris, however, was optimistic and felt confident that he could get along with the SS.

Though only forty-seven, Canaris appeared much older. Because of his snow white hair and wrinkled skin, he was called "The Old Man." His subordinates sometimes referred to him as the White Admiral. Himmler and Heydrich derisively called him Father Christmas.

The word Abwehr literally means defense. It was called that to make it appear less threatening to other countries. The Abwehr that Canaris inherited was extremely small. He was, however, given limitless funds to expand the organization.

Canaris reorganized the Abwehr into two sections, the central section and the foreign group. Under these sections were three groups: Group I — secret intelligence service; Group II — military sabotage; and Group III — counterespionage. Group I had the job of gathering intelligence and conducting espionage operations. Group II's mission was fermenting political insurrections in addition to sabotage behind enemy lines in the event of war. Group III — counterespionage — had the difficult task of breaking enemy codes and ciphers.

After establishing the organizational makeup, Canaris next sought to staff the various groups with highly competent men. To head Group I he appointed Col. Hans Pieckenbrock. For Group II he tapped Helmuth Groscurth, and to lead Group III, Major Bamler was selected. For his second-in-command and head of the central office, Canaris selected Maj. Hans Oster, a man who ultimately led to the admiral's downfall.

One major problem facing the Abwehr was its position in relation to the SD* under the ruthless leadership of Heydrich. The primary question was, Would the Abwehr eventually be absorbed by the Nazi organ or would it be the only politico-military intelligence service. Though Hitler proclaimed that the Abwehr had exclusive responsibility for military intelligence and counterespionage within the armed forces, in reality the Gestapo continued to meddle in military affairs. That problem had brought about the downfall of Patzig. Using the pretext of the illegality of the Roehm Putsch of June 30, 1934, when the Gestapo murdered many of Hitler's political enemies including the SA chief, Ernst Roehm, Patzig unwisely attempted to bring Heydrich down. Field Marshal Blomberg, Reichswehr minister, approached Himmler but the latter threw out the suggestion and Blomberg backed down. Instead, Patzig was dismissed, leaving the jurisdictional problem to his successor, Canaris.

Canaris approached his job in a positive vein, confident that he could work with the Gestapo. The inscrutable Canaris was in his element.

To his staff the Abwehr head was an enigma. He looked colorless, had certain habits that were odd, slept more than appeared necessary and yet always looked tired. He also had an excessive affection for his pet dogs whom he kept with him all day at work and who fouled up the office to the great dismay of his subordinates. They soon discovered, however, that their new chief was a workaholic and that the interests of the Abwehr were always uppermost in his mind.

In order to deal with the central jurisdictional problem, Canaris felt that a face-to-face meeting with

*Reich main security—SS organization.

Himmler was necessary. When they did meet it was cordial and from it came a delimitation of authority between the Gestapo, SD and the Abwehr. Both men agreed upon a system of exchange of information and regular conferences between department heads. Canaris also realized that he had to meet with the steely headed leader of the SD, his former subordinate from the training ship *Berlin*, Reinhard Heydrich. A chance meeting in early 1935 brought them together once more. Though the two had not seen each other for twelve years, they managed to pick up their relationship right where it had left off. It seemed auspicious that the Abwehr head and the chief of the SD were cordial friends. Although on the surface they appeared close friends, it cannot be forgotten that both were competitors in a highly dangerous game of power.

On January 17, 1935, Canaris and Heydrich signed an agreement defining the powers of their respective organizations. Described as functions of the Wehrmacht and thus the Abwehr were: (1) Military espionage and counterespionage, (2) Intelligence work in the Reichswehr, (3) Army safeguards against foreign espionage, and (4) Direction and determination of policy in all matters affecting national defense. The Gestapo and SD powers were geared more in the political field, internal security, police and customs control.

Canaris was satisfied that this document established the Abwehr as the prime espionage and counterespionage organization. In the eyes of his subordinates the Abwehr chief had achieved the impossible and their respect for him soared.

One of Canaris's first assignments was to keep a close watch on any potential military moves by the French, Italian and British in reaction to German rearmament. Canaris alerted his organization, "Times of great international tension are a test of the intelligence service, its organization and mettle. I therefore expect all members of the Abwehr section to do their utmost to meet the extreme demands of these days for the good of the fatherland."[12]

It did not take the Abwehr long to conclude that the major foreign powers would meekly accept German rearmament plans. Rearmament brought deep satisfaction to Canaris for it meant Germany was on the move. Professionally, so was the head of the Abwehr. In May of 1935, he was promoted to the rank of rear admiral.

Recruitment became a prerequisite for the admiral. He wanted agents infiltrating all foreign intelligence services in addition to placing informants in every level of foreign industry. When he had first become head of the Abwehr there had been some 150 men in the organization. By June of 1937, there were 956 and the unit was expanding daily. The ranks of the Abwehr swelled with many former army officers, a number of whom would play a large role in the organization's eventual downfall. The numerous recruits to the ranks eventually made the organization less efficient in many ways and much too unwieldy. Unfortunately, Canaris's personality was not one to inspire so large a group. Thus, much of the Abwehr's future works lacked expertise and occasionally bordered on amateurish.

To run an organization of this size demanded a chief who would be chained to his desk constantly reviewing files, analyses and operational reports. Canaris was not that kind of man and was easily bored and tired by bureaucratic duties. He was an active person who loved to be involved "at the front." He enjoyed travelling incognito to visit his foreign agents. Without his direct leadership, others tended to use the Abwehr in ways unknown to the admiral. Lacking a central director constantly at the helm, the Abwehr ship at times moved dangerously close to shipwreck. One critic commented, "His absences from headquarters were so frequent that . . .

286

Canaris was totally uninformed about many developments. He relied too heavily on his group and subgroup heads to keep the big machine in running order."[13]

On September 8, 1935, Canaris was granted an audience with Hitler. There the admiral presented his initial progress report to the Führer. At the meeting Hitler gave Canaris a complete rundown of his future plans for moving troops into the Rhineland in violation of the Versailles Treaty. He also revealed his plans for expansion into Austria. The admiral told Hitler that the Abwehr had loyal connections in Austria that would prove most helpful when the time came. Hitler showed his pleasure at the news and went on to discuss Czechoslovakia, Poland and the Soviet Union. Canaris confessed that he already had agents in the first two countries but not in Russia. He did not seem overly upset or startled with Hitler's revelations at the time.

Hitler's next maneuver was toward remilitarization of the Rhineland. The Abwehr was asked to learn all they could regarding the potential reaction of the other side to this move. In March of 1936, when German troops crossed the Rhine bridges, the Abwehr reported that the French garrison in the Maginot line had been brought up to wartime strength, that some North African divisions had been transferred from the south of France to the German frontier and that all leave was cancelled for French troops. But that was the extent of the French reaction. War Minister Blomberg was certain that France and England would react militarily to this blatant violation of Versailles and went so far as to advise Hitler to withdraw the German troops. Hitler refused. Luckily for the Führer, the British and French protest never exceeded a written one which allowed Hitler a great moral victory.

Meanwhile, Canaris's organization continued to grow as Hitler's revisionist intentions became more obvious. The Abwehr's chief rival also continued to grow and covet more power. Himmler was elevated to the rank of Reichsführer SS and chief of the German police. As his authority increased so too did that of his principal subordinate, Heydrich.

The Abwehr/Gestapo problem flared once more. On December 21, 1936, a new jurisdictional settlement was concluded. The document was entitled "Principles Governing Cooperation Between the Geheime Staatspolizei and the Abwehr Offices of the Wehrmacht."

In the eyes of Hitler, the Abwehr played an important role and he frequently summoned Canaris to the chancellery for meetings. The admiral himself undertook secret missions on Hitler's behalf, exploring all aspects of potential enemies and establishing a web of spy contacts necessary for the gathering of secret information.

What did Canaris feel toward Hitler? Observers concluded that Hitler and Canaris became rather close during those early days. The admiral was loyal beyond any doubt. As a conservative and a nationalist, he was totally devoted to the state and Hitler stood for the state. Though Canaris despised many aspects of National Socialism, he was mesmerized by the promise of Germany's future greatness under Hitler's leadership.

Canaris felt that two natural allies of Germany were Italy and Spain. He worked diligently to bring Italy into closer relationship with Germany. Until Italy's war with Ethiopia, that proved difficult but with the League of Nations sanctions against Italy, only Germany offered a friendly hand. Using his contacts in that country, Canaris paved the way for the formation of the Axis alliance. His skill in negotiating earned him the respect of War Minister Blomberg.

The Spanish Civil War soon occupied the full attention of the admiral and his organization. Considering himself an expert on Spanish affairs, the civil war came as no surprise to him. Attracted to the ultraconservative view, Canaris favored the forces of the right who approached him in hopes of receiving German aid in the struggle against the republic. Espousing Franco's cause, the wily Canaris convinced Hitler and later Mussolini to send aid. The army leadership, however, was unhappy over the prospect of dispatching troops to Spain. They recognized the international dangers inherent in that provocative action. Canaris, however, was blind to such dangers.

The admiral was a beehive of activity while he cemented Germany's ties with Franco. As the civil war deepened, Canaris increased his involvement. In October of 1936, Blomberg dispatched the Abwehr chief, dressed in civilian clothes, to assess Franco's chances and the extent of further German aid. Canaris and the Spanish generalissimo were quickly drawn to each other since both were conservatives and shared a passionate hatred of Communism. To both men, the civil war represented a crusade. The admiral did all in his power to increase Germany's commitments to Spain. At one meeting Canaris informed Franco that the Reich was prepared to send a Luftwaffe corps to Spain, the famous Condor Legion. Eventually, the admiral became Franco's most important and most indispensable advisor and helpmate.

Meanwhile, Canaris was feeling the growing pressure of the rival SD led by Heydrich. He feared the expansionary pressure of the SD and complained that Heydrich's informants were amateurishly disrupting the Abwehr's work.

All the while, Hitler, through the machinations of Goering, Himmler and Heydrich, brought the army under his control. Over the previous few years the army leadership had constantly placed roadblocks in Hitler's way. In 1938, the Führer received damaging and distasteful information regarding his two army leaders, War Minister Blomberg and Army Chief of Staff Col. Gen. Baron von Fritsch. The former had embarrassed the army and compromised its reputation by marrying a woman of ill repute; Fritsch was accused (falsely) of being a homosexual. Blomberg resigned his position immediately but the unfortunate von Fritsch, aware that he had been falsely accused, sought to salvage his reputation. Canaris became a willing ally of the general and utilized the powerful research organization of the Abwehr to aid in the investigation.

When the admiral first heard about the impending action against Blomberg and Fritsch he was shocked and appalled. Hohne says that the affair caused him to "abandon the illusions of Hitlerism. It was then that Canaris began to turn from Hitler."[14]

The entire affair exposed the rottenness of Nazism. How could the Führer strike out against the army leadership in this manner?

Eagerly, Canaris, aided by Colonel Hossbach and Fritsch's lawyer, went to work on the SS's dossier. The general was unquestionably the victim of an elaborate frame. After an intensive search they managed to locate the actual von Fritsch who had the homosexual relationship. The man was a retired cavalry captain and not the chief of staff. When the case finally went to trial General von Fritsch was completely exonerated and all charges were dismissed. Unfortunately, the damage was already done. Hitler had assumed control of the army during the trial and had also taken over Austria in a bold show of force. Von Fritsch quietly retired from the army only to be given command of a regiment during the Polish campaign. There he perished in combat while leading his troops in action.

Though shaken by the loss of the case, Heydrich managed to ride out the storm but fumed inwardly against his former superior. He began to keep a dossier on the admiral. As for Canaris, he now was able to see clearly the true nature of Germany's leaders.

Although it took some time for Canaris to become aware of the truth of Nazism, his subordinate and chief of staff, Oster, had already learned to despise the methods of the National Socialist movement. Inside the Abwehr he built up a circle of colleagues critical of the regime. Thus the Abwehr, unbeknown to the admiral, was a hotbed of anti-Nazism. In Hohne's words, "Oster's office was a port of call for all those members or associates of the Abwehr who were self-acknowledged opponents of National Socialism."[15]

In the midst of the Fritsch trial, Hitler annexed Austria on March 13, 1938. Two days earlier Canaris assembled his departmental heads at Abwehr headquarters and informed them of Hitler's plans for dealing with the Austrian question. All Abwehr offices were to be manned around the clock. Agents in all foreign countries were alerted in order to observe reaction to the German move. France and Great Britain in particular were closely watched by Abwehr agents.

The night of March 12 was a tense one for Canaris as he closely scrutinized the stream of reports coming in from his agents. All reports indicated that Austria was isolated. No military preparations were reported by the agents in France and Great Britain. In fact, the dispatches left little doubt that Germany's annexation of Austria would be completely unopposed.

Canaris was present in Vienna amid the euphoria of the crowds that emotionally cheered Hitler's triumphant return to Vienna. As a nationalist Canaris could not help being caught up in the excitement.

With the successful Austrian coup, Canaris turned to the task of curbing the abusive powers of the SS. The abortive Fritsch case exposed the depth of that organization's corruption. The admiral was determined to check the evils of such a corrupt institution. He drafted a number of proposals, one of which called for the dismissal of the Gestapo leadership, Himmler and Heydrich in particular. The major obstacle, however, was to get the Wehrmacht leaders to agree to this proposal. No influential army commander had enough courage to recommend to Hitler that a purge of the SS should be carried out. Keitel, Beck, Brauchitsch, von Rundstedt—all declined to sign the document. Thus ended a valiant attempt by Canaris to squash the power of the SS.

On April 1, 1938, Canaris was promoted to vice admiral. He now turned the bulk of his attention toward the question of Czechoslovakia.

Ringing the western part of the Czech state is a province called the Sudetenland. There were three-and-one-half million Germans living there and it was Hitler's stated purpose to annex that territory.

The Abwehr was not adverse to annexation. It was sympathetic to the Sudeten Germans and as an organization went all out to assist in preparations for the annexation, utilizing all its wiles in the process.

The Sudeten crisis raised the specter of a European war in the summer of 1938. Both France and the Soviet Union had pacts with Czechoslovakia calling for an armed attack should its borders be violated. The Russian agreement, however, was contingent upon French moves.

As war with Czechoslovakia became imminent, Hitler made it known to Canaris what was expected of the Abwehr. Czechoslovakia had to be intimidated by propaganda and undermined with threats. Abwehr agents went to work immediately.

Canaris also ordered the creation of combat and sabotage teams that would operate behind enemy lines. This unseen army was given the vital tasks of seizing border towns and occupying bridges and railway stations on the day of the attack.

Canaris was unhappy with the prospect of war, especially a total war. He was not pleased with the policy followed by Hitler for he felt that it was destined to bring Germany to eventual destruction. He therefore became determined to bar Hitler's path to war.

Perhaps Canaris could be described as a schizophrenic. Here was a man who helped create an apparatus which placed a tremendous weapon for conquest in Hitler's hands. Yet, he showed inhibitions with Hitler's intention to prosecute a war. Canaris introduced murderous weapons of sabotage, infiltration and sent German soldiers on suicide missions but now permitted individual officers to conspire against the regime. In the postwar trials of the Nazis, Canaris, though dead, was described by some as possessing a Dr. Jekyll-Mr. Hyde personality.

Initially, Canaris thought that Hitler's saber rattling against Czechoslovakia was merely a bluff to force Prague to grant autonomy to the Sudeten Germans. He became disillusioned as it became clear that Hitler meant war. The admiral attempted various and sundry means to try to halt the avalanche toward war. Once more he attempted to mobilize the army commanders but again was rebuffed by the inertia of the Wehrmacht leadership. Though eliciting support from a number of them, collectively they refused to act.

Canaris also sought support from Germany's ally, Italy. That country's misgivings towards war did manage to shake up some of the reluctant generals, particularly Brauchitsch, the commander in chief who took it upon himself to personally speak to Hitler in an attempt to talk him out of the invasion. All efforts were to no avail. The Führer was adamant.

At the Nuremberg rally of September, 1938, Hitler ranted and raged and threatened invasion in order to free the oppressed Sudeten Germans. Oster was prepared if necessary to eliminate Hitler and his regime by force. He tried to enlist Canaris in his plans for a coup d'etat. The plan appealed to the admiral who promoted Oster by placing him in a more prominent Abwehr position.

The coup de'etat plans included the occupation of the main government center in Berlin, the seizure of all major centers of communications, neutralization of all Gestapo and SS authorities, and the arrest of Hitler. Canaris gave his support for the good of Germany. The coup took on form with the enlistment of Col. Gen. Franz Halder and General Witzleben, both ardent anti-Nazis.

The effort, however, was sabotaged when British Prime Minister Neville Chamberlain flew to Hitler's mountain retreat at Berchtesgarden carrying a plan for peace. Anxious to preserve peace at all cost, Chamberlain sold Czechoslovakia down the river and the Munich conference of September 28-29 sealed the country's fate. Hitler was allowed to occupy the Sudetenland on October 1, 1938.

With the crisis over, Canaris quickly became Mr. Hyde and turned toward Hitler as if he had played no part in the conspiracy. Oster was dismayed at how quickly the admiral seemed to make his peace with Hitler.

Hitler now intended to take over the rump Czecho-Slovak state and tore up all his promises made at Munich. To garner information and to prepare the way for his aggression, Hitler consulted Heydrich and the SD. Canaris's misgivings during the Sudeten crisis apparently had not been forgotten. Unbeknown to the admiral, his rivals were sent to the rump state with the purpose of destroying it. On March 15, 1939, Wehrmacht units crossed the Czech frontier, destroying that country in the process, and establishing the Reich protectorate of Bohemia and Moravia.

Hitler was now free to turn his full attention toward Poland. Once more the war clouds over Europe darkened.

Canaris knew that the road Hitler was travelling would lead Germany to war, a war which he firmly believed was the very last thing the country could afford. Canaris thought that if the Führer knew that the British would come to Poland's aid, it would deter him from embarking on that dangerous course. The admiral tried to make Hitler believe that the British were better prepared for war than they actually were. Despite this, the road to war was blithely followed.

As a loyal German officer, Canaris had no option but to prepare. Agents were given the critical tasks of exploring the strength, dispositions and operational objectives of the Polish armed forces. Others were assigned to infiltrate Poland in civilian clothes and, on the day of the attack, to initiate acts of sabotage behind the Polish front lines and capture strategic points such as the bridge over the Vistula at Dirschau and the Jablunkov Pass in the Beskid Mountains. Their objective was to occupy these key positions in the Polish communications system by surprising and overpowering the defenders before the commencement of hostilities. Still another force of Abwehr agents were directed to infiltrate the German-Polish frontier with orders to instigate an insurrection.

Canaris was enthralled with these cloak and dagger plans. The Mr. Hyde personality in the admiral once more surfaced. A short time earlier the Dr. Jekyll was decrying the road to war. Now, here was Canaris revelling in extraordinary plans for sabotage and infiltration.

Incredibly, Canaris could be Dr. Jekyll and Mr. Hyde at the same time. Preparing for war on the one hand, he attempted to stay the Führer's hand on the other. He hoped to use Italy's fear of war to convince Hitler of the folly of his actions. War with Poland would almost certainly mean war with Britain and Russia. The conclusion of the Soviet-Nazi nonaggression pact on August 23, 1939, however, eliminated the fear of a two-front war.

Prior to the signing of this pact, on August 21, Canaris went to Hitler's mountain retreat where the Führer spoke to all his military chiefs. Canaris left the meeting harboring no illusions about Hitler's intentions. War was inevitable.

On August 25, at 4:05 p.m., Canaris received an order from Keitel to prepare for war on the following day. The Abwehr's sabotage and combat teams left their bases. Then Hitler was quickly handed two setbacks. Poland and Britain signed a long-term military pact and Italy dropped out of the Pact of Steel. Hitler could expect no help from Italy in his struggle with Poland. In addition, the Polish-British pact virtually guaranteed British intervention in the event of an attack on its ally. Canaris hoped that this would cause Hitler to cancel his war plan. Unfortunately, the delay was short-lived. At 5:30 p.m. on August 31, the order for war went out. Canaris was reputed to have said to Hans Gisevius upon hearing the order, "This means the end of Germany."[16]

It was left to Heydrich's SD to kindle the flames of war. SD agents, dressed in Polish uniforms, took up their positions and were prepared to ferment incidents. The next day the Nazi-controlled Volkischer Beobachter reported Polish rebels across the German frontier.

With the beginnning of war, Canaris, though upset with the turn of events, was every bit a patriot and demanded from his subordinates unconditional loyalty to the Führer and Reich.

The admiral's primary task was to serve the army and to smooth its path to eventual victory. Most Abwehr operations were successful. Agents occupied the rail junction at Kalthof, saved industrial installations at Rybnik and seized the valuable coal mines in upper Silesia. Canaris was proud of the performance of his organization. All pessimistic thoughts soon dissolved during those early euphoric days of victory. Soon, however, he was shocked and saddened by reports of SS death squads murdering Jews and Polish intelligentsia. As far as he was concerned, Germany's military achievement was tarnished by the racial extermination policies carried out by the SS.

On September 12, Canaris sought out Hitler in his special command train to present evidence of the atrocities. The admiral was convinced that Hitler would not condone such brutality. Field Marshal Keitel coolly told the Abwehr head not to become involved in that business. While Keitel and Canaris were talking, Hitler entered the compartment and welcomed the admiral. Hitler was specifically interested to know what the French intentions were. Canaris was shocked by Hitler's callousness. Many biographies of Canaris point to this meeting as the actual turning point in Canaris's attitude toward Nazism. The atrocities in Poland left an indelible mark on him. He never recovered from this brutal awakening.

Germany, however, was always foremost in his thoughts. Though he had come to despise the corruption and brutality of Nazi ideology and its perverse leaders, his country was still at war and as a loyal German, that consideration transcended all others.

Still another aspect of the Polish war that horrified Canaris was the Russo-German Treaty which divided Western Europe between Germany and the hated Communists. For him this was a betrayal; a sacrilegious violation of the world order. Canaris felt that the fact that Lithuania was placed in the Soviet sphere was a major step toward renouncing the Baltic as a German sea. Hitler was betraying the crusade against Bolshevism.

With the Polish campaign over, the admiral faced a new problem. Hitler was determined to launch an early offensive in the West if England and France refused to accept the peace proposals he submitted. After receiving Hitler's war directive, the general staff began laying plans for the campaign. Hitler bombarded the Abwehr chief with a bevy of suggestions. He envisioned Abwehr commandos, wearing foreign uniforms, seizing enemy bridges, paratroopers dropping on the Hague with the incredible objective of abducting the entire Dutch cabinet, Abwehr agents dressed as policemen and railwaymen jumping bridge pickets, and glider troops landing on Belgium strong points such as Fort Eben Emael.

Abwehr headquarters buzzed with activity as they prepared to implement Hitler's plans. Dutch uniforms were found and agents were dispatched to reconnoiter the desired targets. All the while Abwehr commando units, called Brandenburgers, trained for lightning strikes at the proposed objectives.

Canaris, however, knew that Germany was following a path that could only lead to its eventual destruction. Though victory came easy in Poland, he was realistic enough to sense that the German economy could not sustain a protracted war. At first the admiral was hopeful that war in the West would not have to be fought. Most of the leading generals were reluctant to initiate the campaign in the West. With their apparent opposition to the campaign, Canaris opined that now might be the ideal time to end the Hitler regime and enact the coup d'etat plans scrapped the previous year.

Colonel Oster and his colleagues were prepared to follow the admiral's lead. Eager for action, Canaris urged Oster (who needed no urging) to mobilize for action. Meanwhile, Canaris attempted to enlist the support of as many generals as he could.

Support was forthcoming from Gen. Ritter von Leeb, the commander of Army Group C and General von Witzleber, commander of the First Army. Most of the other generals were too cautious to openly support the coup although they were sympathetic. Canaris faced insurmountable obstacles. The older army officers, whom he needed if the attempt was to be successful, shrank from the idea of launching a coup d'etat against their supreme commander, particularly while he was scoring one victory after another. Consequently,

298

Canaris became more and more disillusioned.

Canaris knew that Colonel General Halder, chief of the general staff, was against attacking the West, and had tried to enlist his support. Halder, however, was annoyed at Oster's and Canaris's badgering and rejected their advances. Nevertheless, he still left himself open to the possibility of not having to fight. Early in November of 1939, Halder finally made contact with Canaris. The coup plans began to take form at once.

Oster felt that the Western powers should be made aware of the plans for a coup d'etat against the Nazi leadership. He suggested that Pope Pius XII be made the vehicle by which the coup plans could be disseminated to the West. Canaris agreed. The two enlisted the aid of a lawyer with Vatican contacts, Josef Muller, and commissioned him to carry out this vital task.

Plans for the coup continued both at Abwehr headquarters and Halder's headquarters at Zossen. The general had already warned the leading conspirators to hold themselves in readiness for a military coup from November 5 onwards.

The coup plans, however, floundered as the army chief of staff grew fainthearted after his inability to induce Brauchitsch and others to join in the conspiracy. Fearful of Hitler's finding out about the conspiracy, Halder abandoned the conspiratorial ship, thus causing the entire plan to sink.

Soon the two-headed admiral also appeared to abandon his attempt to overthrow the regime. Canaris's Jekyll-Hyde existence was fast becoming extremely dangerous. He was finding it difficult to prepare for war on one hand while with the other planning the Nazi regime's destruction. Having come up against a stone wall with Halder's defection, then being warned of

Oster's many indiscretions,* the admiral abandoned all hope of overthrowing Hitler and his cronies.

Though Canaris officially ordered plans for the coup halted, Oster continued to plot behind his chief's back. The colonel felt that only by a major military setback could the generals be enticed to back a coup d'etat. Ironically, while Canaris worked to avert war because he felt war with the West would destroy Germany, Oster looked forward to it, for only after a military defeat (which he expected) could the hated Hitler regime be ended. Canaris would not and could not consent to such an idea. He was a loyal German first and foremost.

Meanwhile, the Abwehr intellegence machine correctly gauged British intentions regarding Norway. Germany obtained the majority of its iron ore from Sweden. The ore was then shipped to Germany via Narvik in Norway. The Abwehr discovered the British intention of occupying Norway in order to frustrate this iron ore trade.

Canaris brought this information to Grand Admiral Raeder who recognized the seriousness of the threat. In turn, Raeder appealed to Hitler to forestall the British move. The Führer, whose mind was at that moment occupied with plans for the West, paid only scant attention to the threat. By December, however, he began to show more interest in Norway and by the end of January had instructed the OKW to work out a plan for the occupation of Norway and Denmark. Canaris's Abwehr was once again called upon to pave the way for yet another major operation. Information on Norway was scant. Agents were immediately dispatched to find out all they could about the northern lands.

On April 1, 1940, Canaris was promoted to full

*He was carrying with him a list of names of those who joined the conspiracy in hopes of enlisting more to join by showing them the list. If that list ever fell into Gestapo hands, many heads would unquestionably roll.

admiral. On the ninth of the month Germany invaded Norway and the recently promoted admiral insisted on complete loyalty from all his subordinates for the Nazi regime. Mr. Hyde again ruled the Abwehr.

While Canaris busied himself preparing his units for the Norwegian campaign, Oster tried desperately to warn the British of the German intentions but to no avail.

Ironically, Oster, who had attempted to compromise the German plan to the enemy, was delegated to award medals to those Abwehr men who had helped Hitler achieve success in Norway. Once again the Brandenburg units had secured railway bridges and other key centers. Thus Hitler registered another conquest. With each one, the prospect for a coup lessened.

With the German attack in the West soon to begin, Oster attempted everything in his power to warn the Belgians and Dutch of the impending attack. Canaris was not privy to all of Oster's dealings. Warnings or not, it mattered little, for the German blitzkrieg was unleashed on May 10, 1940. Abwehr commando detachments again spearheaded the assault. Canaris was highly impressed by the rapid German gains. His doubts about the offensive vanished quickly as another great victory was earned by the German military machine.

In mid-June, however, disaster struck when Hitler disclosed to Canaris that the attack date for the Western offensive had been betrayed. Both Canaris and Heydrich were ordered to find the traitor or traitors at once. In the Third Reich, treason was considered one of the most heinous crimes. To betray one's fellow soldiers was virtually the worst thing anyone in uniform could do. The hue and cry raised by this revelation shook the very foundations of the Abwehr organization. Opposition to Hitler was one thing, collaboration with the enemy at the expense of one's comrades was abominable.

The admiral immediately suspected Oster's Vatican agent, Josef Muller, and ordered him recalled at once.

After interrogating Muller the admiral knew that both men were guilty. Although he detested what Oster had done, he knew that the motives of his chief of staff and friend were good. The admiral was visibly hurt by Oster's actions and the bond of trust between them was irrevocably severed. He ordered Oster to destroy all links with Muller along with all incriminating evidence and, in particular, any connection with the coup d'etat plans of 1938-40. Unfortunately, Oster's deputy, Dohnanyi, failed to destroy the incriminating evidence but instead hid it in a safe. This action would prove disastrous for all concerned. As for Canaris, it was the last favor he performed for Oster. He severed all his ties with the Resistance and immersed himself deep in his work.

Agents were dispatched to many and sundry places. Canaris was a whirlwind as he directed numerous projects. Outwardly he appeared very much to be one of Hitler's greatest supporters. Spain still remained, as always, his favorite. In July of 1940, he travelled there to explore further schemes. Assisted by a team of experts, he examined the possibility of capturing the Rock of Gibraltar from the British. In German hands, Gibraltar would deny the British access to the Mediterranean. Canaris was extremely enthusiastic about the scheme and sought Franco's support. The admiral's team, meanwhile, went to work reconnoitering the "Rock." Canaris himself lurked near the border in disguise revelling in the role of the master spy.

The complex admiral must have exasperated his friends who were sworn opponents of the Nazi regime. Canaris was dedicating all his talents to the prosecution of the Nazi cause.

While Canaris built Spain into a major Abwehr stronghold, OKW asked him to gauge Britain's war potential. Operation Sea Lion, the invasion of England, was being formulated by the German high command and they desperately needed intelligence data on the British Isles. Canaris did not welcome the assignment;

the Abwehr had no effective network of informants in England. A few were parachuted into England but unbeknownst to Canaris they were quickly captured by the British counterespionage units and turned into double agents.

Canaris was always more anxious to intrigue in Spain because there he had a bevy of agents. Gibraltar was still high on the Abwehr menu for devouring. A plan of attack, code-named Operation Felix, was drawn up and, on August 2, submitted to Keitel. Five days later it was shown to the Führer. Hitler approved of the plan but told Canaris that Franco's help was a prerequisite for the plan's enactment.

Canaris was given the all-important job of convincing Franco of the value of the operation. The Spanish dictator was cautious, however. In June, Franco made some bold claims but by September his tune had changed as Britain continued to fight on. The Spanish leader was reluctant to commit his recently war-torn land to further bloodshed and thus became evasive each time the topic of Gibraltar came up. Hitler decided to force Franco's hand by challenging him face to face. A meeting was set up on October 23, 1940 at the Franco-Spanish border town of Hendaye. The Führer presented his demands that Spain and Germany forge an alliance and that the former should enter the war the following January by attacking Gibraltar. Franco then started to speak and in a short time the eloquent dictator had talked down the German leader. By the time Hitler left, no definitive agreement with Spain had been reached. A frustrated Hitler swore never to get entangled in another debate with Franco. Canaris now knew that Spain had no intention of joining Germany.

Meanwhile, on October 28, 1940, Italian troops invaded Greece via Albania. Canaris and Hitler both opposed the Italian maneuver. They urged Mussolini and Ciano, the Italian foreign minister, not to widen the war in the Balkans. In a short while, however, the

Greeks were pushing the feeble Italians back into Albania. The war situation became so precarious that Hitler offered aid to his partner. Ciano assured Mussolini that the war situation would improve soon and advised against accepting German aid.

Canaris was a busy man. He travelled back to Spain where he continued working on plans for the assault on Gibraltar. But he realized that Franco was in no way willing to help in the attack. Without that help, Operation Felix could never be launched. Hitler again dispatched Canaris with orders to enlist Franco in the cause. However, it was obvious that so long as the British held out, Franco would never join the Axis. The interview with Franco was held on December 7. The anticipated response duly followed: Spain would not join Germany.

Failing in his efforts to convince Franco, Canaris then attempted to bring about the conclusion of the Italo-Greek conflict. The Greek dictator felt himself being tugged from two sides, Canaris on one and the British on the other. The latter wanted the Greek government's permission to send troops to that country to help in the conflict. They could then use Greece as a springboard for attacking Germany from the south. The Greek leader, Metaxes, eventually yielded to British exhortations and in mid-January, 1941, agreed to allow British troops to land in Greece. The very thing that Canaris had hoped to avoid, the widening of the war, seemed inevitable.

By March, German troops were deployed for an attack into the Balkans. The admiral was still hopeful of mediating a settlement but to no avail. Hitler was now bent on a total Balkan war. On April 6, the German army moved up for the attack. Canaris fell into a state of deep depression.

German forces crashed into Yugoslavia while Luftwaffe bombers devastated Belgrade, leaving the city in flames. Canaris flew into Belgrade and saw first-hand the horror of the ruins. He was sickened by the sight and groaned, "I can't take any more of this, we're flying out of here."[17]

A month later the tormented admiral was in Athens. Besides feeling remorse for the failure of his Balkan peace plan, he was doubly troubled over Hitler's invasion plan for the Soviet Union. Though no lover of Communism, Canaris feared that without the surrender of the British first, widening the war to include Russia would give Germany a two-front war, thereby dooming it.

The Abwehr's information on Russia was scant thanks to a Führer order issued after the Nazi-Soviet pact which forbade the Abwehr from conducting any covert activities inside the Soviet Union. This resulted in an intelligence gap. Even though Canaris had been gathering information since the summer of 1940, it was far too little to fully inform the army on Russian dispositions and its war potential.

Canaris was given the vital task of cloaking German intentions from the Russians. Preparations for the invasion (Barbarossa) would continue, but it had to appear to the Russians to be merely a military exercise. Again the admiral was caught in a vise. He did not want the war to widen but felt bound to do his duty. Besides, this assignment was right up his alley. He was a past master at covering tracks, disguising intentions and leading opponents astray. Once more the admiral's schizophrenic personality came to the fore. Though decrying the broadening of the war, he was nevertheless enthusiastic in the performance of his duty.

Canaris issued three basic instructions to his staff: all

branches of the Abwehr must prepare for active counterespionage work against the Soviet Union; foreign intelligence services must be misled so as to suggest that Germany's relations with the Soviet Union were improving, that German attention was instead focused on an attack on Great Britain; and finally, all security measures must be designed to keep secret the preparations for war against the Soviet Union.

As the German army moved to the Soviet frontier, the Russians suspected nothing. The subterfuge worked. Even a warning from Churchill, who picked up the German plans through British code-breaking efforts, failed to convince the Russians.

Meanwhile, Canaris had made contact with the anti-Communists, specifically Ukranian expatriates who had left the Soviet Union in the years following the revolution and were desirous of returning to their homeland once Stalin was overthrown. A true anti-Communist crusading spirit pervaded the admiral's intentions.

He remained profoundly dismayed, however, with the prospect of widening the war while Britain remained undefeated. Nevertheless, feeling duty-bound to his country, he unleashed his Brandenburgers on June 22, 1941. Within a relatively short period of time his combat units were racking up a remarkable record.

Before long Canaris began to see what kind of war this would be. Following in the wake of the victorious combat troops were the Einsatzgruppen, the dreaded death squads. The roundup of Jews, Russians and Ukranians began in earnest. Extermination on a grand scale was the order of the day and the reality of this sickened Canaris.

Though appalled by the actions of Heydrich's death squads, the admiral was reluctant to take action against them. Instead, he permitted those Abwehr officers who were so inclined to assist Jews in trouble so long as that assistance did not reflect on the department. He also condoned the employment of Jews as agents in the Abwehr foreign service in order to place them beyond the reach of the SS. It is recorded that Canaris helped Abwehr offices in Holland to devise a plan for the sneaking of five hundred Jews out of the country. Unfortunately, Heydrich and the new SD chief, Walter Schellenberg, were amassing a file on the admiral listing such activities and were simply waiting for the right time to use it.

As the war situation in Russia deepened, Canaris began to sense his position with Hitler slipping. The Führer hardly sent for his intelligence chief anymore since the scanty intelligence provided by the Abwehr proved of little value to the deteriorating war situation. Canaris's mental state, according to his colleagues, also began to show signs of distress.

In the meantime, his bitter rival, Heydrich, was appointed acting Reich protector of Bohemia and Moravia though retaining control of the RSHA.* Schellenberg moved up to command of the foreign intelligence department which placed him in a position of rivaling that of the Abwehr chief.

In December of 1941, Schellenberg used this opportunity to exploit the weakened position of Canaris and resurrect the old SD-Abwehr jurisdictional battle. A meeting was held in early January, 1942, to bring about a new settlement. The settlement finally settled on limiting the Abwehr to purely military intelligence matters while the RSHA agency's powers swelled.

Canaris's subordinates realized at once what the agreement meant for the Abwehr and immediately drafted a counterproposal which retracted virtually all of the admiral's concessions. Heydrich was infuriated and refused to meet with Canaris but at the insistence

*RSHA—Reichssicherheitshauptamt, the German police and security apparatus under Himmler with the SS and SD among its components.

of the OKW chief, Keitel, another meeting was held on March 1, 1942. Another document was drafted defining the respective positions of the two organizations.

Heydrich was pleased with the new document for the RSHA was granted increased powers. On May 17 Canaris again met with Heydrich in Prague where by mutual agreement they were to review and sign the latest agreement between the two rival intelligence organizations. The conference ended with both chiefs on friendly terms. A few days later, Heydrich lay dying, the victim of Czech assassins. On June 4, the RSHA chief died. It was said that at his funeral Canaris wept.

Meanwhile, the war situation continued to deteriorate. Since December 11, 1941, Germany had been at war with the United States. Now the full weight of the New World was harnessed to that of the Old. Global warfare broadened Canaris's horizons. New plans were hatched in his fertile mind. One was a plot to destroy the Panama Canal. This plan, however, was compromised and subsequently scrapped. Another plan envisioned the sabotaging of Britain's diamond industry in South Africa. Abwehr headquarters hoped to cripple British war production by cutting off its supply of industrial diamonds. Without diamonds, manufacture of the precision tools needed to make weapons of war would be curtailed. In this endeavor the Abwehr agents were at least partially successful. They managed to steal millions of dollars worth of industrial diamonds from a British warehouse in Kimberley, South Africa.

In November of 1942, thanks to the industrial capacity of the United States, a successful invasion of northwest Africa was accomplished. In Russia, the situation at Stalingrad turned from bad to worse as Russian forces completely encircled the German Sixth Army.

Canaris could easily see that there was no way Germany could hope to win the war. Instead, he began to think of methods whereby the country could be saved. Again the Dr. Jekyll admiral sought a way to end hostilities. Peace feelers were sent to the Anglo-Americans but the British foreign office rejected every overture. In fact, British diplomatic missions aboard were under distinct instructions that any peace feelers from military or civilian members of the German Resistance be automatically rejected. The door was shut. President Roosevelt closed it even tighter at the Casablanca Conference in January of 1943 when he called for unconditional surrender. Even so, Canaris persisted for he was determined to save Germany from total destruction.

Using Spain as a meeting place, Canaris continued to attempt to open up negotiations with the Americans. During the summer of 1943, a face-to-face meeting took place with Generals Stuart Menzies, head of the British secret service, and William Donovan, head of the OSS. Here then were the heads of three powerful espionage networks. Canaris presented his counterparts with a peace plan: a cease fire in the West, followed by a coup d'etat against Hitler and the continuation of the war in the East. Menzies and Donovan saw the logic in the plan but Roosevelt crushed any acceptance of Canaris's peace proposal.

The admiral knew that his contact with the British and Americans was treasonous and if revealed could only spell his destruction. Nevertheless, the entire edifice was falling down around him anyway. The Abwehr had failed to warn of the Russian buildup in the Stalingrad area; it was taken by surprise by the Anglo-American landings in North Africa. Other Abwehr plans had also failed.

Even before those failures, in June, 1942, Canaris

was summoned to Hitler's headquarters to explain why there had been so many recent Abwehr failures. Hitler kept him waiting until late in the afternoon. When he finally admitted the admiral to his presence, the Führer flew into a rage. He demanded a total explanation for the failures and bellowed so loudly that he never gave Canaris an opportunity to reply. Bowing his head like a naughty child, the Abwehr chief simply stood there quietly. When he finally was allowed to speak, Hitler refused to listen. Canaris had failed once too often.

Meanwhile, Oster, who had never abandoned his plans for initiating a coup, continued to plot. He made contact with a civilian resister, Fabian von Schlabrendorff who told him that several army group center officers in Russia had banded together and intended to move against the regime as soon as possible. The prime organizer of this group was Col. Henning von Treskow who had devised a plan for assassinating Hitler by blowing him up. To make the coup successful, however, Treskow needed the aid of the Abwehr agencies.

Oster had befriended the head of the general army department, Gen. Friedrich Olbricht. Together with Olbricht, Oster took his earlier coup plans and merged them with those of Treskow. Through 1942 and into 1943, Treskow, Oster and their fellow conspirators prepared to carry out their plan.

In the interim, an Abwehr agent, Wilhelm Schmidhuber, was arrested for misconduct. Schmidhuber was privy to the anti-Nazi activities, not only of Oster, but of many of his co-conspirators as well. If he talked, it would spell disaster for the admiral.

Late in 1942, Schmidhuber was transferred to the cells of the RSHA who quickly realized the value of their prisoner. Schmidhuber represented a time bomb which could explode and bring the Abwehr down with it. The blow fell when, in an effort to save his own skin, Schmidhuber talked. During his initial interrogation he spoke of the intelligence links between the Abwehr and the Vatican. Little by little the RSHA was able to put all the pieces of the puzzle together.

The evidence against the Abwehr and Canaris was overwhelming. Incredibly, when the RSHA reports were forwarded to Himmler he asked that Canaris be left alone.

Why did Himmler persist in covering up for Canaris? Did Canaris have something incriminating on the SS head? Was Himmler awed by the admiral's reputation? Himmler's attitude was a mystery to those who sought Canaris's downfall. Perhaps Himmler was simply waiting for the appropriate time when he would be able to absorb the Abwehr into the SS. Only time would reveal his true motives. Nevertheless, he ordered Schellenberg to keep the file handy.

Despite the ongoing investigations, Oster continued to plot for the overthrow of the Nazis. In March, 1943, an attempt to blow Hitler up while he was on a flight failed. Later in that same month another attempt at assassination while Hitler was visiting the Berlin armory also misfired.

The axe finally fell on April 5, 1943 when Gestapo agents invaded Abwehr headquarters and strode up to Canaris armed with a search warrant and arrest order for Oster's deputy, Dohnanyi. The admiral accompanied the Gestapo men to Dohnanyi's office. A search of the office uncovered piles of incriminating evidence. Here was proof linking Oster and the Abwehr to actions against the state.

Though he was not arrested, Canaris feared that the incriminating evidence would eventually reflect on him. He fell into a deep state of depression and completely dissociated himself from the incarcerated Oster.

Investigations into the extent of the Abwehr's treasonable actitivies continued on through the spring and summer of 1943. Once again, through the intervention of Himmler, Canaris was exonerated and completely freed of any complicity in the acts of his subordinates. Schellenberg was incensed with the admiral's rehabilitation as it again thwarted his dream of combining the Abwehr with his own organization to form one all-powerful intelligence service. As part of the rehabilitation, Canaris was directed by Keitel to replace the heads of all sections and to improve the Abwehr's standard of performance. The main substance of the organization, however, remained intact.

On July 25, Mussolini was overthrown and a new Italian government formed around Field Marshal Pietro Badoglio. Keitel urgently needed specific information regarding intentions. Would Badoglio remain committed to the Axis? Canaris flew to Venice on July 29 for a meeting with the head of the Italian military intelligence section, Gen. Ceasare Ame. Ame secretly confided that Italy was furtively seeking a way to get out of the Axis by surrendering to the Allies. Canaris swore that he would not inform Berlin of Italy's true intention but instead would report that Italy intended to fight on.

The admiral hoped that the Italian defection would convince Germany's military leaders that the time had come to neutralize Hitler and to offer the Allies a cease fire. He attempted to use his influence to prevent German troops from being sent into northern Italy where they could react quickly to an Italian surrender. Canaris emphasized Italy's loyalty and its desire to remain in the Axis, hoping in this way to prevent reinforcements being dispatched to northern Italy.

Schellenberg, however, was not buying Canaris's report and dispatched his own agents to Ame in an effort to ascertain the true feelings of the Italians. These agents quickly discovered what actually had transpired at the meeting between Ame and Canaris. The SD chief was convinced that at last he had enough evidence against Canaris. Accordingly, Schellenberg drafted a report relating the admiral's treasonable actions of misleading the German government about Italy's true intentions.

Schellenberg had the backing of Heydrich's successor, RSHA Chief Ernst Kaltenbrunner. Kaltenbrunner brought the report to Himmler who ordered the report left behind. Once more the wily Canaris had squirmed off the hook by writing a report that explicitly stated Italy's true attitude. His fancy footwork in this operation marked his last victory over the RSHA.

Meanwhile, blunders and failures continued to plague the Abwehr. The fact that all its British agents were turned into double agents caused Germany to receive a large volume of false information. In November of 1943, another project ended in a bitter failure. Actually this project was hatched in the evil minds of Schellenberg and Kaltenbrunner. It was a plan to assassinate the "Big Three": Roosevelt, Stalin and Churchill. Having come into possession of information regarding a Big Three gathering in Tehran, the two SS thugs brought Canaris into the conspiracy.

Schellenberg did not allow his hatred for Canaris to stand in the way. He needed the assistance of the Abwehr agents in the Middle East, particularly those in Iran where the Abwehr was headed by the very competent Schulze-Holthus. Hitler held out high hopes for the plan and anxiously maintained close contact with Schellenberg regarding its progress.

The SD and the Abwehr organized four units to carry out this ambitious project, code-named Long Jump. Throughout the early fall of 1943, the operation became the main project of both rival secret services. Hitler was filled with hope that if the plan was successful, new life would be given to Germany.

One of the major questions was who would lead the assassination squads. Almost immediately the choice fell to the man who at the time was considered the most dangerous man in Europe, SS Col. Otto Skorzeny. He studied the plans and quickly rejected them for security reasons. He attempted to contact agents in Iran for more information but could not receive a response. Skorzeny was then able to discover that the Allies had been tipped off by the Soviet espionage center in Switzerland.

Skorzeny was right on target. The Allies did know of the German plan. The assassination teams would never have been able to get close to the Big Three. Security around them was unusually heavy. The plot fizzled out to the immense dismay of the Führer.

The performance of the Abwehr continued to decrease in quality. Blunder followed blunder. On January 21, 1944, Canaris was again in Rome where he visited the headquarters of Field Marshal Albert Kesselring. The commander in chief southwest wished to know everything about Allied intentions. Did they plan to launch an attack behind the main German defensive position, the Gustav Line? Canaris assured Kesselring that there was absolutely no danger of another landing in the near future. Less than ten hours later Allied forces waded ashore at Anzio and took the Germans completely by surprise. General Westphal, Kesselring's chief of staff, swore never to trust the Abwehr again. Canaris's organization had failed once more. Hitler demanded answers.

At this point Hitler began to seriously contemplate replacing Canaris. At a conference with Himmler on February 9 the Führer alluded to this possibility. Foreign Minister von Ribbentrop, who held a long-standing grudge against the Abwehr, backed Hitler enthusiastically.

On February 11, Hitler made his move against Canaris. He ordered Himmler to unify the Abwehr with the SD thereby creating a single intelligence service, something Himmler had dreamed of for a long time.

OKW Chief Keitel and Col. Gen. Alfred Jodl were given responsibility for breaking the news to Canaris. Using the argument that the critical military situation coupled with the Abwehr's manifold failures of the past had caused Hitler to streamline the secret intelligence services, the generals ordered the admiral to Burg Lauenstein, a castle in southern Germany where he was directed to hold himself in readiness until the Führer reassigned him.

The castle resembled a place of exile more than anything else. While Canaris was there, the dismantling of the Abwehr by the SS continued in earnest. Little by little the establishment created by Canaris was dissolved and parcelled out among various SS departments.

By June, Canaris was still at Lauenstein but continued to hold out hope that Hitler would find suitable employment for him. At the end of the month he was allowed to go to Berlin and on July 1 was assigned as the new head of the special staff for mercantile warfare and economic combat measures. Though it was a lofty sounding position, in reality the office had very little power and a small staff of officers unfit for combat duty.

Canaris's rehabilitation coincided with the deeper diminution of territory held by the Third Reich. On June 6 the long-awaited cross-channel invasion was launched by the Allies. This was followed on June 22 by a Soviet offensive which swept the Russians deeper into Germany's eastern empire.

The recent setbacks had again given impetus to the conspirators in the army. One particular conspirator, Col. Count Klaus Shenk von Stauffenberg was prepared to assassinate Hitler to save Germany from total catastrophe. At the beginning of July Stauffenberg's plans were revealed to Canaris. Though considered an outsider, the admiral was grateful to the conspirators — Freytag, Schrader and Sack — for bringing him up to date on their plans.

July 20, 1944 was the day that the conspirators plan was put into effect. On that fateful day the one-eyed Stauffenberg* went to Hitler's headquarters near Rastenburg in East Prussia armed with a time bomb. The plot failed when the explosion failed to kill Hitler. The bungled attempt resulted in one of history's greatest orgies of revenge and reprisal.

Canaris, though aware of the plot, was not privy to the date. For him, July 20 was a day like any other. Not until 5:00 p.m. when he heard of the day's events did he realize that the coup was doomed to failure. He went immediately to his office where he had his adjutant draft a telegram to the Führer congratulating him on his miraculous escape.

Canaris knew that the regime would retaliate brutally. He therefore quickly destroyed any incriminating evidence in his files. Meanwhile, the SS began to crush the conspirators. Gestapo squads combed every

*He was wounded in North Africa, losing an eye and the use of his right hand.

corner of the Reich searching out any and every Resistance member or sympathizer. The admiral held out hopes that he would be spared because he had taken no active part in the plot.

One of the arrested conspirators was Col. Georg Hansen, the man who had led the rump Abwehr while it was being dismantled by the SS after Canaris's dismissal. A note written by Hansen was found containing the following statement: "I regard Canaris as the spiritual instigator of the revolutionary movement that led to July 20. . . . Canaris made an important personal contribution to this by maintaining the requisite contacts abroad."[18]

This note proved devastating to the admiral. Gestapo Chief Heinrich Himmler turned the evidence over to Schellenberg. Canaris was ordered taken into custody.

The Gestapo made every effort to prove that Canaris had known of the plot, if not personally involved in it. Oster was harshly interrogated with typical Gestapo thoroughness and brutality. After three torturous days, he made a partial confession. In his statements Canaris was portrayed as a tired defeatist. This was enough to confine the admiral to the SS dungeons for further interrogation.

At his own interrogation, Canaris demonstrated some of his former skill. He made every effort to sever his link to Oster and the other conspirators. The admiral handled each allegation with precision. Though the others, including Oster, spoke against him, Canaris was able to challenge their statements.

Finally, the Gestapo located the final pieces of evidence. Through interrogation they learned of papers hidden in a safe in an underground shelter in one of the former Abwehr headquarters in Zossen. In the safe were all the papers ordered destroyed by

Canaris years before. The papers contained precise details of every conspiracy from the mid-1930s onward. Unfortunately, the Gestapo also found carbon copies of some pages from Canaris's long-sought-after diary.

Canaris's subsequent treatment remains a puzzle. Why wasn't he stripped of his rank, hurled before the people's court and then herded to the gallows as so many others were? Why was he still addressed as admiral? This was an enigma. Perhaps even in his distress an aura continued to surround his person.

Perhaps all the evidence was still inconclusive. Maybe the Gestapo considered the admiral more valuable alive than dead. Unfortunately, the answer to this puzzle will probably remain a mystery.

Nothing, however, could raise the admiral's ire more than being branded a traitor. He eloquently defended himself but the noose around his neck was tightening. Though still inspiring a trace of respect, Canaris continued to receive the effects of his persecutor's rage. Initially, his prestige saved him from physical maltreatment. The Gestapo devised many ways of breaking his spirit such as cutting his food rations by one-third, disturbing his sleep with incessant security checks, forcing him to do undignified chores such as cleaning the toilets. In the interim, through the torture of fellow prisoners, the Gestapo continued to extract additional damning evidence against the admiral.

By February of 1945 the Third Reich found itself being squeezed by the Russians from the east and the British and Americans from the west. Hitler's gamble in the Ardennes, having failed in January, propelled the Western Allies toward the Rhine which they reached by March.

Meanwhile, one of the incessant Allied bombing

raids had destroyed part of the Gestapo prison in Berlin early in February. It was decided to transfer the prisoners to Flossenburg Concentration Camp where the interrogations could be continued safe from the hazards of bombing.

At Flossenburg the treatment of Canaris disintegrated. Two SS guards escorted him to his new cell. They pushed the admiral inside, handcuffed him to the walls and shackled his ankles in chains. Canaris's only hope now was that the Nazi regime would collapse before the Gestapo could complete their case against him.

The admiral's hopes were dashed, however, on April 4, 1945, when his long-lost diary was located and promptly turned over to the RSHA. Kaltenbrunner delivered the diaries to Hitler in his underground bunker in Berlin. The Führer read a few passages, paused, and grew angry. For years, he said, he had been deluded by this traitor in his midst. The plotters, Hitler insisted, had to be destroyed at once.

The SS were given a free hand to begin the executions. Cloaking the actions with a veil of legality, summary trials began after April 6 and continued for a week. The sham trials were quickly followed by hangings. Dohnanyi, Oster, Pastor Bonhoeffer and, of course, Canaris went to the gallows. Still attempting to defend himself, Canaris argued his case to the end but to no avail. He was found guilty of high treason.

Back at his cell after the verdict, Canaris tapped out a message on the wall in morse code to a fellow prisoner. That message became his final one:

Badly mishandled . . . nose broken . . . I die for my fatherland. I have a clear conscience. I only did my duty to my country when I tried to oppose the criminal folly of Hitler leading Germany to destruction.[19]

In the early morning hours of April 9, 1945, the condemned men were ordered to undress. Then, naked, they were led to the gallows. After the execution their bodies were cremated.

Thus ended the enigmatic life of Adm. Wilhelm Canaris. Was he a traitor to Germany? Probably not. He was first and foremost a patriotic German. Till his last day he continued to cling to the ideal of an authoritarian nation-state. His early acceptance of Hitler and the Nazi regime stemmed from his preference for that type of state. However, when the brutality of the regime became evident, as a German whose background and tradition placed his country before all other considerations, Hitler included, he acted against the government. To Canaris, Hitler did not equal the state even though that was a Nazi belief. If the good of the state meant Hitler's overthrow, then so be it.

Canaris did not betray Germany. He was incapable of doing so. If he gave false information it was either because he was fooled by Allied deception or he felt, as in the case of Italy's secret surrender, that it would convince others to overthrow Nazism.

Unfortunately, Canaris's death came one week before he would have been rescued. It was his most fervent hope that with the overthrow of the regime, a new, better, decent Germany would emerge. Unhappily, he did not survive to aid in its construction.

Introduction

Notes

1. Patrick Beesly, *Very Special Intelligence*, pp. 63-64
2. *Ibid*, p. 70

Bibliography

1. Beesly, Patrick. *Very Special Intelligence*. Hamish Hamilton, London, 1977.
2. Bennett, Ralph. *Ultra In The West*. Charles Scribner's Sons, New York, 1979.
3. Calvocoressi, Peter. *Top Secret Ultra*. Pantheon Books, New York, 1980.
4. Garlinski, Jozef, *The Enigma War*. Charles Scribner's Sons, New York, 1979.
5. Hinsley, F.H., et al. *British Intelligence in the Second World War, Vol. I*. Cambridge University Press, New York, 1979.
6. Hinsley, F.H. et al. *British Intelligence in the Second World War, Vol. II*. Her Majesty's Stationery Office, London, 1981.
7. Johnson, Brian. *The Secret War*. Metheum, New York, 1978.
8. Jones, R.V., *The Wizard War*. Coward, McCann & Geoghegan, New York, 1978.
9. Kahn, David. *The Code Breakers*. Weidenfeld and Nicholson, London, 1967.
10. Lewin, Ronald. *Ultra Goes To War*. McGraw Hill Book Co., New York, 1978.
11. Pfannes, C. & V. Salamone. *The Great Commanders of World War II Volume I: The British*. Zebra Books, New York, 1981.

12. Weichman, Gordon. *The Hut Six Story*. McGraw Hill Book Co., New York, 1982.
13. Winterbotham, F.W. *The Ultra Secret*. Harper & Row, New York, 1974.

Chapter One

Notes

1. Richard Humble. *Hitler's High Seas Fleet*. p. 10.
2. *Ibid*, p. 23.
3. Eugene Davidson. *The Trial of the Germans*. p. 371.
4. Cajus Bekker. *Hitler's Naval War*. p. 32.
5. *Ibid*, p. 34.
6. Edward Von der Porten. *The German Navy in World War II*. p. 29.
7. Bekker, *op. cit*. p. 70.
8. Von der Porten. *op. cit*. p. 44.
9. Humble. *op. cit*. p. 49.
10. *Ibid*, p. 57.
11. *Ibid*, p. 75.
12. Von der Porten, *op. cit*., p. 108.
13. Humble, *op. cit*., p. 114.
14. *Ibid*, p. 121.
15. Bekker, *op. cit*., p. 292.
16. *Ibid*, p. 293.
17. *Ibid*, p. 293.
18. *Ibid*, p. 299.
19. Davidson, *op. cit*., p. 383.

Bibliography

1. Ansel, Walter. *Hitler and the Middle Sea*. Duke University Press, Durham, 1972.
2. Beesly, Patrick. *Very Special Intelligence*. Hamish Hamilton, London, 1977.

3. Bekker, Cajus. *Defeat at Sea*. Henry Holt & Co., New York, 1955.

4. Bekker, Cajus. *Hitler's Naval War*. Doubleday & Co., New York, 1974.

5. Bekker, Cajus. *The German Navy 1939-1945*. Dial Press, New York, 1974.

6. Broome, Jack. *Convoy to Scatter*. William Kimber, London, 1972.

7. Connell, C.G. *Arctic Destroyers*. William Kimber, London, 1982.

8. Davidson, Eugene. *The Trial of the Germans*. Collier Books, New York, 1966.

9. Doenitz, Karl. *Memoirs*. World Publishing Co., Cleveland, 1959.

10. Frank, W. and E. Rogge. *The German Raider Atlantis*. Ballantine Books, New York, 1956.

11. Humble, Richard. *Hitler's High Seas Fleet*. Ballantine Books, New York, 1971.

12. Irving, David. *The Destruction of Convoy PQ17*. Simon and Schuster, New York, 1968.

13. Kennedy, Ludovic. *Pursuit*. Viking Press, New York, 1974.

14. Kennedy, Ludovic. *The Death of the Tirpitz*. Little Brown & Co., Boston, 1979.

15. Macintyre, Donald. *The Naval War Against Hitler*. Charles Scribner's Sons, New York, 1971.

16. Pope, Dudley. *73 North*. J.P. Lippincott & Co., New York, 1958.

17. Potter, John. *Fiasco*. Stein and Day, New York, 1970.

18. Raeder, Erich. *My Life*. U.S. Naval Institute, Annapolis, 1960.

19. Roskill, S.W. *White Ensign*. U.S. Naval Institute, Annapolis, 1960.

20. Showell, Jok. *The German Navy in World War II*. U.S. Naval Institute, Annapolis, 1979.

21. Von der Porten, Edward. *The German Navy in World War II*. Galahad Books, New York, 1969.

22. Warlimont, Walter. *Inside Hitler's Headquarters*. Frederick A. Praeger, New York, 1964.

Chapter Two

Notes

1. Dudley Pope, *Graf Spee*, p. 62.
2. *Ibid*, p. 68.
3. *Ibid*, p. 88.
4. *Ibid*, p. 115.
5. Michael Powell, *Death in the South Atlantic*, pp. 180-181.
6. Pope, *op. cit.*, p. 210.
7. *Ibid*, p. 237.

Bibliography

1. Bekker, Cajus, *Hitler's Naval War*. Doubleday & Co., New York, 1974.
2. Bekker, Cajus, *Defeat at Sea*. Henry Holt & Co., New York, 1953.
Bennett, Geoffrey, *Battle of the River Plate*. Ian Allen Ltd., London, 1972.
4. Dem Porten, Edward von, *The German Navy in World War II*. Thomas Y. Crowell, New York, 1969.
5. Frischauer, W. & R. Jackson, *The Altmark Affair*. The MacMillan Co., New York, 1955.
6. Lenton, H. & J. Colledge, *British & Dominion Warships of WW II*. Ian Allen Ltd., London, 1964.
7. Hoyt, Edwin, *Kreuzerkrieg*. World Publishing Co., New York, 1967.
8. Humble, Richard, *Hitler's High Seas Fleet*. Ballantine Books, New York, 1971.
9. Macintyre, Donald, *The Naval War Against Hitler*. Charles Scribner's Sons, New York, 1971.
10. Martiensen, Anthony, *Hitler and His Admirals*. E.P. Dutton & Co., New York, 1949.
11. Pope, Dudley, *Graf Spee, The Life and Death of a Raider*. J.P. Lippincott & Co., 1957.

12. Powell, Michael, *Death in the South Atlantic*. Ace Books, New York, 1956.

13. Rowher, J. & Hummelchen, G., *Chronology of the War at Sea Vol. I*. Arco, New York, 1972.

14. Ruge, Friedrich, *Der Seekrieg*. U.S. Naval Institute, Annapolis, 1957.

15. Taylor, J.C., *German Warships of WW II*. Doubleday & Co., New York, 1967.

16. Vian, Philip, *Action This Day*. Frederick Miller Ltd., London, 1960.

Chapter Three

Notes

1. T. Krancke & H. Brennecke, *Pocket Battleship*, p. 62.
2. George Pollock, *The Jervis Bay*, p. 86.
3. Krancke & Brennecke, *op. cit.*, p. 88.
4. *Ibid*, p. 231.
5. Dudley Pope, *73 North*, p. 242.
6. *Ibid*, p. 249.
7. *Ibid*, p. 251.

Bibliography

1. Bekker, Cajus, *Defeat at Sea*. Henry Holt & Co., New York, 1953.

2. Bekker, Cajus, *Hitler's Naval War*. Doubleday & Co., New York, 1974.

3. Dem Porten, Edward von, *The German Navy in World War II*. Thomas Y. Crowell, New York, 1969.

4. Doenitz, Karl, *Memoirs*. World Publishing Co., New York, 1959.

5. Hoyt, Edwin, *Raider 16*. World Publishing Co., New York, 1970.

6. Humble, Richard, *Hitler's High Seas Fleet*. Ballantine Books, New York, 1971.

7. Krancke, T. & H. Brennecke, *Pocket Battleship*. W.W. Norton & Co., New York, 1958.

8. Lenton, H. & J. Colledge, *British & Dominion Warships of WW II*. Ian Allen Ltd., London, 1964.

9. MacIntyre, Donald, *The Naval War Against Hitler*. Charles Scribner's Sons, New York, 1971.

10. Martiensen, Anthony, *Hitler and His Admirals*. E.P. Dutton & Co., New York, 1949.

11. Moulton, J.L., *Warfare in Three Dimensions*. Ohio University Press, Athens, 1967.

12. Pollock, George, *The Jervis Bay*. William Kimber, London, 1959.

13. Pope, Dudley, *73 North*. J.P. Lippincott & Co., New York, 1959.

14. Ruge, Friedrich, *Der Seekrieg*. U.S. Naval Institute, Annapolis, 1957.

15. Taylor, J.C., *German Warships of WW II*. Doubleday & Co., New York, 1967.

16. Warlimont, Walter, *Inside Hitler's Headquarters*. Frederich A. Praeger, New York, 1964.

Chapter Four

Notes

1. Karl Doenitz, *Memoirs*, p. 167.

2. Ludovic Kennedy, *Pursuit*, p. 29.

3. Richard Garrett, *Scharnhorst & Gneisenau*, p. 43.

4. *Ibid*, p. 68.

5. Cajus Bekker, *Hitler's Naval War*, p. 218.

6. *Ibid*, p. 219.

7. Burkard von Mullenheim-Rechberg, *Battleship Bismarck*, p. 110.

8. *Ibid*, p. 142.

9. *Ibid*, p. 150.

10. B.B. Schofield, *Loss of the Bismarck*, p. 56.

11. *Ibid*, p. 65.

Bibliography

1. Bekker, Cajus, *Defeat at Sea*. Henry Holt & Co., New York, 1953.
2. Bekker, Cajus, *Hitler's Naval War*. Doubleday & Co., New York, 1974.
3. Bradford, Ernle, *The Mighty Hood*. World Publishing Co., Cleveland, 1959.
4. Dem Porten, Edward von, *The German Navy in World War II*. Thomas Y. Crowell, New York, 1969.
5. Doenitz, Karl, *Memoirs*. World Publishing Co., Cleveland, 1959.
6. Forrester, C.S., *The Last Nine Days of the Bismarck*. Little, Brown & Co., Boston, 1958.
7. Grenfell, Russell, *The Bismarck Episode*. MacMillan & Co., New York, 1948.
8. Hoyt, Edwin, *Sunk By The Bismarck*. Stein and Day, New York, 1977.
9. Humble, Richard, *Hitler's High Seas Fleet*. Ballantine Books, New York, 1971.
10. Kennedy, Ludovic, *Pursuit*. Viking Press, New York, 1974.
11. Schofield, B.B., *Loss of the Bismarck*. Ian Allen Ltd., London, 1972.
12. Lenton, H. & J. Colledge, *British & Dominion Warships of WWII*. Ian Allen Ltd., London, 1964.
13. Moulton, J.L., *Warfare in Three Dimensions*. Ohio University Press, Athens, 1967.
14. Mullenhein-Rechberg, Burkard von, *Battleship Bismarck*. U.S. Naval Institute, Annapolis, 1980.
15. Taylor, J.C., *German Warships of WW II*. Doubleday & Co., New York, 1967.
16. Garrett, Richard, *Scharnhorst & Gneisenau*. Hippocrene Books, New York, 1978.

Chapter Five

Notes

1. Adolf Galland, *The First and the Last*, p. 89.
2. John Potter, *Fiasco*, p. 23.
3. *Ibid*, p. 54.
4. *Ibid*, p. 61.
5. Richard Garrett, *Scharnhorst and Gneisenau*, p. 104.
6. Terrence Robertson, *Channel Dash*, p. 169.
7. *Ibid*, p. 167.
8. Potter, *op. cit.*, p. 200.
9. *Ibid*, p. 189.
10. Robertson, *op. cit.*, p. 167.

Bibliography

1. Bekker, Cajus, *Defeat at Sea*. Henry Holt & Co., New York, 1953.
2. Bekker, Cajus, *Hitler's Naval War*. Doubleday & Co., New York, 1974.
3. Busch, Fritz-Otto, *The Story of the Prinz Eugen*. Robert Hole Ltd., London, 1960.
4. Busch, Fritz-Otto, *Holocaust at Sea—Drama of the Scharnhorst*. Rinehart & Co., New York, 1956.
5. Galland, Adolf, *The First and the Last*. Henry Holt & Co., New York, 1954.
6. Garrett, Richard, *Scharnhorst and Gneismau*. Hippocrene Books, New York, 1978.
7. Humble, Richard, *Hitler's High Seas Fleet*. Ballantine Books, New York, 1971.
8. Lamb, Charles, *To War in a Stringbag*. Nelson Doubleday Inc., Garden City, 1980.
9. MacIntyre, Donald, *The Naval War Against Hitler*. Charles Scribner's Sons, New York, 1971.
10. Peillard, Leonce, *Sink the Tirpitz*. G.P. Putnam's Sons, New York, 1968.
11. Potter, John, *Fiasco*. Stein and Day, New York, 1970.

12. Robertson, Terrence, *Channel Dash*. E.P. Dutton & Co., New York, 1958.
13. Ruge, Friedrich, *Der Seekrieg*. U.S. Naval Institute, Annapolis, 1957.
14. Taylor, J.C., *German Warships of World War II*. Doubleday & Co., New York, 1967.
15. Watts, A.J., *Loss of the Scharnhorst*. Ian Allen Ltd., London, 1970.

Chapter Six

Notes

1. Michael Carver, Ed., *The War Lords*, p. 473.
2. *Ibid*, p. 474.
3. Admiral Karl Doenitz, *Ten Years and Twenty Days*, p. 44.
4. Eugene Davidson, *The Trial of the Germans*, p. 396.
5. *Ibid*, p. 396.
6. David Mason, *U-Boat*, p. 58.
7. *Ibid*, p. 96.
8. Davidson, *op. cit.*, p. 409.
9. Maurice Matloff, *Strategic Planning for Coalition Warfare*, p. 26.
10. Doenitz, *op. cit.*, p. 299.
11. *Ibid*, p. 311.
12. *Ibid*, p. 312.
13. Mason, *op. cit.*, p. 108.
14. *Ibid*, p. 120.
15. Richard Humble, *Hitler's High Seas Fleet*, p. 143.
16. Mason, *op. cit.*, p. 138.
17. Humble, *op. cit.*, p. 156.
18. Doenitz, *op. cit.*, p. 439.
19. *Ibid*, p. 441.
20. *Ibid*, p. 461.
21. Carver, *op. cit.*, p. 483.

Bibliography

1. Ansel, Walter, *Hitler and the Middle Sea*. Duke University Press, North Carolina, 1972.
2. Beesly, Patrick, *Very Special Intelligence*. Hamish Hamilton, London, 1977.
3. Bekker, Cajus, *Hitler's Naval War*. Doubleday & Co., New York, 1974.
4. Bekker, Cajus, *The German Navy, 1939-1945*. Dial Press, New York, 1974.
5. Brennecke, Jochen, *The Hunters and the Hunted*. Pyramid Books, New York, 1957.
6. Buchheim, Lother-Gunther, *U-Boat War*. Alfred A. Knopf, New York, 1978.
7. Carver, Michael, Ed., *The War Lords*. Little Brown & Co., Boston, 1976.
8. Davidson, Eugene, *The Trial of the Germans*. Collier Books, New York, 1966.
9. Doenitz, Karl, *Memoirs: Ten Years and Twenty Days*. World Publishing Co., Cleveland, 1959.
10. Frank, Wolfgang, *The Sea Wolves*. Rinehart & Co., New York, 1955.
11. Gasaway, E.B., *Grey Wolf, Grey Sea*. Ballantine Books, New York, 1970.
12. Gilbert, G.M., *Nuremberg Diary*. New American Library, New York, 1961.
13. Hughes, Terry & John, Costello, *The Battle of the Atlantic*. Dial Press, New York, 1977.
14. Humble, Richard, *Hitler's High Seas Fleet*. Ballantine Books, New York, 1971.
15. Irving, David, *The Destruction of Convoy PQ17*. Simon and Schuster, New York, 1968.
16. Kennedy, Ludovic, *Pursuit*. Viking Press, New York, 1974.
17. Kennedy, Ludovic, *The Death of the Tirpitz*. Little Brown & Co., Boston, 1979.
18. MacIntyre, Donald, *The Naval War Against Hitler*. Charles Scribner's Sons, New York, 1971.

19. MacIntyre, Donald, *U-Boat Killer*. W.W. Norton & Co., New York, 1955.

20. Mason, David, *U-Boat: The Secret Menace*. Ballantine Books, New York, 1968.

21. Matloff, M., *Strategic Planning for Coalition Warfare 1943-1944*. Office of the Chief of Military History, Washington, D.C., 1959.

22. Morison, Samuel, *The Two-Ocean War*. Little Brown & Co., Boston, 1963.

23. Morison, Samuel, *History of U.S. Naval Operations in WW II., Vol. I, The Battle of the Atlantic*. Little Brown & Co., Boston, 1970.

24. Morison, Samuel, *History of U.S. Naval Operations in WW II., Vol. X, The Atlantic Battle Won*. Little Brown & Co., Boston, 1975.

25. Pfannes, C. & V. Salamone, *The Great Commanders of World War II, Vol. I: The Germans*. Zebra Books, New York, 1980.

26. Pope, Dudley, *73 North*. J.P. Lippincott Co., Philadelphia, 1958.

27. Potter, John, *Fiasco*. Stein and Day, New York, 1970.

28. Roskill, S.W., *White Ensign*. U.S. Naval Institute, Annapolis, 1960.

29. Schaeffer, Heinz, *U-Boat 977*. W.W. Norton & Co., New York, 1952.

30. Showell, Jak P., *The German Navy in World War II*. Naval Institute Press, Annapolis, 1979.

31. Speer, Albert, *Spandau: The Secret Diaries*. MacMillan Publishing, New York, 1976.

32. von der Porten, Edward, *The German Navy in World War II*. Thomas Y. Crowell, New York, 1969.

33. Werner, Herbert, *Iron Coffins*. Holt, Rinehart & Winston, New York, 1969.

Chapter Seven

Notes

1. Anthony Cave-Brown, *Wild Bill Donovan, The Last Hero*, p. 128.
2. *Ibid*, p. 129.
3. *Ibid*, p. 129.
4. *Ibid*, p. 129.
5. *Ibid*, p. 129.
6. *Ibid*, p. 129.
7. *Ibid*, pp. 130-131.
8. Heinz Hohne, *Canaris*, p. 93.
9. *Ibid*, p. 103.
10. Charles Whiting, *Canaris*, p. 25.
11. *Ibid*, p. 29.
12. Hohne, *op. cit.*, p. 185.
13. *Ibid*, p. 198.
14. *Ibid*, p. 258.
15. *Ibid*, p. 262.
16. *Ibid*, p. 352.
17. *Ibid*, p. 448.
18. *Ibid*, p. 570.
19. Ian Colvin, *Master Spy*, p. 248.

Bibliography

1. Bazna, Elyesa, *I Was Cicero*. Harper & Row, New York, 1962.
2. Cave-Brown, Anthony, *Bodyguard of Lies*. Harper & Row, New York, 1975.
3. Cave-Brown, Anthony, *The Secret War Report of the O.S.S.* A Berkley Medallion Book, New York, 1976.

4. Cave-Brown, Anthony, *Wild Bill Donovan, The Last Hero*. Times Books, New York, 1982.

5. Colvin, Ian, *Master Spy*. McGraw-Hill Book Co., New York, 1951.

6. Delarue, Jacques, *The Gestapo: A History of Horror*. Dell Books, New York, 1964.

7. Deutsch, Harold C., *Hitler and His Generals*. University of Minnesota Press, Minneapolis, 1974.

8. Dulles, Allen, *Germany's Underground*. The MacMillan Co., New York, 1947.

9. Farago, Ladislas, *The Game of the Foxes*. David McKay Co., New York, 1971.

10. Fitzgibbon, Constantine, *20 July*. W.W. Norton, New York, 1956.

11. Gehlen, Reinhard, *The Service*. World Publishing Times Mirror, New York, 1972.

12. Grunberger, Richard, *The 12-Year Reich*. Holt, Rinehart, and Winston, New York, 1971.

13. Hilton, Stanley, *Hitler's Secret War in South America 1939-1945*. Ballantine Books, New York, 1981.

14. Hoffman, Peter, *The History of the German Resistance 1933-1945*. The MIT Press, Mass., 1977.

15. Hohne, Heinz, *The Order of the Death's Head*. Coward-McCann, New York, 1970.

16. Hohne, Heinz, *Canaris*. Doubleday & Co., New York, 1979.

17. Hoyt, Edwin, *Kreuzerkrieg*. World Publishing Co., Cleveland, 1968.

18. Kahn, David, *Hitler's Spies*. MacMillan, New York, 1978.

19. Manvell, Roger & Fraenkel, Heinrich, *The July Plot*. Pan Books Ltd, London, 1964.

20. Masterman, J.C., *The Double Cross System*. Yale University Press, New Haven, 1972.

21. Persico, Joseph, *Piercing the Reich*. Viking Press, New York, 1979.

22. Pfannes, C. & Salamone, V., *The Great Commanders of World War II Volume I, The Germans*. Zebra Books, New York, 1980.

23. Schellenberg, Walter, *The Labyrinth*. Harper Brothers, New York, 1956.

24. Speer, Albert, *Inside the Third Reich*. MacMillan & Co., New York, 1970.

25. Speer, Albert, *Infiltration*. MacMillan & Co., New York, 1981.

26. Whiting, Charles, *Canaris*. Ballantine Books, New York, 1973.

27. Wykes, Alan, *Heydrich*. Ballantine Books, New York, 1973.

THE BEST IN ADVENTURES FROM ZEBRA

GUNSHIPS #2: FIRE FORCE (1159, $2.50)
by Jack Hamilton Teed
A few G.I.s, driven crazy by the war-torn hell of Vietnam, had banded into brutal killing squads who didn't care whom they shot ... ~~John~~ Hardin, tapped for the job of wiping out these ~~...d of~~ misfits into a fight-

GUNSHIPS #3: COBRA KILL (1462, $2.50)
by Jack Hamilton Teed
Having taken something from the wreckage of the downed Cobra gunship, the Cong force melted back into the jungle. Colonel John Hardin was going to find out what the Cong had taken — even if it killed him!

THE BLACK EAGLES #4: PUNGI PATROL (1389, $2.50)
by John Lansing
A team of specially trained East German agents — disguised as U.S. soldiers — is slaughtering helpless Vietnamese villagers to discredit America. The Black Eagles, the elite jungle fighters, have been ordered to stop the butchers before our own allies turn against us!

THE BLACK EAGLES #5:
SAIGON SLAUGTHER (1476, $2.50)
Pulled off active operations after having been decimated by the NVA, the Eagles fight their own private war of survival in the streets of Saigon — battling the enemy assassins who've been sent to finish them off!

Available wherever paperbacks are sold, or order direct from the Publisher. Send cover price plus 50¢ per copy for mailing and handling to Zebra Books, Dept. 1756, 475 Park Avenue South, New York, N.Y. 10016. DO NOT SEND CASH.

THE SURVIVALIST SERIES
by Jerry Ahern